Political Clubs
in New York

Norman M. Adler
Blanche Davis Blank

foreword by
Roy V. Peel

The Praeger Special Studies program—utilizing the most modern and efficient book production techniques and a selective worldwide distribution network—makes available to the academic, government, and business communities significant, timely research in U.S. and international economic, social, and political development.

Political Clubs
in New York

PRAEGER SPECIAL STUDIES IN U.S. ECONOMIC, SOCIAL, AND POLITICAL ISSUES

Praeger Publishers   New York   Washington   London

Library of Congress Cataloging in Publication Data

Adler, Norman, 1942-
  Political clubs in New York.

  (Praeger special studies in U.S. economic, social,
and political issues)
  Continues R. V. Peel's The political clubs of New
York City published in 1935.
  Includes bibliographical references and index.
  1. New York (City)—Clubs.   2. New York (City)—
Politics and government.   3. Political clubs.
I. Blank, Blanche Davis, 1923-   joint author.
II. Peel, Roy Victor, 1896-   The political clubs
of New York City.   III. Title.
JK2295.N74P4   1975   329'.0211'097471   72-89642
ISBN 0-275-28852-8

PRAEGER PUBLISHERS
111 Fourth Avenue, New York, N.Y. 10003, U.S.A.

Published in the United States of America in 1975
by Praeger Publishers, Inc.

Printed in the United States of America

To our parents
Pearl and Louis Adler
Mathilda Markendorff and Joseph B. Davis

ACKNOWLEDGMENTS

Our sincere thanks to all those whose tireless talents helped to create and sustain our work:

Madi Adler and Bud Blank—our spouses who sympathized and
    survived.
Frank Feigert and Roberta Siegel—who critiqued at convention
The Thomas Hunter Fund—for patronizing and paying
Russ Matteson—for matrices and manipulations
Mike Mische—for bibliography and briefings
William V. Pickett—for conversation and confidences
Edward Rogowsky—for recognizing and reporting
Mike Speer—for reading and reviewing
Susan Said—for typing and translating
Joseph Vitoritti—for scanning and scheduling
Our students—for visiting and validating, especially Fran Toneatta
    and Harold Sullivan
Eugene Bochman and Librarians of the New York City Municipal
    Reference Service—for references and other research resources
Nat Cippolina—for coding and clarifying, our chief standby and all
    purpose aide who has been part of this project throughout its
    life. He has been absolutely invaluable and indispensible
and, of course,
Roy V. Peel—who initiated and inspired.

When I was informed by Dean Blanche D. Blank and Professor
Norman Adler that they wanted me to write this introduction to their
work on New York City's political clubs, which they had designed
as a revision of my Political Clubs of New York City (1935), and
a modernization of this earlier work, I felt both grateful and honored.
From what Dean Blank told me about their plans, from the critical papers on the earlier work that she showed me, as well as the
copies of research forms she gave me, I knew that Blank and Adler
would produce a survey of great value. From Dean Blank's textbook,[1]
I learned that her values were the same as mine, but that her approach
would be somewhat different. Blank and Adler want to expose the am-
biguities and ambivalences in our structure of myths, and reveal "the
contradictory values embodied in the American Constitution." It
would probably be fair to say that Blank and Adler use a modified
"systems" and "behavioral" approach, something like that charac-
terizing the work of my friends Bert Gross and Ralph Goldman.[2]
But the Blank-Adler study is the only modern survey of clubs. My
own study has been praised by many scholars without any comment
on the method I employed. I can say here that my style of observation and analysis was influenced by Charles E. Merriam, whose
approach was what F. D. Wormuth called Verstehen.[3] How I came
to choose this study of political clubs and how I organized my inquiry
I shall come to below. All scholars are influenced by early experiences and environment as well as by their teachers and associates.
Revolutionaries and innovators, such as Thomas Paine, Karl Marx,
Charles Beard, and Thorstein Veblen gave their biographers some
problems in explication. But most scholars develop interests, pref-
erences, and capacities that are easily accounted for.
I derived my special concerns and methods of study from
Merriam, the distinguished political scientist at the University of
Chicago, whose influence over colleagues and students during the
1920s and 1930s is easily recognized in the works of many (among
them H. F. Cosnell, H. D. Lasswell, Joseph P. Harris, C. O.
Johnson, V. O. Key, Pearl Robertson, Sonya Forthal, Al Lepowsky,
Elizabeth Weber, Frank Stuart, Herman Beyle, C. H. Woody, Martha
Stevenson), from other political science professors, such as Leonard
D. White and Quincy Wright who gave their graduate students insights
into administration and world affairs. It was also my good fortune
to study history under such eminent men as A. C. McLaughlin,

Wm. E. Dodd, and G. Scherill—and to learn about economics from John H. Williams and Paul Douglas. While I was in Chicago, two graduate students in sociology (later professors) produced studies in social disorganizations, which were of value in analyzing and comparing community behaviors.[4]

My master's thesis in history was a study of Sovereignty in the Territorial Waters, which could have been a political science topic. My doctoral dissertation in Political Science was a study of James G. Blaine, and this involved some close examination of political trends in New York, the critical state in the 1884 election.

It was Merriam's advice that I examine carefully the entire political system in the New York Metropolitan area, where I had spent two years prior to the year in which I completed my graduate work. Why did I choose clubs as the chief object of research? Partly because I grew up in a neighborhood in Des Moines, a "model city" which in my youth adopted a reform style of urban government where the entire city was one political unit. In Chicago, I had seen how important were the wards, which were nearly coterminal with neighborhoods, such as Hyde Park. In New York City I soon learned that the basic units were assembly districts, and that each had a club for each party that was official; and I soon learned that there were minor clubs of various types.

My political preferences in 1928, 1930, and 1932 were Democratic, and I participated enthusiastically in support of Al Smith in 1928, and Franklin Roosevelt in all three years. This helped me gain entry to Democratic circles in all five boroughs in New York's greater city. With Thomas C. Donnelly, I wrote analyses of the 1928 and 1932 national campaigns. At the same time, I was engaged in a number of other studies in addition to the study of political clubs. Also, from 1926 to 1936, I made three trips abroad, two of which consisted of visits to the leading capitals of Europe, where there were some clubs of interest, but, except for the working men's clubs of London, not as numerous or varied as the district clubs in New York City. However, at home and abroad I found much literature on the history of political clubs, including several books cited in my 1935 volume.

Part of my interest in cities, communities or neighborhoods, precincts, districts, and metropolises was due to my early experiences, in childhood up through high school and at college and university, and my travels. My childhood home lay in a well-defined neighborhood, and in various ways I came to recognize other neighborhoods, such as Grand View, the South Bottoms and Grand Avenue (the date district). While I was a child, Des Moines adopted the commission plank known as the Des Moines Plan, which put local council and mayoralty elections on a citywide basis. As most people know, it was at this time that throughout the country the old alderman district system began to decline—but not in New York City, in which there was reformed aldermanic, assembly, county, and other districts with independent electoral functions.

Wherever I traveled in the United States and abroad I found a great variety of urban structures and divisions, some that were combined electoral, demographic, geographic and economic areas, and some that were not.

I had a great interest in the need for proper integrated communities before I learned about foreign efforts in London, Stockholm, and other places to create model neighborhoods and communes. I recognized that people who lived in neighborhoods, such as Hyde Park in Chicago, Riverdale in New York City, or Encino in Los Angeles, could not use all the different electoral districts to integrate main political preferences. The commission and manager-council system were attempts to get real majority rule. The P.R. voting system, for a time in New York, offered some hope for fair representation for a number of political constellations.

But when I made the 1935 study I had to accept the assembly district as the basic political unit, and to indicate how ethnic, religious, economic, and social elite clubs and disorderly (or illegal) institutions had members—or clients—scattered over a larger area. Outside of New York City (and even there to some extent) community integration was fostered by schools and churches rather than by political clubs.

Most of my academic colleagues agreed that our cities were becoming unbearably large.[5] Even President Roosevelt in his first inaugural address pleaded for a decentralization of urban population.[6] He recommended several measures to accomplish this goal, but the New Deal Program, which covered all phases of national life and structure as well as world relations, was too broad and comprehensive for F.D.R. to make much headway in this endeavor. Neither the old Tammany regime nor the new LaGuardia Fusion government made any attempt at revolution in city life.

It is noteworthy that the second great "Fusion" mayor, John V. Lindsay, who served from 1966 until 1974, attributed the city's ills to the stubborn controls over the authority of the municipal government by the New York State Government, as Plunkitt had said in 1899.[7] As the urban situation grew worse hundreds of writers and statesmen suggested reforms, mostly financial, such as "revenue-sharing" or the creation of "garden cities" and "new cities," such as Levittown or Reston. My own contribution in 1933 was to urge the reorganization of the nation on regional lines, a proposal later expanded upon by the National Resources Committee in Regional Factors in National Planning (1935).[8]

Inasmuch as Hitler had risen to power in Germany, I felt
obliged, as did most of my fellow political scientists, to study the
causes for the rise of Nazism and to estimate what effect the Fascist
Revolution would have on our foreign policy. Part of my staff helped
me assemble data on Germany. There were German clubs in the
city, all relatively quiet. But a German friend invited me to a picnic
in Westchester, presided over by a Tammany bigwig (a doctor), and
I was astonished to detect the pro-Nazi sentiment which prevailed.

In 1974 Blank and Adler are not likely to have noticed any under-
currents of Nazi sympathy. But there remains today an obvious distaste for our "war" in Southeast Asia, which may have caused unrest
in the clubs. The mayor (Lindsay) was certainly antiwar, and a critical number of citizens knew this when they voted for him. Outside of
of the war issue, which was very different between 1933 and 1945,
when LaGuardia favored America's use of force to stop aggression,
and from 1966 to 1973, when Lindsay practically became an outright
pacifist, for obvious reasons, the two New York City leaders were
much alike. Both were, in youth, Republicans, both used Republican
aid to overcome the faulty tendencies in Tammany Hall, and after
two terms in office, both even supporting liberal Democratic doc-
trines. And, most of the time, both men were highly regarded by
independent reform leaders. But further than that we must not go,
because the contemporary period is (or was) the "age of protest,"
whereas the earlier period witnessed a higher degree of consensus
on national, state, and local issues.

What I wanted to learn from 1927 to 1935 was how local clubs
of all varieties caused some voters to be loyal to the "organizations,"
and others to respond favorably to appeals for reform or a chance
for exponents of new ideologies. After I began my study at Chicago,
I made two trips to Europe, visited clubs in all the great cities
(London, Stockholm, Berlin, Prague, Vienna, Paris and Brussels).
After I obtained my master's degree at the University of Chicago,
I spent parts of two years at New York University, and became ac-
quainted with many local leaders of both major and minor parties.
At Chicago, I was permitted to participate in the Merriam-Gosnell
study of Non-Voting, and living in Chicago in the twenties, I could
not fail to observe the antics of the crooked Mayor Thompson and
Governor Small's political machines, or note what the reformers
Merriam, Ickes, Richberg, and others were doing to restore good
government.

America's social histories, and reruns of old movies keep the
present generation informed of the evils of crime, rackets, and gangs
during the Prohibition Era. When I was living in Chicago during the
twenties, there were speakeasies everywhere, and dominating illegal
activities of all kinds, there were the Capone and other rival mobs.

Most honest, temperate, and decent people were not much disturbed. Murders and other violence were manifestations of intergang rivalries. Ordinary citizens were relatively safe. In New York City, with its complex and intricate political club patterns, the Tammany clubs were the chief offenders, along with their elected officials and bureaucracy, in protecting the gangsters. When political clubs catered to the thirsts of their members, it was to provide them with amenities, which were freely offered elsewhere. However, I found that the Tammany leaders were more closely identified with the gangsters than the Republicans and, of course, the independent reform leaders.

My associates and I found much wrongdoing in the clubs, but what we found was simultaneously, or later, finally exposed by Judge Seabury in three investigations, and by such law officers as Thomas E. Dewey. As to prostitution, our investigators found that this was an activity carried on in private quarters, protected by the dominant political machine, the police, and even the courts. In some areas, mostly Manhattan, the Bronx and Brooklyn, machine bosses were found to be guilty of bribery, protection, and the use of gangsters in protecting vice. In the 1920s and 1930s the drug problem was one of tremendous concern, but played no role in the life of the clubs. Our charts of delinquency dealt with other crimes and misdemeanors. What Seabury, Dewey, LaGuardia, and other champions of justice found in the way of relations between politicians and criminals we did not put on charts, but we had the data by names of felons and miscreants.

Some of the work on political clubs and other projects I engaged in during the years from 1927 to 1939 I did on my own except that in the case of the two campaign books, Donnelly and I shared the burden. Actually I had the help of about twenty students who represented communities scattered all over the area. I outlined programs for them. Their work was supervised by Nichols T. Rogers and Mario Vaccaro, both of whom later became lawyers.

Besides visits to nearly all the clubs by me, with Rogers or Vaccaro driving, or by others, we had files of historical data on New York City in our office; also reports by public or social service agencies on population and industrial distributions, economic levels, crime and disorder, concentrations of ethnic and religious groups, transit and recreational facilities, etc. We should have printed more of them. One for example, showed that the neighborhood where I lived in Brooklyn, called "Midwood," once was a Dutch Town. Our ethnic maps showed rather accurately where Jews, Germans, Italians, etc., dwelt. It also showed that east of Negro Harlem, there was a small Finnish colony and it revealed how Slavic, Italian, Greek, and other minorities were distributed.

We did have some estimates on numbers of members of clubs, and of characteristics, but except for minor clubs we did not publish the figures. Except when there were special programs, the regular attendants at the club were male adults. Naturally the women's clubs catered only to adult females. As to the average wealth of members, I and my aides found that the active members represented pretty much the "purchasing power" of the communities, which information was made public by the leading newspapers who had a cooperative enterprise to abolish this data from census publications. Naturally the 15th & 10th Congressional Districts of Manhattan included the wealthiest inhabitants—and the poorest areas were in downtown Manhattan[9] and some outlying areas of the other boroughs. What I and my associates should have done was to publish maps showing neighborhoods by popular name: for example, Yorkville, Greenpoint, Riverdale, Harlem. The club names usually indicated the neighborhood, although some indicated only the Assembly District, or some present or past leader. Many had Indian names—just as the names of the states of Iowa, South Dakota, and Utah were of Indian origin. Still we could have included a map showing the locations of the more important clubs.

Even today, the clubs—better than churches whose members maintain residences far away from their church—are the centers of community action. This was not true of the elite clubs and unions, the reform organizations (Commonwealth, City Club, Citizen's Union, etc.), or the fraternal orders.

I don't think that Blank and Adler have visted as many clubs of all kinds as I and my chief aides, Rogers, Vaccaro, Lazar, did in the 1930-37 period, nor do I have the impression that they have participated so actively in the Lindsay campaigns as I did along with Barry, Berle, Blanshard, Forbes and Sayre, in the LaGuardia reform years. But Blank and Adler have made available in paper and enlightening form all the data on social, environmental, economic, moral, and psychological behaviors—which I took for granted that everyone knew or should have known. The contemporary Watergate hearings reveal how difficult it is to learn the truth about the motives and ideals of suspected wrongdoers. The great advantages which the investigators of the thirties had was that there was no television— a medium of presentation and communication which has grave faults, as Marshall McLuhan has pointed out. However, what Blank and Adler have done is to encourage us to reconsider the viability of metropolitan, social and political institutions.

Notes

1. Blanche D. Blank, American Government and Politics (Chicago: Aldine, 1973).

2. B. Gross, ed., Social Intelligence (Boston: 1969); R. M. Goldman, Contemporary Perspectives (New York: 1972); Also see W. J. Crotty, ed., Approaches to the Study. (Boston: 1968).

3. F. D. Wormuth, "Matched Dependent Behavioralism; the Cargo Cult in Political Science," Western Political Quarterly, December 1967.

4. These were H. Zarbaugh, The Gold Coast and the Slum, and F. Thraser, The Gang.

5. See W. A. Bobson, ed., Great Cities (1954; C. M. Green and T. R. Dye, ed.; A. K. Campbell, ed. M. S. Stehman, Jr., ed. et al. On New York, see W. S. Sayre and H. Kaufman, Governing New York City (1960).

6. See E. H. Kevinsky & J. Park, My Friends (Buffalo: Foster and Stewart, 1946), pp. 2-3.

7. See W. L. Riordan, Plunkitt of Tammany Hall (New York: Knopf, 1948) Reprint, introduction by R. V. Peel pp. 28 ff. and J. V. Lindsay, The City (New York: Norton, 1969).

8. On my proposal, see: comments by W. B. Graces, various works; Roy V. Peel, Ch XXII in J. N. Andrews and C. A. Marsden, Tomorrow in the Making (New York: Whickelsey House, 1939) R. V. Peel, State Government Today (Albuquerque: U of N. Mex., 1948) with references. For modern ideas, see proposals by R. G. Tugwell, etc.

9. See the maps in the 1935 book, political boundaries, frontispiece, purchasing power, p. 47, Industrial distributions, p. 51 and delinquency p. 24.

CONTENTS

LIST OF TABLES AND FIGURES

Political Clubs
in New York

1

**POLITICAL
CLUBS**

To write about American politics is to write about the principles and practices of democracy. That is why many political scientists who have observed American political parties in the twentieth century have been concerned with such matters as the responsiveness of the parties, participation in them, and their ideological cohesiveness. There was a time in American history when the parties seemed to belong to their adherents; the political machine was a grassroots organization that brought a multitude of constituents into its membership or sphere of contact:

Participation in politics was not only open but conceivably could be meaningful in an easily observed way. Indeed, one needed special qualifications to become a machine politician, but none of them served as ascriptive 'tickets of admission' like education, wealth, or high social status. The question of citizen efficacy in mass, impersonal surroundings was almost as salient in nineteenth-century urban America as it is today. The machine provided knowable, workable, and accessible routes for use in bringing about some change in one's immediate environment through governmental action. While the machine was utterly inappropriate as an institution for mass social change, it was exceedingly useful as a means for achieving personal ends. Millions of ignorant, illiterate immigrants became citizens and voters almost immediately after leaving the steerage of their ship.[1]

Nowadays we hear the frequent complaint that politics, and politicians, have lost touch with the people, and, what is more serious, the people have lost direct contact with politics.

How can we speak of democracy when there is little relationship between the vehicle by which a candidate is brought to the voters and the voters themselves ? In an era when special consultants may be hired to launch a political campaign, finance it, choose the viewpoint that it presents to the public, and, finally, advise the newly elected official what to do, the alienation of voters is well on its way to becoming complete. The impact of such events as Watergate has not caused this feeling of isolation, but has confirmed what was already suspected: politics is one thing and citizens are another.

A movement is underway to close up this gap, through the restructuring of government and the development of new forms of political access for the public. But this is taking place in the dark, and without an understanding of past models, or an appreciation of the ways in which existing institutions function, we cannot hope to develop new institutions that will endure. Yet the need to feel that one can participate in politics is important if democracy is to survive. The continuing erosion of voter identification with political parties may eventually lead to the demise of party politics, with no system developed to replace it. Already at the local level, where the political machine once had a considerable impact, "the thousands of inactive precinct workers and unfilled precinct positions"[2] today foreshadow the impending demise of community partisan politics as a citizens' activity. The vacuum that would result from such a demise would be filled by men engaged in politics as a business, rather than by citizens engaged in political affairs.

The discipline of political science seems to be abandoning its sneering rejection of the sentiment that once led to such books as Toward a More Responsible Two-Party System,[3] which sought to view the subject of parties within the broader context of developing revised forms for maintaining popular democracy. Many political scientists of the so-called Chicago school of studying parties in the 1930s held that the study of parties was tied closely to a concern for renewing democracy. We believe that an examination of political clubs is a step in the same direction. As Roy V. Peel pointed out:

> Since this form of political organization has survived
> the centuries as the natural and inevitable expression
> of community political needs, it cannot be thrust aside
> but must be understood and accommodated to the designs
> of those who would adjust the social and political poten-
> tialities of man to his new conditions, his expanding
> opportunities and his newly perceived standards.[4]

Clearly a form of political organization is needed to restore the relationship between local citizens and their government. Perhaps the key to that restoration lies within the concept and practice of club politics.

The term "political clubs" may be foreign to some people, because these clubs do not exist in many parts of the country, and where they do exist they are not always visible. They have existed in New York City for a long time. Yet in 1974 we know little more about them than we learned from Roy V. Peel's book Political Clubs of New York City, written some forty years earlier. It might seem strange that, at a time when many political commentators are forecasting the demise of American political parties, we have undertaken to study political clubs. To some commentators the clubs already appear to have died, with several obituaries having been written for them. Six years ago Theodore Lowi observed that "by 1961 the clubhouses and districts had been replaced almost altogether by new types of units."[5] Yet as Mark Twain was said to have written about his own prematurely published obituary, reports of death are greatly exaggerated.

We did not decide by accident to study the reputedly moribund political clubs. We were led to the clubs by Peel's work. His 1935 book provided a landmark in the study of local political organization, and became the definitive book on the subject of the local urban political club. It ran counter to almost all of the political science studies of its time, not focusing on a single case or on a combination of cases, but ranging across all parties and factions. And in an age when empiricism was considered to be a radical experimental technique, the study was truly an empirical one, with Peel and his investigators visiting hundreds of political clubs and conducting thousands of interviews.

Political clubs invite analysis by their very position in politics. They hold the same extralegal status of the political groups that Leon Epstein wrote about in his study of Wisconsin state politics.[6] Sorauf, in describing the status of the groups studied by Epstein, noted the following:

> The "regular" Republicans found it easier to operate through their voluntary party organization than through the carefully regulated statutory organization. The Democrats . . . followed suit in the Forties and Fifties. At present, therefore, both parties operate through these duplicating but separate voluntary organizations which parallel—county organization for county organization—the statutory organizational structure . . . both control the statutory organizations,

3

keeping them docile and using them only to perform
the mandated statutory activities.[7]

Similarly the political clubs of New York City dominate and manipu-
late legally mandated forms of political organization while themselves remaining outside state and local regulation. The 1973
edition of the New York State Election Law contains 387 pages of
definitions, restrictions, calendars, prescriptions, and forms that
apply to the operation of electoral politics. Forty-two of the law's
602 sections deal directly with political parties and their officers;
there is no mention of political clubs. Moreover, the political
committees that are described in the law rarely meet, and their
meetings are brief. As Peel observed . . . "the fundamental primary unit of political regimentation is the club, not provided for
either by state law or by party rule, but universally acknowledged
as the unit-cell in the organization of the major political parties."[8]
The political structure in both Wisconsin and New York appears to
function this way, with little notice taken of the club function.
     What is a political club? It is a voluntary organization, whose
members mutually identify with, and expect to gain benefit from, a
certain political party or faction. The club has officers, bylaws,
regular meetings, rituals, an institutional purpose, and a certain
degree of face-to-face contact with voters. Frequently a person
must formally apply for membership and be voted into the club.
The manifest business of the political club is to work in behalf of
its party, by recruiting and supporting candidates for public and
party office. The club's functions may also include social, fraternal, economic, communal, legal, and ethnic activities. These
activities may temporarily, or permanently, overshadow the
political activities.
     In some cities, of which New York is a prime example, political
clubs are ubiquitous. There is hardly a community in New York
City that does not claim one or more clubs engaged more or less
actively in the business of politics. And there are few politicians,
regardless of the office they seek or the resources they have at
their disposal, who do not court the support and endorsement of
the political clubs of their party.
     Political clubs are an integral part of the electoral process.
In New York City the political clubs are where politics is happening.
That is why New Yorkers want to know about these clubs and why
we have chosen to study them.

The Literature

     It is not altogether clear why political scientists generally have
abandoned the literary study of party organization below the national

4

level. Joseph Schlesinger, in his bibliographic essay on political organization literature, noted that "it is remarkable how little the study of party organization per se ... has developed beyond its state at the turn of the century." [9] Writing in the field has concentrated its attention on the national parties, with only some work done on state parties. The few works that have dealt in any way with local parties have been either historical or concerned with personalities. Dayton McKean and J. T. Salter represent the latter approach, while M. R. Werner's history of New York City's Tammany Hall is illustrative of the former. [10]

The remaining studies have emphasized party personnel rather than party structure. Two predominant schools have evolved, separated generally by time: "machine" literature and "grassroots" literature. Robert H. Salisbury listed the "machine" writers as Peel (we do not consider Peel a "machine" writer), Harold Gosnell, Salter and Frank R. Kent. Certainly Sonya Forthal and, more recently, Harvey Wheeler belong in this group as well, as does the lesser-known work of William Bennett Munro. [11] Salisbury noted:

Their studies portrayed an urban political organization, established at the ward of assembly-district level, purposefully carrying on the essential tasks of attracting precinct workers to the party: organizing, disciplining, and rewarding their labors and, by providing the base of the party hierarchy, doing the ultimate task of the party—making face-to-face contacts with the electorate in quest of votes. The postulated model was highly rational. The tangible organizational objectives of votes was achieved in order that the equally tangible rewards of jobs and other perquisities could be enjoyed by the members. Whatever social functions might be provided by organization were instrumental in attracting workers and in satisfying prospective electoral supporters. The organization was populated by male politicians, often first- or second-generation Americans, little interested in the large questions of national and international policy, but preoccupied with career opportunities in local and state government or government related jobs. The organizational type was likely to be of somewhat higher status than the population he sought to deliver at the polls, but in education, occupation, and above all, style of life, he managed to remain reasonably close to "his people." [12]

What all of the "machine" studies have in common, as well, is a failure to place the activities of politicians in an organizational setting. Either the political organization is equated with the vote-getting, selfserving activities of individuals, or it is some monolithic monster, of an unspecified breed and lineage, for whom all ward heelers work. Organizational structure and components, as well as internal differences in style, format, rules and regulations, are all absent from "machine" studies. The reason for this is that these studies were caricatures rather than the products of systematic observation. They were done in an age when common-sense notions of existing institutions were considered sufficient as a data base. They leave us word pictures, a sense of what the political machines are like, but little idea of how politicians worked in groups to control both government and the electoral process through local political parties.

After a hiatus of several decades a new and rather substantial literature developed, mostly in the sixties, dealing with what the authors called "grassroot activists" in political parties.[13] This new literature described the local political activists on the basis of their demographic characteristics, their motives for participating in party politics, their activities, and their beliefs and disciplines. Precinct captains, county chairmen, and members of legally defined statutory committees of local parties were studied in Missouri, North Carolina, Michigan, New Jersey, California, and other states. These studies culminated in Samuel Eldersveld's elaborate study of what he termed the "stratarchical" party system in Detroit.[14] Just as we regard Peel as an exception to the "machine" studies, we consider Eldersveld an exception to the "grassroot" studies.

Because most local politicians perform the bulk of their activities alone, away from any physical party headquarters, and beyond all but the most casual supervision, the "grassroots" studies tend to see individual behavior as collective party behavior. Undoubtedly in opposition to the notion of the party as a monolith, which was so popular with those who wrote about the machines, the "grassroots" writers generally studied the behavior of men and women working in their own neighborhoods, and called that behavior the functioning of the political party. Generally unobserved, because they are not a part of the activities of many of these "grassroots" politicians, were such phenomena of big-city politics as regularized meetings, reports to and from party leaders, social interaction among active participants, and the like. While the "machine" studies focused on New York, Chicago, Philadelphia and Jersey City, the "grassroots" studies looked at smaller cities outside the mainstream of organization politics as Gosnell and Salter had known it.

Most of these studies report not what precinct workers and local committeemen do or achieve, but what they say they do and achieve. There is no direct observation, no evidence of output, and no other data in the studies except the results of a mailed questionnaire or, in rare cases, an interview. The environment of political activity is seen as being regional (northeast or southwest) or demographic (rural, lower class, Italian-American, or blue collar), rather than situational (neighborhood or physical setting for political work) or historical (seen against the backdrop of those who did political work in years past). Except for the Eldersveld work, there is no indication that factions exist, or that there is a hierarchy of command or a clientele. The social environment that dictates and limits the configuration of relationships between the activist and the voter, or between the activist and his role, or among competing and cooperating political workers, is not studied. Attention is centered on the local party's recruitment function, its voter contact function, and its organizational maintenance function. The concept of the local party as a structure is totally absent from just about every "grassroots" study. As one might expect, therefore, the "grassroots" writers find it impossible either to discuss the effect of structural linkages on the practice of politics or to speak of the impact of the structure of environment (physical, ideological, or legal) on party output. Membership in the party is seen in functional terms—so many positions unfilled or so many voters uncontacted—rather than in terms of the reasons for a dearth of activists or a decline in the activity of activists. The relative impact of party organization form or tradition, and the reinforcement of practices and relationships, are unexplored factors in "grassroots" studies.

There is an absence of what Heinz Eulau and Kenneth Prewitt call "contextual analysis," involving, in Harold Lasswell's terms, "the principle of situational reference." [15] As Lasswell and Abraham Kaplan noted, "Empirical significance requires that the propositions of social science, rather than affirming unqualifiedly universal invariances, state relations between variables assuming different social contexts." [16]

Sorauf, who summarized the significance of many of the "grassroots" studies, noted that "the major political party as an organization is a mechanism for uniting adherents in the pursuit of general goals of hierarchies (priorities) of goals. It recruits and mobilizes the resources and skills for political action." [17] What is absent from many of the personnel-oriented studies of local politics, in both the "machine" and "grassroots" forms, is a description of the nuts and bolts of that mechanism (the major political party). One cannot criticize a study for not doing what it never intended to do. On the other hand, there is a serious

7

scarcity in the literature of political parties of the sort of descriptive writing that is commonplace in the study of hospitals, mental institutions, corporations, and assembly lines. It is a strange failing, since structures are invariably easier to observe, describe, and understand than are functions. As Eulau and Prewitt noted, "If . . . structures are more easily identifiable than the functions they perform, structural analysis recommends itself as a first step."[18] In saying this they take issue with the main body of party organization writers who would probably agree with V. O. Key, who noted "to understand party organization one must keep in mind the functions of party."[19] Key added, "How are the political activists, however large or small their number, to perform functions of the party? This is in essence the problem of party organization."[20] Key is not alone in stating this. Lee F. Anderson discusses numerous opportunities to apply organization theory to the study of political organizations.[21] Every one of these attempts begins with a functional approach, whether it is Kaufman's theory of organization, "built around the concept of functional requirements," or Perrow's "tasks every organization must accomplish if it is to maintain itself."[22]

Occasionally over the past decade a work has appeared that touches on the structure and composition of local political clubs. James Q. Wilson's comparison of the political reform movements in New York, Illinois, and California is basically a journalistic approach to political club life.[23] It is frequently unsystematic and usually impressionistic, leaving the reader with a false notion that all New York reform clubs are alike. In each of the three states studied (New York, Illinois, and California) Wilson uses a handful of clubs from which to generalize on the behavior of all clubs. He offers little discussion on the non-reform organizations that make up the bulk of the clubs, nor on the Republican and third parties. What Wilson has done, however, other than "discovering" the amateur Democratic movement of the sixties for political scientists (generally the last ones to know), is to provide a number of hypotheses regarding the differences among types of political structures and participants. He compares reformers and regulars, insurgents and noninsurgents, and various forms of political participation. His use of demographic data to create "profiles" of amateur Democrats is a useful, if somewhat inaccurate, indicator of who leads political movements and who participates in them. Whatever the shortcomings of Wilson's book, he has contributed to our understanding of what the clubs are and what they do. His book gives us a feeling that the club to which amateurs belong plays as much a part in molding their participation as they do in molding the club. We see the variety of clubs as an outgrowth of the communities

in which they function. We have a better understanding of the interaction of the people, environment, election law, and ideology that
facilitates the performance of party functions, and, at the same time,
frustrates it.

Methodology

We began with the idea of replicating, as closely as possible,
the original Peel study. However, this presented several difficulties.
First, we did not have access to Peel's research design, and his book
gave us few clues. Second, we could not ascertain the nature of his
research instrument (we later discovered that there had been no such
instrument). We had no idea what questions his research team had
developed to generate his findings. Third, we did not have the easy,
informal access to many political organizations that Peel had gained.
He had been an influential figure in city reform politics, and a well-
known denizen of the political subculture of New York.

Responding to these problems, we reversed the direction which
most graduate students are instructed to take in pursuing research.
We isolated what we took to be Peel's principal findings, devised
certain hypotheses which we believed would lead to such findings,
developed a methodology that seemed to reflect the original, and
then created an instrument that was suitable for such research.
Two techniques were employed: (1) guided observation of meetings
and environments of political clubs, and (2) interviews with key club
officials. Our research team was instructed to describe (in the
first part of the research instrument) the characteristics of the
political club and its environs, recording their observations on a
Guttman-scaled device (see Appendix A). They observed the condition, decor, and structure (type of building) of the clubhouse;
activities occurring both on an evening when a meeting was held
and on an evening when no meeting was held; and the location of the
clubhouse in the community. Part two of the research instrument
contained an interview schedule to be conducted with an officer of
the club (generally the president), including both open- and closed-
end questions. Topics covered in the interview included club
finances, activities, regulations and bylaws, size, composition,
history, and relations with affiliates and with the community.

Initially we identified approximately three hundred political
clubs in the five boroughs of New York City. Peel had looked at
suburban clubs as well, but we did not have the resources to do so.
Three of the four principal political parties of the city have active
political clubs: the Democratic, Republican, and Conservative.
The smallest of New York's parties, the Liberal party, has very
few clubs, and those that do exist appear to be connected with

9

dissent or insurgent factions within the party. Apparently it is a source of embarrassment to the Liberal party's leaders that there are so few organized clubs among enrolled members of what purports to be a liberal, democratic party. We made repeated attempts to get lists of Liberal clubs and leaders, but our efforts ended in frustration. Finally we received a list of "people who will give you information on the party." We never did get a list of the party's local leaders, by assembly district, or a list of clubhouses and meeting places. Liberal party control seems to rest in very few hands, and the absence of local political clubs ensures that no faction will arise to seriously challenge that control. The fears of the party's leaders are not groundless. Wherever we did find Liberal clubs—generally in the boroughs of Queens and Richmond—we also found a small but flourishing cadre of insurgent Liberals working against the central leadership of the party. Ironically, the more recently organized, and organizationally cautious, Conservative party opened up all of their clubhouses to us, and provided copies of bylaws, constitutions, and budgets. These were never forthcoming from the Liberals.

Since there is no regulation requiring clubs to register with a regulatory agency, or to be licensed, or even incorporated (although many of them eventually do incorporate because of their precarious financial condition), there is no single source from which to get complete lists of the clubs. In addition the county organizations of the respective parties maintain lists of only their regular clubs: those clubs that have elected district leaders. Therefore, to find about the remaining clubs, we employed a variety of resources, including telephone directories, lists of insurgent and reform coalitions, (such as the New Democratic Coalition (NDC), an alliance of reform-type clubs in New York City that, incidentally, have only the vaguest notion of where their constituent clubs are located, and who leads the clubs) and key political observers. Since clubs continually come and go, and since some small insurgent clubs carry on their business far from the view of well-informed observers and outside of any particular coalition or organization, it is possible that several clubs exist in each of the parties that we did not identify. Thus a total of 268 clubs were covered by our study, through interviews and on-the-spot observation.

Thirty-one clubs contained in our lists turned out to be phantom clubs that are either one-man operations, simply an office with a name on the door, or a listed telephone which no one ever answers. Lewis Bowman and G. R. Boynton had a similar experience in a study of partisan activity in North Carolina, in one community they found "no trace of several persons who were listed officially as (party) chairmen; the names seemed to be fictitious."[24] They provided no explanation for this strange phenomenon. We found it difficult to explain as well. An analysis of New York's phantom clubs shows that both the Republican and Democratic parties have them, and that there are reform, regular, and insurgent phantoms operating in several sections of the city. In several cases these mystery clubs may be set up for an intended future political activity. By maintaining an organization name, and the pretense of operating in a community, nonexistent clubs provide an incipient vehicle for future influence by those who control them. A few of them are akin to rotten boroughs, with their so-called officers given votes or voice in the party or faction councils, and trotted out as representatives of partisans in communities that the clubs purport to serve. Finally there are those clubs whose members have left the community, lost interest, or shifted allegiance. Possibly the club was founded and dominated by one ethnic group that never made the effort (or made the effort and failed) to absorb a newly arrived group in a transitional neighborhood. In either case a few hardy souls hold onto control of such clubs for old times' sake, or with the romantic hope that someday they will attract new members and once again assume the position of influence they previously held. Whatever the circumstance, we concluded that approximately 15 percent of all clubs supposedly operating in New York City do not actually operate.

We tried to be as faithful as possible to the original Peel work, because of our belief that too little replication is done in political science. In this, our discipline has suffered, due to the inevitable changes that time brings about. However, both the advantages of new technology and the changes that have occurred in the presentation of scholarly data have made this book different from Peel's. For one thing hindsight is often more effective than foresight—we asked certain questions, about who participates in club life, how members are chosen for the clubs, what written rules govern club business, etc., that Peel did not ask. Second, we capitalized on research skills developed since Peel did his study, including those of research design, instrument design, and guides to observation that make much of our data more precise than Peel's was. Third, the blessings of computer technology (and the attendant difficulties) have made it easier to gather material and compare data in a variety of categories than it was 40 years ago. Of course none of these advantages necessarily make our study more valuable than the Peel work.

Peel was an inside dopester par excellence who had all the assets and liabilities which that term implies. As noted previously, he had a good deal of informal access that we did not have. In addition he was able to collect the sort of information that people may provide to a close acquaintance, but never to an interviewer. He knew intuitively many things about the clubs, and his "verstehen" is a continuing source of data throughout his book. On the other hand he wrote frequently of what he knew rather than what he saw. He avoided counting whenever he could and often generalized about things for which he did not present a shred of evidence. He was opinionated in a way that only a man with regular contact with the good and the bad of a complex institution can be. Often he gave his readers his opinions rather than his understanding.

In the end Peel's work presents a reasonably clear picture of what the political clubs of New York City were like in the twenties and thirties. In addition it gives numerous testable hypotheses about why clubs were what they were and why they acted as they did. The columns of numbers that would neatly lie alongside those generated by our study are, for the most part, nonexistent. The comparison between things past and things present must be made on Peel's terms rather than our own—a usual occurrence—when you compare what you know with what your predecessors have given you.

If the picture that we have drawn of political clubs in 1974 is clearer in quantitative terms than Peel's was, it is probably more fuzzy in qualitative terms. The end result of extensive interviewing and observation of approximately one thousand clubs in 1927, and almost three hundred clubs in 1974, may simply serve to tell the reader more about this phenomenon of political organization. It may explain what clubs were then, what they are now, and how they have changed. Although we have tried to avoid casual explanations, the present study, viewed against the earlier work, may provide an understanding of why things are different. Beyond that the possibility for employing this understanding to effect positive change becomes both a challenge and a hope.

About the Book

In the chapters that follow we tried to parallel Peel's approach to political clubs. He was concerned chiefly with three areas: the position and scope of clubs, the activities of clubs, and their aims. Chapter 2 of our book deals with the history of New York City's political clubs. The clubs of New York date back to the American revolution, and these roots have had an impact on the clubs present form and activities. Chapter 3, titled "What is a Club?", describes the structure of clubs in terms of their formal organization, their bylaws and regulations, their day-to-day operations, and their place in the formal and informal networks of the city's political parties. Chapter 4 contains information relating to the membership of clubs that is not found in the Peel book. Peel foresaw that this void would raise problems for those observers interested in the role of clubs in the community. He provided the following suggestions, in a footnote to his concluding chapter, for those who would be inclined to pursue his inquiry further:

Membership of clubs:
(a) classification of grades and types of membership
(b) ratios of active to total club members; of elect members to party members (enrolled voters; supporters); of club members to total residents of district; of club members to total citizens qualified for membership
(c) participation of various grades and types of members and non-members in various types of activities
(d) reasons for affiliation with clubs [25]

To this we added information on the socioeconomic, racial, ethnic, and nationality characteristics of club members. We explored the means by which members are selected, the length of membership in various types of clubs, and the role that special groups play in clubs (such as officeholders, judges, patronage positionholders, community activists, etc.).

Chapter 5 describes the quarters that house the political clubs. Peel believed that locating clubs in a permanent physical setting contributed to their stability:

No association can exist without some means of effecting, intensifying, and guaranteeing unity. Unity is not an end in itself; it is a means to one or several ends. But it is vital, and hence religious organizations have temples, business associations have meeting places, and political clubs have quarters. In the absence of a regular place of meeting, there must be either a journal or some other regular method of communication, or a poll of members, or some common symbol of identity. [26]

Most of the political clubs we studied had permanent quarters in 1973. We explored these physical environments, describing their facilities and relating these to the activities of the clubs. Chapter 5 also describes the place of the political club in the community that it serves, in terms of its physical distance from important structures and centers of community activity.

Chapter 6, titled "Club Activities", compares the activities of clubs operating in 1974 with those of Peel's study. Social, political, communal, and service activities are both catalogued and described. Political clubs have adopted various styles of activity, ranging from intensely community-service-oriented clubs to those that concentrate on the social life of their own membership when they are not involved in political campaigning. Several theses relating to political styles and ideological orientations are explored, among parties and factions, and over time.

The finances of political clubs are discussed in Chapter 7. In view of the Watergate scandal and other evidences of dishonesty in political budgeting, the facts surrounding political funding take on added interest. Data is provided on club income and expenditures, and political budgeting is studied in clubs operating in a variety of settings and circumstances, including reform clubs that have close ties with established political figures, third party clubs, etc.

Chapter 8 adopts a theme popular in many earlier works on political organization, "Regulars and Reformers: Cycle or Stance." Clubs that exist outside of the regular county political organizations (the so-called machines) are viewed as a separate class. The causes of club defections and splintering are discussed as well as the agreements and disagreements, and the fractures and common purposes, that develop among reform clubs. Peel provided a wealth of information of insurgent groups of the twenties and thirties with which to compare current information.

By 1932 Peel had investigated 750 "nationality" clubs and 32 "racial" clubs in New York City and its environs. Identified by "name, traditions, language (sometimes) and leadership,"[27] these clubs were the unique outgrowth of the heterogeneity in New York that had been spurred by the city's growing immigrant population. New York is no less heterogeneous today than it was then, but the grandchildren of those immigrants now run the city's politics, and the purely ethnic clubs have all but disappeared. We identified and studied the ethnic activities that are a general part of club operations, and discussions of this and other aspects of ethnic influence in the clubs can be found throughout the book. However, we did not devote an entire chapter to the topic, as Peel did, because pure nationality clubs are not part of the mainstream of club politics, but rather museum pieces of a bygone era in New York City's party affairs.

We have avoided dealing with minor parties and what Peel termed "quasi-political associations." The latter category included such disparate groups as the Original Hound Guards of Greenwich Village, the Jewish Theatrical Guild, and the Grand Street Boys. Almost without exception New York City's minor (as opposed to third) parties no longer have enough members to support political clubs. The few minor clubs that exist are secretive, occasionally clandestine, and generally not engaged in political operations as they once were. The quasi-political groups may still exist, but it would take researchers with the intimate knowledge and access that Peel had to discern them. We did not make such an effort, because we suspect that almost all community-based civic, social, and service organizations fall into the quasi-political category at one time or another. If we use Peel's definition that they "hover on the edge of politics, or . . . participate more actively and effectively in the political process than do the regular political organizations,"[28] they undoubtedly would number in the thousands. This staggers the imagination, and our limited resources as well.

Notes

1. Eugene Lewis, The Urban Political System (Hinsdale, Ill: The Dryden Press, 1973), p. 65.
2. Sorauf, Party and Politics in America, (Boston: Little, Brown, 1968) p. 107.
3. Committee on Political Parties of the American Political Science Association, Toward A More Responsible Two-Party System (New York: Rinehart, 1950).
4. Roy V. Peel, The Political Clubs of New York, (ed. rev. New York: Ira S. Friedman, 1968), p. 22.
5. Theodore Lowi, "Machine Politics: Old and New," The Public Interest No. 9 (Fall 1967).
6. Leon D. Epstein, Politics in Wisconsin (Madison: University of Wisconsin Press, 1958).
7. Sorauf, op. cit., p. 73.
8. Peel, op. cit., pp. 61-62.
9. Joseph Schlesinger, "Political Party Organization," in James G. March, Handbook of Organizations (Chicago: Rand McNally, 1965), p. 764.
10. Dayton McKean, The Boss: The Hague Machine in Action (Boston: Houghton, Mifflin, 1940); J. T. Salter, Boss Rule: Portraits In City Politics (New York: McGraw-Hill, 1935); M. R. Werner, Tammany Hall (New York: Doubleday, 1928).

11. Sonya Forthal, Cogwheels of Democracy: A Study of the Precinct Captain (New York: William Fredrick Press, 1946); Harvey Wheeler, "Yesterday's Robin Hood: The Rise and Fall of Baltimore's Trenton Democratic Club," American Quarterly (Winter 1957); William Bennett Munroe, Personality in Politics: Reforms, Bosses and Leaders: What They Do and How They Do It (New York; Macmillan, 1924); Samuel P. Orth, The Boss and the Machine (New Haven: Yale University Press, 1919); Paul Bartholomew, Profile of a Precinct Committeeman (Dobbs Ferry, N.Y.: Oceana Publications, 1968); Harold Gosnell, Machine Politics: Chicago Model (Chicago: University of Chicago Press, 1937); Frank R. Kent, The Great Game of Politics (New York: Doubleday, 1923); Gustavus Myers, The History of Tammany Hall (New York: Boni and Liveright, 1917); William E. Mosher, "Party and Government Control at the Grass Roots," National Municipal Review, No. 24 (January 1935).

12. Robert H. Salisbury, "The Urban Party Organization Member," Public Opinion Quarterly, No. 29 (Winter 1965): 551.

13. David Gutmann, "Bigtown Politics: Grass Roots Level: The Precinct Captain Gets Out the Vote," Commentary, No. 17 (February 1954); Lewis Bowman and G. T. Boynton, "Recruitment Patterns Among Local Party Officials: A Model and Some Preliminary Findings in Selected Locales," American Political Science Review, No. 6 (September 1966); Richard T. Frost, "Stability and Change in Local Politics," Public Opinion Quarterly, No. 25 (1961); William J. Keefe and William C. Seyler, "Precinct Politicians in Pittsburgh," Social Science, No. 35 (1960); Gerald Pomper, "New Jersey County Chairmen," Western Political Quarterly, No. 18 (March 1965); Salisbury, "The Urban Party Organization Member," Public Opinion Quarterly (1963); Thomas A. Flinn and Fred Wirt, "Local Party Leaders: Groups of Like-Minded Men," Midwest Journal of Political Science, No. 9 (February 1965); Blanche D. Blank, Robert S. Hirschfield and Bert Swanson, "A Profile of Political Activity in Manhattan," Western Political Quarterly, September 1962; M. Margaret Conway and Frank Feigert, "Motivation, Incentive Systems, and the Political Party Organization," American Political Science Review, December 1968; Peter H. Rossi and Phillips Cutright, "Party Organization in Primary Election," American Journal of Sociology, No. 64 (November 1968); Rossi and Cutright, "Grass Roots Politicians and the Vote," American Sociological Review, No. 23 (April 1958).

14. Samuel Eldersveld, Political Parties: A Behavioral Analysis (Chicago; Rand McNally, 1964).

15. Harold Lasswell and Abraham Kaplan, Power and Society (New Haven: Yale University Press, 1950), quoted in Heinz Eulau

and Kenneth Prewitt, Labyrinths of Democracy: Adaptations, Linkages, Representation and Policies in Urban Politics (Indianapolis: Bobbs-Merrill, 1973) pp. 48-49.

16. Ibid.

17. Sorauf, op. cit. p. 82.

18. Eulau and Prewitt, op. cit. p. 49.

19. V. O. Key, Jr., Politics, Parties and Pressure Groups, 5th. ed. (New York: Thomas Y. Crowell, 1964), p. 314.

20. Ibid., pp. 314-15.

21. Lee F. Anderson, "Organizational Theory and the Study of State and Local Parties," in William J. Crotty, ed., Approaches to the Study of Party Organization (Boston: Allyn and Bacon, 1968).

22. Ibid., p. 385.

23. James Q. Wilson, The Amateur Democrat (Chicago: University of Chicago Press, 1962).

24. Bowman and Boynton, op. cit., p. 125.

25. Peel, op. cit. p. 325.

26. Ibid., p. 15.

27. Ibid., p. 251.

28. Ibid., p. 306.

2

THE EVOLUTION
OF THE CLUB:
FROM PEEL TO
THE PRESENT

Roy Peel began his study of the organization and operations of New York City's political clubs at a time when they had passed their zenith. Between that time, in the late 1920s and the 1970s, the clubs moved from a position of primacy in the city's politics and influence to a peripheral position in city affairs. The proliferation of clubs that Peel interpreted as a sign of organizational health was instead an indication of the sickness of the body politic. It was as if the city's parties, having been invaded by some pestilence, had generated greater and greater numbers of antibodies. The end result was that the patient survived the sickness, but nearly died from the cure.

Beginning on the afternoon of April 25, 1924, when Charles Francis Murphy died peacefully in his bed, the clubs moved inexorably out of the magic circle of prosperity that they had occupied for more than fifty years. Murphy was called the "Grand Sachem" of Tammany Hall, the leader of the New York County (Manhattan) Democratic party, and the last political boss who had citywide influence and almost total control of his organization. His death created chaos in his own borough, and its shock waves were felt throughout the city. Half a dozen so-called leaders followed Murphy as the Manhattan Democratic chief, and none of them could fill his shoes. Insurgents, seeing their opportunity, created hundreds of spin-off, revolt, and independent, clubs. There was no one able to discipline these clubs, to deal with their demands, and to bring pressure upon their leaders to cease the destructive warfare that was making a shambles of a well-oiled political machine. The cooperation among the city's Democratic county leaders, which Murphy had wrested from them by will and wile, dissolved. "Edward J. Flynn, the Bronx leader, and John H. McCooey, the Brooklyn chief, were not prepared to take orders from the likes of George W. Olvany, who now assumed the reigns of

18

Tammany."[1] To whatever extent the Democrats had acted in concert prior to 1924, there now existed a splintering that was to have a lasting effect on clubs and their leaders throughout the five boroughs.

Three years after the death of Murphy came the imprisonment in 1927 of Queens County Democratic leader Maurice Connolly. In a borough where loyalties to towns and villages had made any political organization a shaky business at best, the Connolly machine had maintained a temporary peace for almost a decade. His abrupt departure brought about the collapse of the Queens County Democratic party. The vacuum was filled by reform Borough President George U. Harvey of Queens. "Non-partisan Harvey Clubs were formed from north shore to south shore, and the papier-mache crusader was swept into office."[2] Scores of political clubs were piled upon the multitude that already existed (frequently under the guise of civic or self-help associations) in the fractious borough of Queens.

> At one time it was estimated that there were more
> civic associations in Queens than speakeasies in
> Manhattan, and that may have been so; certainly
> there were more than a statistician could keep
> track of or in mind. Every petty rising politi-
> cian joined a civic association or formed his own
> to get his name in print. It was easy enough. A
> few reams of printed stationery and a fancy name
> such as "the 158th Place Taxpayers Group" em-
> powered the politician to pass whereas resolutions
> every Wednesday night.[3]

The tradition in Queens was never one of organization, but rather of revolt. Connolly's death exacerbated that situation.

Until 1932 Brooklyn had maintained a stable party system among its Democratic clubs. That stability had been achieved by Brooklyn Democratic leader, John H. McCooey, who single-handedly ran the entire borough. There were 60 regular Democratic clubs[4] that were franchised by the Brooklyn boss to run their districts, collect whatever they could in the way of graft and protection money, and deal with the local populace. Revolt was uncommon, if not rare, and whatever patronage was available was divided fairly among clubs and leaders. As was the case in the other boroughs:

> Nothing was too big and nothing too small for the
> district leaders and wardheelers . . . . Politicians
> in the upper stratum of power took their cut on such
> ambitious projects as the leasing of piers, the pur-
> chase of real estate, . . . the granting of franchises;

it was almost impossible to engage in private business
without in some manner rendering unto Caesar the
things that weren't Caesar's. Appointments and
nominations to the bench were often bought and sold,
the quoted prices running from $10,000 . . . up to
$100,000.[5]

Everything was going well for the Brookly Democratic clubs
until (in 1932) McCooey erred seriously. Witholding his Brooklyn
delegation's support for the Democratic presidential nomination
of Franklin D. Roosevelt until the last minute, he found himself
ignored by the party after the national elections. Despite the 320,000
vote plurality that Brooklyn gave to the Democratic national ticket,
McCooey did not obtain a single federal patronage appointment during
his remaining days as county leader. At his death his once prominent
organization of powerful Brooklyn clubs was besieged by insurgency
and revolt.

Only in the Bronx, where Edward Flynn was the leader, did
the clubs withstand the ravages of political disorder that marked the
decade beginning in 1924; the clubs in the Bronx flourished under the
benign dictatorship of the shrewd Flynn. Flynn's clubs were similar
to McCooey's in that they controlled the county. And unlike McCooey,
Flynn knew a winner when he saw one, and immediately supported
Roosevelt. As a result of his support he became the source for most
of the federal patronage in the city after 1932, sharing these duties
with Eddy Ahearn, a lower Manhattan district leader and a Roosevelt
agent. It is thus understandable that Peel found fewer clubs in the
Bronx than in the other boroughs, and that the Bronx clubs were powerful political monopolies that tolerated no rebellion and allowed
little opposition.

As to the Republican clubs of this period, in most of the city
their existence was a gesture of futility, and their survival a testi-
mony to the power of patronage to sustain a second party in a one-party
town. Republican clubs of the twenties and thirties left few records.
They spawned no intraparty battles, stimulated few reform or splinter
groups, and limited their activities to social and charitable events
and the unenviable noncontests that served to populate their ranks with
the largest array of losers ever to be assembled in any long-standing
political organization. They suffered the fate of all permanent losers:
that of being a corporal's guard, and never being considered either as
an imitator or an insurgent. After the Roosevelt victory the Republican clubs dwindled in number and strength even further than before,
and only a few sturdy groups remained scattered throughout the city.

The Great Depression fell upon the nation two years after Peel
began his study. The depression left an imprint on political clubs

that lasted for several years; and it is not clear from reading Peel whether he understood that a large part of what he saw and wrote of the clubs was a direct response to the depression. The proliferation of clubs that took place was a product of the breakup of three powerful political machines; it was also a product of the lean times, as men turned in desperation to political warfare and to political associations aimed at redressing their harsh circumstances. Socialist clubs mushroomed in response to the calamity brought about by a capitalist order, as did Communist, Socialist Labor, and Fascist groups. Everwhere the clubs took on additional responsibilities as charitable societies. Peel called the clubs' welfare activities the "best known of all the functions of political clubs."[6] Many groups that came together to relieve poverty and provide mutual assistance were soon turned into political clubs by leaders who saw an opportunity to cash in on both the availability of an organization and the gratitude of those people they had helped. In other cases veteran politicians exploited such groups, luring them into political activity with the frequently false promises of jobs, influence, and money. Few sections of the city were secure enough to resist such machinations, and the number of clubs grew as the impact of the depression was felt increasingly in the city.

Roosevelt's victory and the influence of the depression, combined with the weakening of the county political organizations, led to the election of a reform mayor—Fiorello LaGuardia—in New York in 1934. It was LaGuardia who called the denizens of the clubhouses "bums" and "clubhouse loafers"[7] and who administered the final blow to the faltering clubhouses and their leaders. Within a decade of his victory LaGuardia saw the Society of St. Tammany (or Columbian Order of New York City) hold its last meeting in its ornate clubhouses at 17th Street and Union Square, a victim of financial bankruptcy. "During the first LaGuardia term alone, membership in Tammany clubs dropped seventy percent. With no jobs in the patronage pipeline, there was little incentive to contribute to the organization."[8] In the second year of his incumbency LaGuardia could read with relish of the ouster of John Curry as leader of Tammany—the first time in the history of that organization that "a Chief had been scalped by his own braves."[9] And by 1943, every city magistrate in New York had been appointed by a fusion mayor (LaGuardia) rather than by a Democratic mayor.[10]

The Democrats came upon hard days, with City Hall all but eliminated as a source of patronage, and with the Federal government providing funds for the Bronx clubs and a few Manhattan clubs. Any hope of renewed jobs and favors was crushed by the passage in 1940 of the Hatch Act, which prohibited federal employees from holding political positions or contributing to political organizations. When

District Attorney Thomas E. Dewey was elected governor of New York State, and held that office throughout the forties, the last vestige of income was shut off from the majority of Democratic clubs.

Into this gap stepped several powerful gangsters, whose funds made up, in part, for those funds lost by the local party officials, and whose muscle enforced their decisions with frightening finality. From the day in 1931 when two of Lucky Luciano's gunmen visited the old Tweed courthouse behind City Hall to inform City Clerk and Democratic District Leader Harry Perry that he was to step aside so that Albert Marinelli could take control of the party leadership in the area around Manhattan's Mott Street, Tammany and the Brooklyn organization were not free of mob influence for more than two decades.[11] Frank Costello, the gang leader identified as a kingpin of crime in New York City, became Tammany's financial angel. This position helped him to dictate the selection of prospective Tammany chieftains, beginning with Congressman Michael Kennedy, who defeated Sheriff Dan Finn, Jr. in the race for county leader in 1942,[12] and carrying through the successive leaderships of Edward V. Loughlin, Frank Sampson, Hugo Rogers, and, some observers say, Carmine DeSapio.[13]

It was not a case of criminals and political clubs being unknown to one another at other times. Luciano and James J. Hines, Harlem's Democratic boss, had been in connivance since the mid-twenties in the area north of Central Park. In addition small-time hoodlums had infiltrated clubs, or established their own, for many years. The period from the early thirties through the mid-fifties, however, saw the advent of powerful mobs in the city and the complete domination of the Democratic party by these mobs in at least two counties (New York and Kings). The late forties were called "the era of the dirtiest politics of Tammany's long, sullied history."[14] One observer estimated that by the end of the forties, "nearly one-half of Tammany's clubs were controlled by the rackets."[15] In Brooklyn the notorious mobster Joe Adonis held a life-and-death grip on both the Democratic and Republican parties.

Alliances between criminals and politicians crossed party and factional lines. Even the leftist American Labor party congressman from East Harlem, Vito Marcantonio, resisted pressure from other parties because of his relationship with Thomas Luchese, known to the crime community as Three Finger Brown. It was the Marcantonio-Luchese alliance that led, according to Warren Moscow, to the placing of Vincent Impellitteri on the citywide ticket by Mayor William O'Dwyer in 1949.[16] It is not clear as to what extent criminal elements were involved in the clubs in Queens and the Bronx, but informants have indicated that these boroughs were not completely free of such involvement.

22

The number of clubs ebbed and flowed throughout the 1930s and 1940s, with World War II eclipsing the Depression, and the battles over who should occupy City Hall and the five borough halls forcing the creation or demise of certain clubs. In 1946, one year after regaining the mayoralty for the Democrats, after a twelve-year famine, O'Dwyer took on the county Democratic leaders, ousted Loughlin, Clarence Neal, and Bert Stand from their positions of power in Tammany, and began building strength through his own clubs and followers. This led to an increase in the overall number of clubs, but also to the death of a few clubs, and to some changes in who controlled the destiny of the clubs.

Midway in his second term as mayor O'Dwyer resigned, on the heels of a City Hall scandal, and became U.S. Ambassador to Mexico. He was replaced by Vincent Impellitteri; and subsequently a special election brought the new acting mayor into conflict with some of the city's most powerful Democrats. Impellitteri won the election, and he made Frank Sampson, a veteran DeSapio opponent, his patronage secretary, and forced further changes in the number and composition of Bronx, Manhattan, and Brooklyn clubs. [17] By the end of the forties the only peace and tranquility that existed anywhere in the city was found in the outer-borough Republican clubs, where state patronage, perennial defeat, and seasoned leadership all contributed to a placid cadre of nonargumentative party members.

Out of the tumultuous forties came an unhappy generation of "wealthy young men and women, who had time as well as money" [18] to devote to the formation of a political club of their own in the posh Silk Stocking District of Manhattan's East Side. In 1949 these liberal and concerned Democrats established the Lexington Democratic Club, which became the seedbed of what was to be a flourishing reform movement within the Democratic party. Disgusted with the criminally-tainted traditional Democratic clubs, these reform Democrats competed against the regular Grover Cleveland Club in their area, and eventually won out. They took their example from the short-lived Fair Deal Democrats, who had helped to elect Franklin D. Roosevelt, Jr. to Congress against the wishes of the local party organization. The influence of the Lexington Democratic Club, their financial largesse, and their simple message that politics could be fun served to nurture new clubs throughout Manhattan. Among these clubs the Village Independent Democrats stood out on the strength of their militancy and commitment. The VID, as it was called, followed the pattern of many of the new clubs, drawing its initial membership from "energetic groups of young Democrats, largely middle-class, who were active in Citizens for Stevenson," [19] in 1952 and 1956, and who became disenchanted with the lack of support given their favorite by the established clubs of the period.

As the reform movement spread, first in Manhattan, and later in the Bronx and Brooklyn, dozens of new clubs were spawned. They fostered hundreds of primary contests, many under the sponsorship of Senator Herbert Lehman, Mrs. Eleanor Roosevelt, and former U.S. Secretary of the Air Force Thomas K. Finletter. By 1960 they had organized themselves into the Committee for Democratic Voters (CDV), and had developed 18 affiliated clubs with a claimed membership of nine thousand. Four years later the CDV reported a total of 47 clubs with almost eighteen thousand members. In addition several dozen other clubs were in the process of becoming affiliated with, or being organized around, the reform banner.[20]

The sudden success of reform politics was spurred by Mayor Robert F. Wagner, who disassociated himself from his former allies in the county Democratic organizations during his 1961 bid for a third term, and embraced the fledgling reform movement, supporting its candidates and adopting portions of its program. However, the alliance was short-lived and stormy. By November 1962, the eight Bronx reform clubs had broken off relations with the mayor's Bronx Reorganizing Committee;[21] in Manhattan the mayor and the reformers were having similar difficulties. However, the Wagner-CDV alliance spawned a Brooklyn reform movement that led to the elction of Thomas R. Jones as the first black district leader in the Bedford Stuyvesant section, and to the creation of several new clubs.[22] In the November, 1962 primaries the reform clubs generated 68 primary fights for public office, as well as "thousands of contests for election of party officials—posts that normally go to the organization men by default."[23] From 1962 until the seventies reformers continued to organize and expand in numbers and influence, culminating in their key participation in the two mayoral victories of John V. Lindsay in 1965 and 1969.

By the time the seventies had dawned the political clubs of New York had seen many changes. The once renowned Tammany Hall had gone completely out of business during the short leadership tenure of Edward Costikyan in the mid-sixties, and it was to be known henceforth only by its legal name, the New York County Democratic Committee. Lindsay, the city's second reform mayor, was to occupy City Hall for two terms, spawning a new group of political clubs that were called John V. Lindsay Associations. Despite the energies of the new Democratic reformers, or perhaps partly because of them, the aggregate total of clubs had dwindled to a fourth of the number that had been counted by Peel. A new political party, with clubs in all five boroughs, was created out of the conservative unrest in the Republican party, gaining legal recognition as the Conservative party after polling 121,000 votes in the 1962 gubernatorial election.[24]

It is hard to believe that the clubs of New York City had not developed until around 1890. Their rapid development in the respective districts was centered around saloons and gambling houses, and later, after passage of the 18th Amendment to the United States Constitution, took place within the walls of private clubhouses. These clubs represented the city's first effort at political decentralization. The rise of the clubs, their popular acceptance, and their ubiquitous nature were evidence of their importance to all classes of constituents in all types of communities. Their character rapidly evolved from social and fraternal societies, such as the Whig clubs and the St. Tammany societies, to the political associations and charitable leagues that they had become by the time Peel studied them. They hit hard times as they followed their natural inclinations toward gaining further independence from county leaders, after the restraint of strong leadership had been lifted. In so doing they multiplied in number, but suffered a decline in their influence, resources, followers, and discipline. In the end they were fair game for the political vultures that habitually prey on groups that are weak and vulnerable to exploitation; and the clubs generally succumbed.

However, the establishment of CDV, the Conservative party, and the John V. Lindsay Associations provided new evidence that the clubs had not outlived their usefulness. The club activities, programs, and purposes that we shall describe in the following chapters respond to needs that are as contemporary as the most recent election or as historical as the first club-type organization in America. The colonial caucuses of the early eighteenth century practiced politics in a way that is not much different from practices employed by the clubs of the nineteenth and twentieth centuries:

> Mr. Samuel Adam's father and twenty others, one or two
> from the north end of town, where all the ship business
> is carried on, used to meet, make a caucus, and lay
> their plans for introducing certain person into places
> of trust and power. When they had settled it, they
> separated, and each used their particular influence
> within his own circle. He and his friends would
> furnish themselves with ballots, including the names
> of the parties fixed upon, which they distributed on
> the day of election. By acting in concert together
> with a careful and extensive distribution of ballots
> they generally carried the elections to their own mind. [25]

With the addition of certain amenities, along with the questionable benefit of modern technology, that is precisely what political clubs did when Peel studied them, and that is what they do today.

Notes

1. Louis Eisenstein and Elliot Rosenberg, A Stripe of Tammany's Tiger (New York: Robert Speller and Sons, 1966), 43.

2. Milton Mackaye, The Tin Box Parade (New York: Robert M. McBride and Company, 1934), 180.

3. Ibid., 165.

4. Roy V. Peel, The Political Clubs of New York, rev. ed. (New York: Ira S. Friedman, 1968), 42.

5. Mackaye, op. cit., 26.

6. Peel, op. cit., 205.

7. Eisenstein and Rosenberg, op. cit., 103.

8. Alfred Connable and Edward Silberfarb, Tigers of Tammany (New York: Holt, Rinehart and Winston, 1967), 292.

9. Ibid., 286.

10. Warren Moscow, The Last of the Big Time Bosses: The Life and Times of Carmine DeSapio and the Decline and Fall of Tammany Hall (New York: Stein and Day, 1971), 50.

11. Ibid.

12. Eisenstein and Rosenberg, op. cit., 147.

13. Moscow op. cit., 56; George Wolf and Joseph DiMona, Frank Costello: Prime Minister of the Underworld (New York: Wm. Morrow Co., 1974).

14. Moscow, op. cit., 65.

15. Connable and Silberfarb op. cit., 309.

16. Moscow, op. cit., 63.

17. Connable and Silberfarb, op. cit., 318.

18. Moscow, op. cit., 136.

19. Connable and Silberfarb op. cit., 330.

20. 1964 Report of the Executive Director: New York Committee for Democratic Voters.

21. New York Post, Nov. 29, 1962.

22. New York World Telegram and Sun, Sept. 7, 1962.

23. New York Herald Tribune, Sept. 7, 1962

24. New York World Telegram and Sun, Nov. 29, 1962.

25. Samuel Orth, The Boss and the Machine (New Haven: Yale University Press, 1919), 20.

3

Political clubs have much in common with garden clubs and private clubs, and less in common with fan clubs and book clubs. All clubs are voluntary associations of individuals who have mutual interests or characteristics. Some clubs are self-governing, a characteristic seldom found in book or fan clubs. In addition clubs provide some opportunity for face-to-face relationships. That usually dictates that members live near each other, and that there not be so many members as to render it impossible to provide a setting for their personal interaction.

In many ways the political club is a phenomenon of urban settings—an observation made by Peel in 1931, and still accurate today. [1] It is hard to conceive of any club in a rural setting, unless such a club is marked by a discontinuity in its membership's inter-action, and by an absence of any but the most difficult circumstances for face-to-face meetings. Peel described the political club as a unit-cell in a larger political organization, designed with a political purpose, and territorial in nature. He noted: "It is a neighborhood unit, it generally has quarters, either owned or leased, it is more or less permanent in character and it serves a fairly definite number of interests."[2] Edward Costikyan, the one-time leader of the New York County Democratic Executive Committee (previously called Tammany Hall), described the New York political club as follows:

> Every local political leader in an urban area must have
> a permanent headquarters to which supporters and
> suppliants alike may go to see him. In New York
> county, there are in normal circumstances thirty-
> three such local headquarters. They are the regular
> Democratic clubs of their respective areas. Each

club pays for its own rent, telephone bills, mailing, insurance, typewriters, addressograph and adressograph plates. It must pay for whatever social events it sponsors, and for its own charities. The hardest organization in the world to manage and lead is such a volunteer organization. Neither its executives or envelope stuffers are paid. [3]

Costikyan's description notwithstanding, political clubs are not limited to serving the needs of district leaders. The clubs come in all shapes, sizes, ideological stances, partisan affiliations, and purposes. However, there are several characteristics that all clubs share in common:

Political clubs are voluntary organizations. That is, people join them because they want to, and remain in them only so long as they want to. This creates certain problems for the officers, as Costikyan indicated. The chief problem is that voluntarism and the requirements of professional political activity do not necessarily go together. If anything, the clubs are more of an expression of genuine voluntary association today than they were when Peel studied them. This is due to the present lack of widespread patronage opportunities that existed in earlier times. Members of clubs once felt it mandatory to join, and impossible to quit without losing their jobs. Today that feeling is less in evidence, and a member's commitment probably is measured more in terms of potential, rather than actual, reward.

Political clubs in neighborhood organizations. The compactness of urban life facilitates the establishment of clubs whose membership is drawn from a single community, or from contiguous communities where members live or work. Members usually walk to their meetings, or go by public transportation or car in trips that take five to ten minutes. Because most New York City neighborhoods are relatively homogeneous in ethnic and racial terms, this leads to homogeneity in club membership as well.

Political clubs are partisan political organizations. Each club is identified with a political party, and usually includes the party name in its own (the New Democratic Club, the Patrick Henry Conservative Club). Where the clubs represent factional interests as well, those are also often a part of the club name (the Bronx-Pelham Reform Democratic Club, the Independent Democrats of Flatbush). Peel observed that "it is for the purpose of recruiting a stable personnel in the interests of the party organization that political clubs are formed."[4] While that did not appear to be altogether true in 1973, there is no doubt that politics is the primary business of political clubs, and that the provision of manpower for political activities is their chief contribution to party organizations. New York City clubs do not occupy a unique position in terms of their purpose, for Currin V. Shields noted that in California "the purpose of a local party club is to promote the election of Democratic candidates for public office."[5] However, the use of clubs as a source of manpower for political activities is not commonplace among most state and local parties in the United States.

Political clubs are nonofficial unit-cells of parties and party factions. As we noted earlier, the clubs are neither recognized for purposes of election law, nor are they the institution that represents the political party in the local district, the state, or the nation. Moreover, where any New York City political party is in operation in the local community, it is rarely by virtue of its formal committee structures (election district members of the county committees, county executive committee members, members of the state committee, or national committeemen), but rather through the activities of the local club. And, it is frequently the clubs that recruit candidates for whatever party positions the law provides; these candidates usually emerge from the membership ranks of the club.

Political clubs are a physical entity in their communities. While there has been a tendency in recent years to view political parties simply in functional terms, the political club in New York is a physical entity in the community. This in some ways fulfills Schlesinger's concept of a party nucleus. The club is the building block on which the complex organization of city party politics is constructed. However, Schlesinger sees the party nucleus exclusively in terms of activity. "A nucleus may be a very simple array of activities involving only a candidate and a few supporters, or it may be multiple activities involved in an assault on the presidency."[6] The political club is comprised of workers that usually operate throughout the year from a clubroom or clubhouse, or meet regularly in a school, a house of worship, or a community center, and rent campaign headquarters for each election. Chairs, tables, flags, pictures, signs, and other relatively permanent trappings are part of the club. Housekeeping duties, the obligation to pay rent, upkeep, insurance and electricity and telephone bills, and the responsibility of opening the club facility, closing it, and manning it, influence the nature of the club, what it does, and how it is perceived by its constituents, neighbors, partisans, and members. Also, along with a club headquarters comes a sense of the need for formal organization, house rules, a constitution, bylaws, the necessity for regular meetings, a format for handling visitors (and encouraging visitors), and a relatively elaborate division of labor that has little or nothing to do with the manifest political role of the club.

While all political clubs show the attributes listed above, there are other characteristics that many, if not all, clubs have in common. Political clubs (1) hold meetings on a regular basis throughout the year; (2) provide opportunities for social activity for their members; (3) provide a wide range of services to the local community that include: housing "clinics" to which apartment dwellers in rent-controlled or rent-stabilized buildings come for advice in dealing with their landlords or with the city's enormous rent-control bureaucracy; free legal advice from younger lawyers in the club; assistance in dealing with such other bureaucracies as social security, welfare, and the New York City Housing Authority; and counseling on school problems, domestic relations, and a host of other personal difficulties that constituents face, and (4) work for the election of public and party officials, especially at the state assembly-district level.

The importance of the social factor in the survival and success of the clubs is not entirely clear. Peel noted that "although the political motive is the controlling primary factor in club organization, the social motive is never absent."[7] The desire for a convenient place to attend social functions or meet with neighbors has traditionally motivated people to join the clubs. In 1919 Samuel P. Orth observed "in every assembly district there are headquarters and a clubhouse, where the voters can go in the evening and enjoy a smoke, a bottle, and a more or less quiet game."[8] Endorsing this view of the club, Stephen A. Mitchell noted: ". . . the political club of earlier days was not merely a place where public favors were privately dispensed. It was also a place where people met and heard the news about the neighborhood and politics. It was from this headquarters that neighbors received invitations to friendly social affairs, and political events. . . ."[9] While studying two political clubs in Manhattan's Greenwich Village, Vernon Goetcheus was told by a leader of one of the clubs, the Tamawa Democratic Club, that members come to the club "mainly for social reasons. They are not the type to play bridge once a week, but the ladies for instance just like to get together and talk while licking envelopes. They like to get known in the community. . . . They are organization-minded people."[10] These observations appear to be consistent with our knowledge of what motivates or attracts political activists nationwide, whether they are in political clubs or not. "At a general level, almost all of the reported research on the motivations of party activists find that large numbers of them reply that they 'like people' or that they 'like politics.'"[11]

It is doubtful whether the social motivation is enough to keep a club alive if other specifically political incentives are withdrawn. What brings club members together initially is the desire to interact in a political context, rather than in a fraternal or recreational context. If political clubs multiply the incentives to participate by adding other activities, so as to monopolize the time and attention of their members, this does not obviate the central political motives for affiliation in most people. In his discussion of reform Democratic clubs in New York in the early sixties, James Q. Wilson noted, ". . .

if the clubs should cease to define themselves as organizations devoted to liberalism or reformism or similar worthy causes, they could
not for long sustain the interest of any but the handful who simply
enjoy the company of others or like being district leader."[12] This,
Wilson noted, despite the fact that "in the new style political clubs the
attractiveness of the social life and friendship circles is explicit."[13]

With regard to the appropriate function of the local political
organization, Schlesinger suggested that "the basic unit of party
organization is the collective effort devoted to the capture of a single
public office."[14] As noted above, he termed this unit a nucleus.
He added, "For a true nucleus to exist, there must be the expectation
that at some time, if not in the immediate future, organizational
activity will lead to the capture of the nuclear office."[15] Since he
does not expand on what that would involve, we can assume that the
nucleus performs sufficient service if it survives just so long as it
is needed for its single task, and no longer. Peel disagreed:

> Although in a democratic commonwealth it is usually
> believed that political activity signifies campaign and
> electoral activity, very few clubs organize for pur-
> poses solely concerned with voting at the general
> elections. Such clubs as organize for these purposes
> are classified by the regular club members as 'fly
> by night' or 'mushroom' organizations.[16]

In Peel's view such clubs as those organized by James A.
Farley under the general rubric of the "Good Neighborhood League"
for the purposes of the 1932 and 1936 presidential campaigns,[17]
after which they faded into oblivion, were considered "mushrooms."
Schlesinger would consider them "nuclei." On the other hand,
Republican clubs that survive in the West Bronx's solid Democratic
neighborhoods year after year, keeping their doors open to constituents and participating in elections which they cannot hope to win,
would not count for Schlesinger, but would have served functions
for Peel.

We are inclined to side with Peel in this disagreement.
Furthermore, there are political clubs that do very little campaigning
for candidates running for public office, choosing instead to concentrate on the factional battles within their party. Such clubs sponsor
candidates for district leader, state committeeman, and county
committeeman, virtually ignoring legislative and administrative
contests. Usually they choose this course because they cannot
muster the resources to compete for office in expensive races,
but are able to expend the modest sums necessary to win a district
leader's contest. While it is difficult to get reliable figures on the

31

cost of running for public office, it is virtually impossible to get such figures for party positions. Informants indicate that for districts of comparable size candidates for assemblyman or district leader, for example, spend anywhere from five to ten times the amount that party office candidates spend. One reason for this may be that party positions are nonsalaried, and another, that they are less prestigious in most districts.

Number and Distribution of Clubs

The universe that Peel covered from 1927 to 1933 included 1,177 individual clubs within New York City's boundaries, as well as a number of suburban groups. He attempted also to examine a collection of clubs that he termed "quasi-political" (see Chapter 1). Thus his overall total was 2,819 clubs in the entire New York City metropolitan area. Of these he claimed to have observed (through his aides) some twelve hundred different clubs. His city universe included 354 Republican clubs, 703 Democratic clubs, and other clubs.

By 1972 these numbers had dwindled substantially: New York City had approximately three hundred political clubs among its parties, although our researchers were able to identify only 268 of these as active, continually functioning organizations. We estimated the aggregate membership of the clubs at some 112,000, although not all of these were dues-paying members. Peel made no attempt to estimate the total membership of clubs. In our study 62 percent of the clubs called themselves Democratic clubs, 26 percent Republican, and 10 percent Conservative; the remaining 2 percent were clubs associated with the Liberal party, the John V. Lindsay Associations, the assorted minor parties, including the Black Panthers, the Progressive Labor party, and independent groups. Communist, Socialist, and Socialist Labor party clubs, important at the time of Peel's study, are no longer visible in New York. Where these groups do exist they are small groups that meet in the homes of members, are usually marked by a membership of advanced age, and are no longer actively engaged in electoral activity or community service.

As Costikyan noted, "by 1965, the Liberal Party no longer had district clubs, district leaders, or election district captains in most parts of New York City."[18] The John V. Lindsay Associations, usually numbering one in each borough, performed political functions on behalf of Mayor Lindsay. Most of their members were former Republicans who transferred their enrollment to the Democratic party when the Mayor became a Democrat.

The geographic distribution of the clubs is interesting for two reasons: (1) it does not entirely follow the population trends of the five boroughs, and (2) by and large the parties have maintained roughly similar distributions both in each borough and citywide. The reason for the former is not entirely clear, but the latter is caused, no doubt, by the continuing dominance of the Democratic party in city politics. The result is that whatever political competition occurs in New York City generally occurs within the Democratic primary, rather than among parties in the general election. Democratic clubs representing a variety of factions and interests have arisen to participate in primary contests, while other parties' clubs have atrophied from a lack of opportunity to seriously contest for public office in many sections of the city.

Brooklyn was the most populous borough in the city in 1972, just as it was in 1932. Yet in terms of its ranking in number of clubs, Brooklyn was second to Queens in 1972—the same as in Peel's day. Queens has risen from third place to second place among the boroughs, in terms of population. Yet the ranking of the boroughs according to the number of clubs in each borough is the same for both years (1932 and 1972): Queens, Brooklyn, Manhattan, Bronx, and Richmond (see Table 3.1). Perhaps this can be explained by the vestigial town setup in Queens. Unlike citizens in the rest of the city, residents of Queens always refer to their homes as being located in a community, rather than in a borough or on a street. At one time Queens (in the same manner as Nassau and Suffolk counties) was made up of numerous towns and villages, including Laurelton, Flushing, Queens Village, and Bayside. These communities, while now joined with other neighborhoods in assembly, state senate, congressional and other categories of districts (and frequently divided among more than one district) continue to have separate political clubs that represent the communal identification of the residents. Queens is the only borough that customarily divides every assembly district into two executive districts for purposes of electing party officials. In addition only in Queens is there considered to be a viable two-party system. This is a result of both the heterogeneity of the borough's residents, in terms of their ethnic background, race, and class, and the prevalence of communities of one and two-family homes— unusual in a city where most people are housed in multiple dwellings. In a neighborhood of six- or seven-story buildings, for example, an assembly district may not extend for more than forty square blocks. In a neighborhood of private homes, on the other hand, it may cover an area five times that size. For clubs to be convenient to constituents it is necessary in some communities that more than one club represent an area. However, this does not explain the multiple districts in

Manhattan (in one assembly district there are four executive districts). That is the result of historical factors unrelated to geographic propinquity.

Although the number of New York's political clubs has diminished drastically, the citywide percentages of clubs representing the respective parties have remained approximately the same (see Table 3.2). For Republicans, the percentage of total clubs was 30 percent in 1932 and 28 percent in 1972, and for Democrats the figure was 60 percent in 1932 and 59 percent in 1972. Figures for the individual boroughs show a sharp drop in the percentage of Republican clubs in Queens (from 46 percent in 1932 to 27 percent in 1972) and a substantial decline in the proportion of Democratic clubs in Richmond (from 80 percent in 1932 to 50 percent in 1972). Both third parties and minor parties, which we classified as "other," increased their proportion of the total number of clubs from 11 percent in 1932 to 14 percent in 1972. This occurred despite the withering away of leftist parties in New York. A recent phenomenon has been the growth of the New York City Conservative party, and their dominance of third-party politics. Most of the Conservative clubs are relatively new, with some having been in operation for less than two years. During the thirties there were very few right-wing political clubs. However, Peel recalls that "there were several Fascist/Nazi clubs in Yorkville (once a predominantly German section of the upper East Side of Manhattan) . . . Some German clubs had large numbers—a preponderance—of [German-American Nazi] Bund members."[19] In 1972 the city's political left was almost completely unrepresented by clubs; the same was true for the extreme right.

TABLE 3.1

Population of New York City and Number of Political Clubs, By Borough—1932-1972

	1932		1972	
Borough	Population (million)	Number of Clubs	Population (million)	Number of Clubs
Brooklyn	2.5	360	2.6	73
Manhattan	1.8	220	1.5	68
Queens	1.79	404	1.98	77
Bronx	1.25	140	1.47	35
Richmond	0.158	56	0.295	10

Source: For 1932 figures, Roy V. Peel's The Political Clubs of New York (New York: Ira S. Friedman, 1968, rev. ed.), p. 22. 1972 figures from research by the authors.

TABLE 3.2

Percent and Number of Political Clubs Representing Various Parties, Citywide and by Borough—1932 and 1972

Party	Citywide		Manhattan		Bronx		Queens		Brooklyn		Richmond	
	1932	1972	1932	1972	1932	1972	1932	1972	1932	1972	1932	1972
Republican	30	28	27	34	17	40	46	27	21	19	16	20
	(354)	(74)	(60)	(23)	(24)	(14)	(186)	(21)	(77)	(14)	(9)	(2)
Democratic	60	59	53	59	67	57	51	57	66	62	80	50
	(703)	(154)	(117)	(40)	(94)	(20)	(208)	(44)	(239)	(45)	(45)	(5)
Other*	11	14	19	7	16	3	3	16	12	18	4	30
	(120)	(35)	(43)	(5)	(22)	(1)	(9)	(12)	(44)	(14)	(2)	(3)
Total	100	100	19	26	12	13	34	29	31	28	5	4
	(1,177)	(263)	(220)	(68)	(140)	(35)	(404)	(77)	(360)	(73)	(56)	(10)

*Includes in 1932, Socialist, Communist, and Socialist Labor parties, and, in 1972, Liberal and Conservative parties.

Note: Number of members is indicated in parentheses; data for 1932 comes from Roy V. Peel, The Political Clubs of New York (New York: Ira S. Friedman, 1968), appendix; data for 1972 compiled by the authors based on clubs for which complete information was available.

Size of Clubs

Clubs vary in size from very small to extremely large. These extremes represent a very small proportion of the universe, however, with only 6 percent of all clubs having less than fifty members and 6 percent having more than one thousand members. Fourteen percent of the clubs have between fifty and one hundred members. The largest category is comprised of clubs with membership ranging from 101-250; 30 percent of New York City's political clubs may be found in this group. The average-size club has 490 members. However, this figure is distorted because of the presence of a handful of extremely large clubs. A typical club in the city is likely to have 195 members rather than the larger figure indicated by the mean. It is noteworthy that 92 percent of the clubs with more than one thousand members are Democratic clubs.

We would like to have compared the size of present-day clubs with those that Peel studied. However, no such data is available, although we believe that clubs are smaller today than they were 40 years ago. The following table gives the percentage of total clubs for each of the seven size categories that we studied:

Size of Club	Percent of Total Clubs
Less than 50 members	6
50 - 100	14
101 - 250	30
251 - 500	27
501 - 750	12
751 - 1,000	5
1,000 or more	6

Durability of Clubs

Peel mentioned nothing about how long political clubs generally remain in existence; in this respect, he is no different from other writers. We searched the previous literature, and were unable to find a single statement relating to the durability of political organizations. Our own findings indicate that, while clubs come and go, the majority of New York City clubs are extremely durable. True, the number of clubs has declined sharply since 1932, as we mentioned previously. However, of the 264 clubs for which we have accurate data on this item, more than half have been in existence for more than a decade, and 45 percent have been operating for sixteen years or more. The following table shows our findings with respect to the number and percent of clubs in 1972 that had been in operation for varying periods of years:

Years in Operation	Number of Clubs	Percent of Clubs*
Less than 1	3	1
1-3	26	10
4-6	78	29
7-10	22	8
11-15	16	6
16 or more	119	45

*Percentages total 99 percent due to rounding.

The Club and the Party Organization

To paraphrase Woodrow Wilson, when one speaks of party organization in New York City one speaks of clubs. While there are some places in the city where a particular political party is unrepresented by a political club, on the whole parties and clubs are interchangeable. In forty years the organization of political parties has changed very little in New York City. The following description, given by Peel 40 years ago, is basically true today:

Within each county [New York's boroughs are counties, as well] there are a number of assembly districts presided over by an Assembly District Leader. The leader's headquarters are at the office of the regular organization political club. The subdivisions of the assembly district are created by the Board of Elections and are known as Election Districts. The party members living within the election district are represented on the County Committee by the members of the Election District Committee. The agent of the assembly district leader within the election district is the captain, who is appointed by and responsible to the district leader. . . . In each county there is a county leader, chosen by the majority vote of the members of the executive district committees [the district leaders]. To him is delegated the power to make decisions concerning matters of party or public policy, the latter function being of vast importance when the party controls the city administration.[20]

The institutions that make up the political party are (1) the enrolled voters, residing in election districts created by the Board of Elections for purposes of administering the election laws; (2) the county committee, comprised of committeemen elected directly by enrolled voters to represent each election district, and a county chairman elected by the committeemen; (3) the county executive committee, comprised of male and female district leaders, elected by enrolled voters in each executive district (which may be an entire assembly district, or—at the discretion of the county committee—a part thereof, and headed by the county leader, elected by the district leaders; (4) the state committee, made up of two state committeemen (one male, one female) from each assembly district, elected directly by the voters in the assembly district, and headed by the state chairman, elected by the members of the state committee; (5) the district judicial convention, made up of judicial delegates, elected directly by enrolled voters in each assembly district, who meet prior to general elections for purposes of selecting the party's candidates for state supreme court judge; and (6) the political club, comprised of enrolled voters, and headed by officers elected by the club members. (See Figure 3.1.) Of the six the political club is the only institution unregulated by election law.

A registered voter may become a member of a political party by "enrolling," a process described in the election law as follows:

> The voter shall then [after filling out a form and receiving an enrollment number] enter a voting booth and . . . may make with a pencil . . . or pen . . . a cross X mark . . . within a circle underneath the emblem of the party of his election. . . . If a voter declines to enroll, he may return the blank unmarked. . . .[21]

The enrollment blank bears an affidavit, and the registered voter's signature legally commits him to support the party he chooses (see Figure 3.2). "The term 'party' means any political organization which at the last preceding election for governor polled at least 50,000 votes for governor."[22] Those that do not qualify are known as "independent bodies," and they operate under a different set of regulations than do the established parties. New York State has four parties, according to the election law—the Republican, Democratic, Conservative, and Liberal parties. In New York's closed primary system the voter enrolled in any one of these four is licensed to cast an exclusive vote in that party's primaries. In 1973 (as was not the case in Peel's era) the enrolled voter directly chose most party officials as well. The chief official among these

38

FIGURE 3.1

Organization of County (Borough) Politics in New York City

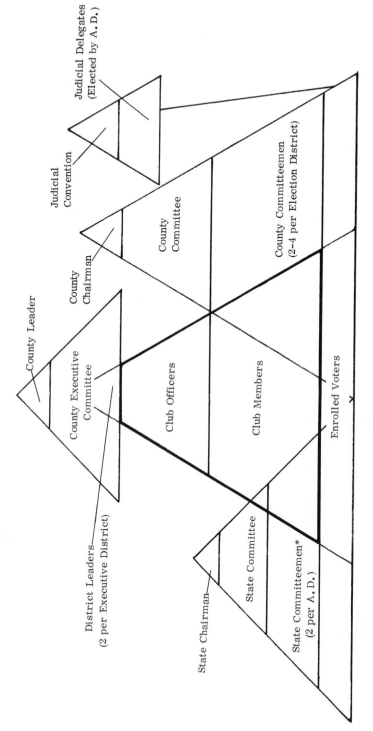

*Note: In Brooklyn the district leader serves also as state committeeman.

FIGURE 3.2

New York State Election Law Enrollment Form for Voters.

"I, ..., do solemnly declare
that I am a qualified voter of the election district in which I have
been registered, and that my resident address is ....
.... (the resident address of the
voter as it appears in the register, is to be here inserted); that I
am in general sympathy with the principles of the party which I
have designated by my mark hereunder; and that it is my intention
to support generally at the next general election, state or national,
the nominees of such party for state or national offices.
.... party.

(Insert emblem.)   (Insert emblem.)

is the district leader, formerly elected by members of the county
committee in each district, but now elected directly.

In 1932 Peel wrote the following about the county committee:

> Strictly speaking, a committee is a directory body
> and, as such, should contain no more than nine to
> fifteen members. But the size of New York's
> political committees belies their designation.
> The New York County Committee [Manhattan]
> of the Democratic party consists of more than
> 13,000 members. Obviously, such a huge body
> could never act on its own initiative. [23]

The nature of the county committees has changed very little over the
past four decades; they are somewhat smaller than they once were,
and somewhat less influential. Their importance to the political
process may be gauged by their place in Costikyan's book on New
York City party politics, in which a footnote (p. 32) contains the
longest explanation that we found concerning function of the county
committee:

The County Committee consisted of three or four
Democrats per election district. Until 1955, the
county committeemen from each assembly district
elected the district leaders. After 1955, the district
leaders were elected directly by the enrolled
Democrats in the district, but the county committeemen remained as the theoretical ultimate source of
party power.

In fact, the County Committee delegated most
of its power to the district leaders, under the party
rules, and, except for a few vestigial functions,
meets once every two years to elect officers and
readopt or amend the party rules.[24]

Today the New York County Committee (Manhattan) contains
3,395 members, or one-fourth the number of members it had
in former years. Its chairmanship has passed from the high-
powered professional politician-lawyers and brokers of
Tammany days to a medical school dean. What more can we say?

Unlike California, where "there is no standard geographic
unit in which clubs are organized,"[25] the New York political
club usually is based on an assembly district:

The Assembly Districts have long been the smallest
political subdivisions in the state in which there are
contests for elective office. . . . Assembly Districts
could thus be easily managed from a political clubhouse and were thus highly convenient units for party
organization. . . . Until 1938, state assemblymen
were elected annually. Consequently, the party units
in their district were almost constantly ready for
action. They had a continuity, a cohesion, a steady
state of preparedness, in contrast with the campaign
organization for less frequently contested offices,
that made them the most effective and natural shock
troops for candidates from all constituencies to
employ.[26]

The clubs form the base from which all local campaigns are launched.
Club members dominate the slates of candidates for county committee
and judicial delegate positions. District leaders are spawned by
clubhouses, and the leaders derive both their campaign manpower
and year-round workers from the clubhouses. State committee

candidates belong to the clubs, and seek the endorsement and active
support of club members in their campaigns. It is a rare district
that elects any public or local party official outside of the political
club structure. The influence of clubs is not the same, however.
The influence of the political club is related to both its electoral
success and the population of its district. Big clubs, clubs that have
helped elect a substantial number of officeholders, and clubs from
large or heavily Democratic districts are able to exert pressure
when they are engaged in selecting candidates from districts larger
than their own (councilmen, congressmen, judges, state senators,
and delegates to national conventions).[27] A regular club participates
in the informal councils of its party, working through its district
leaders. Reform clubs operate through their own organization,
the county Democratic coalition, or the citywide New Democratic
Coalition, when they are selecting candidates that run in areas
larger than a single assembly district. In either case, regular
or reform, political clubs affiliate with the countywide organization
that suits their particular needs and purposes. There are clearcut
cases, such as in the Bronx, where there has been almost no
overlap—the regulars hold almost all of the district leadership
positions, and the county executive committee is the regular
organization. The one or two regular clubs in the Bronx that do
not have district leaders gain their input through informal discussions
with the county leader. The reformers have their own organization—
the Bronx Committee for Democratic Voters. Regularly scheduled
meetings, formal votes of affiliation, countywide conventions, and
established bylaws mark the structure of this federation of reform
clubs. The few reform district leaders in the Bronx, while attending
meetings of the county executive committee, participate in the work
of CDV as well.

The county executive committee, as noted above, is comprised
of male and female district leaders elected in primaries by enrolled
members of their party; the ranks from which these leaders come are
called the executive members of the club. In some boroughs the
political clubs of some parties also refer to their district leaders
as executive members of the club. Each county (or borough) has its
own executive committee. The term of office for district leaders is
usually two years.

Almost without exception district leaders are club leaders
as well. Their influence in the clubs varies, depending upon the type
of club, the depth of other leadership, and the resources available
to the district leader. Traditional clubs in all parties have always
placed the district leader in the pivotal decision-making position so
far as important matters are concerned.

Peel described the leaders as "the heirs of the old ward bosses. Each one wields extraordinary power over his district. Theoretically, he concerns himself with political matters only, but by common report he is the economic overlord, the social arbiter, the unofficial agent of the government, and the patron of the community. . . . The district leader appoints the captains, one for each election district. The captains are the nuclei of the club-organization, the personal representatives of the boss in the neighborhoods and his emissaries."[28] While the leader no longer holds the central position in the district that Peel attributed to him, he is still important in some areas of the city in terms of the party organization. As Wallace S. Sayre and Herbert Kaufman noted:

> District Leaders recruit, mobilize, deploy, supervise, and encourage their captains and keep them under control by holding out the promise of reward (and by threat of deprivation of expected rewards). The leaders thus manage the manpower with which primary and general election campaigns are conducted, which gives them powerful instruments . . . for bargaining with other party officers and candidates and office-holders who want and need the votes the district organizations seem to be able to carry.[29]

For these reasons Sayre and Kaufman believed that "the center of political gravity in the parties"[30] was located in the members of the county executive committee. The committee, in theory, becomes a "joint-chiefs-of-staff" for the party, and is presided over by the county leader (selected by the membership). Each chief presides over the activist captains of the neighborhood election districts, who campaign and deliver the voters to the polls.

The contradiction inherent in this system is that while the members of the executive committee are elected by enrolled party members, their power resides in their command of political activists, who are usually club members. There are a number of leaders, in Democratic reform clubs, who are selected by the members, but do not command them. These men and women are generally leaders in name only, although they continue to cast their vote on the executive committee. As Sayre and Kaufman pointed out, "The position of a District Leader rests in large degree on his command of a political club."[31] It follows that the county executive committee is no more powerful than the district leaders that serve it. Even in those clubs where the district leader is the de facto leader he is no embodiment of the leader that Peel studied. For one thing he has fewer manpower resources at his command. Peel reported that there were 3,495 captains in the Democratic party at the time of his study. [32] There were 76 district leaders under whom these captains served, which means that each leader had approximately 46 captains working for him. Each captain was said to have had at least one deputy, plus several assistants. At the least that meant that some one hundred party workers gave year-round service to the leader, usually because they were salaried employees of the city, borough, or state governments, or were employed by a business owned or influenced by the leader. Very few leaders can count on this sort of manpower today. The ability to maintain a viable party organization, manned by active captains, is limited to a small number of district leaders. The rest rely on a hodge-podge of captains (who sometimes work, but often do not), volunteers, relatives, friends of candidates for office, and club members who sometimes have to be bribed, cajoled, and threatened with unspoken disasters. Another reason why the district leader is less powerful today is that he no longer commands the material resources—jobs, money, and favors—that he once commanded. Whatever services the district leader offers today are pitifully small compared to those which his predecessors offered in similar situations. The county leaders, the political bosses of the city, underscored the present-day weakness of the district leaders just prior to the 1973 mayoral election:

> One of those "bosses," Frank Rosetti, the Manhattan Democratic leader, conceded that 'the organization doesn't have that much input' in the current election. His Brooklyn counterpart, Meade H. Esposito, reinforced that view with his estimate that only 25% of Democratic district captains worked at their jobs of disseminating literature and getting out Democratic voters on Election Day.
> Matthew J. Troy, Jr., the Queens Democratic leader, said he was relying increasingly on women to take up the slack left by the male captains, who don't want to ring doorbells or man card tables with campaign literature outside Queens Boulevard department stores. "The men do the talking and the women do the walking," Mr. Troy said.
> Most of the Democratic organizations either have to hire youngsters or persuade young Democrats to start the organization version of the pre-campaign

blitz—the distribution of probably one million pieces
of Beame literature at subway stations, shopping
areas and some homes over the week-end.[33]

Voting on the county executive committee is based on assembly
districts. If there is more than one executive district within an
assembly district, the leaders of those districts cast partial votes.
Whether leaders come from powerful clubs or weak ones, or
whether they deliver the voters to the polls on election day or they
don't, has no effect on their voting strength.

Governing the Clubs: Constitutions

The clubs are designed (as we noted previously) so that people
with common interests can maintain regular contact. This contact
is achieved through the development of a structure. However, most
people do not invent a new structure when they organize a club;
they adopt a familiar form that seems to work well for them.
Generally one of the first pieces of business in the formation of a
political club is the establishment of a committee to draft a
constitution similar in many respects to the U.S. Constitution.
Of the 261 clubs responding to our question, "Does your club have
a constitution?" 90 percent answered affirmatively, with little
variation showing up among the parties.

Peel provided no information on the constitutional basis for
political clubs in the thirties. It is hard to imagine the old-time
leaders writing constitutions, or their membership demanding them.
However, when we cross-tabulated the age of various clubs in 1973
with the existence of a constitution, we found little or no difference
between the older clubs (many of which date back forty years or
more) and the new ones; constitutions are as ubiquitous as campaign
literature in the political clubhouses of New York City. Perhaps
the advent of constitutional government is recent in the old-line
clubs. We have no evidence by which to judge. Whatever the case,
written club constitutions are here to stay.

The relative importance of the constitution in the day-to-day
operations of the club, however, is another matter. When asked, as
a follow-up question, whether copies of the constitution were made
available to members who requested them, slightly more than one-
third of clubs with constitutions said no. In such cases (where copies
are not made available) a constitution probably has no impact at all
on the operations of a club. Combining as one category those clubs

that do not have constitutions and those that do not make them available, and labelling this category "constitution absent," we found that 43 percent of all clubs fall into this category. Our experience leads us to believe that at least some of the clubs have a constitution, and distribute copies to members, yet function on a basis other than that set forth in the document. As we will indicate below, the "constitution of leadership" is far more important to the operations of political clubs than the constitution as a document.

There is little, if any, variation of the content of club constitutions: they all contain preambles and provisions for officers, executive boards, and elections. Without exception the officers provided for are alike—president, one or more vice-presidents, one or more secretaries, and a treasurer (or some financial officer). Executive boards, existing in almost every club, are elected for terms of office varying from one to three years. The number of prescribed meetings of a club's entire membership varies somewhat. The usual requirement is that there be an annual meeting, at which some, or all, officers are elected. Some clubs have constitutions that require semiannual, quarterly, or bi-monthly meetings, but we could find no pattern in this requirement. Democratic reform clubs have constitutional requirements that are somewhat different from other clubs. We will discuss these differences in chapter eight.

Robert's Rules of Order is the common guide to club meetings, as prescribed in the club's constitution: its rules appear to have been honored more in breach however, than in everyday practice, so far as we could determine. Rarely do the constitutions go beyond the establishment of general classifications and requirements. In this sense they are more like the federal constitution than the constitution of the city and the state of New York, both of which are famous for their detail. The most specific item found in a number of club constitutions was the rate of dues; second, the number required for a quorum of the general membership (a copy of a typical club constitution is contained in Appendix C).

Governing the Clubs: Leaders

Peel found an extensive cadre of leaders in the political clubs of his day:

The hierarchy of officers in clubs is extensive. A newspaper clipping in our files fills two columns

46

merely to enumerate the members of committees
and officers of Sherrif McQuade's Fifteenth Assembly
District (Kings) Democratic Club. Excepting the
members of the board of governors, none of the
officers in any club has any real authority. His
position is only a recognition, a not too subtle
flattering of the ego.[34]

In 1961 Goetcheus found that the Village Independent Democrats had
a president, three vice-presidents, various sercretaries, and an
executive committee consisting of elected officers plus 29 members-
at-large elected by the club membership. In addition "there were
eight committees active in March, 1961: the Newsletter Committee,
the Community Action Committee, the Housing Committee, the
Flight Committee (concerning the organization of a flight to Europe
for club members), the Ad Hoc Constitution Committee, the Social
Committee, the Community Service Committee (which at that time
was arranging a series of polio shots for community residents),
and the Membership Committee."[35] Each committee had at least
a chairman and a secretary, as well as several members. That
would probably be enough officers to fill two columns in any newspaper today.

    Although there are a few clubs so small that the potential
for leadership in them is somewhat limited, we found hardly a club
that did not elect or select anywhere from 25 to 40 officers, board
members and committee chairmen. Goetcheus considered the
multitude of elected officials a symptom of "the democratic
functioning of the club."[36] Unless every club we studied is demo-
cratically run, and we find this impossible to believe, a long list
of officers is not necessarily evidence of democratic operations.
Peel's judgement (noted above) was probably closer to the truth—
that there is a "not too subtle flattering of the ego" involved in many
of the officer appointments in political clubs.

    In an attempt to discover where influence lies in political
clubs, we asked our respondents, "Are there any members of the
club who, because of personal attributes, appeal, prestige or
reputation are able to exert a great deal of influence over the other
members without benefit of holding office?" Approximately one-third
of our respondents indicated that there were one or more influential
members who were not officeholders. However, some of the more
influential clubs that responded affirmatively to this question
answered in terms of what important officials belonged to, or visited,
the club, rather than which persons influenced the decision-making
processes. Still other respondents thought that we were excluding
district leaders from those who hold office: approximately 20

percent of all those who answered yes listed either a present or former district leader as one who exerts a great deal of influence on club decisions.

In this regard one respondent said: "We have an elected Democratic leader. The result is that he influences state assemblymen, councilmen, and of course, club members." Another respondent noted: "The club president has a great deal of power over the other members. . . . This is mainly due to the fact that he has an excellent reputation, a great deal of prestige and has served the community for many years. He has run for district leader, but he lost." One of our project observers noted: "When I attended the meeting I could not help believing that the people were being led by the District Leader and his co-leader without being able to participate in introducing their views on certain issues."

Among those respondents who listed someone besides an officeholder as being influential in their club, the president of one club, with a large membership of blue-collar workers, suggested that the reasons for the "informal" power structure within the club were, "Professional people have more insight of politics and tend to influence our members." An official of a club on the Lower East Side of Manhattan noted: "Joel Silver, the assistant rent commissioner [of New York City], is very influential." A Manhattan Democratic Club official said: "One individual . . . a former aide to a Congressman . . . influences because he is knowledgeable and the club is made up of amateurs."

On the whole, we would have to agree with the observation of one respondent who noted, "Some of the members in the clubs do have prestige and a reputation but they don't exert a great deal of influence over the majority of members without holding office."

Almost without exception, political clubs have an executive board, and the board is elected by the members. Of 268 clubs responding, almost 96 percent said they had some sort of executive board. Of these, almost 85 percent elected the board through a vote of the full membership. We found that Republican clubs were less likely to have elected boards (75 percent had them) than Democratic clubs (83 percent), with Conservative clubs in the middle (81 percent). And those clubs (of all parties) that reported they did not elect their boards had them appointed by club officers. However, only 3 percent were appointed in this way. Other methods of selecting an executive board included the selection of new members by incumbent members, appointments by the district leader, the appointment of each club member to the board for a specified period of time (restricted to very small clubs), self-selection (in relatively new clubs the cadre of members that formed the club served as the executive board because

TABLE 3.3

Number of Clubs That Use Various Methods of Choosing Executive Board, by Average Tenure of Board

Method of Choosing	Less Than 1	1-2	3-4	5	More Than 5	Other	Total
Election by all club members	6	73	44	10	80	5	218
Election by less than all club members	—	1	—	—	—	—	1
Appointment by officers	1	2	—	—	3	2	8
Others	—	9	6	3	14	9	41
Total	7	85	50	13	97	16	268

TABLE 3.4

Number of Clubs with Various Years of Tenure for Executive Board Members, by Party

Party	Less Than 1	1-2	3-4	5	More Than 5	Other	Total
Democratic	5	55	33	7	55	9	164
Republican	1	19	11	4	25	7	67
Conservative	—	5	6	1	14	—	26
Total	6	79	50	12	94	16	257

these members were there first), selections by a nominating committee or selection committee, and appointments by the club's executive officer (see Table 3.3).

Members of executive boards tend to reflect their clubs in matters of ideology, ethnicity, and socioeconomic status. Although the overwhelming majority of clubs hold elections for officers and executive board members annually, there is a tendency for board membership to be relatively stable. Regardless of how the boards are selected, and regardless of what party a club represents, there is a uniform pattern in the tenure of board members. Slightly less than half of the clubs reported an average tenure among all board members of five years or more; this was despite the fact that approximately 6 percent of all clubs (10 percent of Republican clubs) do not permit board members to succeed themselves, and that some of the clubs reporting had not been in continuous existence for five years or more (see Table 3.4).

Clubs reporting tended to cluster in two categories, in terms of the tenure of executive board members: tenure of one to two years, and tenure of more than five years. The only substantial deviation from this clustering was in the Conservative party, where 20 percent were in the one-to-two-year category (as opposed to a norm for all parties of approximately 31 percent), while 54 percent were in the category of five years or more (as opposed to a norm of 37 percent). As we indicated previously, most clubs tend to have a group of activists that is much smaller than their total membership. These activists generally are highly stable members of the club, frequently with long-time residences in the community, and so they are the people elected to executive boards. Conservative clubs, which tend to be somewhat smaller, and somewhat newer, clearly rely on a continuing cadre of activists that do not readily yield their control of club activities. Conservatives tend to be more cohesive, more tightly organized, and less open to factional battles than other parties. This is the case probably because they are a more recent addition to the political scene, and are more embattled electorally, with a considerably smaller following than either Republicans or Democrats.

Obviously some percentage of political clubs have a high rate of turnover among board members. In some cases this is the result of the internecine warfare that is common in political clubs. The frequent redistricting of political boundary lines that has occurred in recent years also contributed to board turnover as some members have shifted their allegiance from one club to another, bringing with them new activists and new candidates for club leadership. In addition some clubs are in highly mobile residential communities, where shifts in population can lead to frequent shifts in the leadership of all organizations. Because club executive boards tend to be rather large (boards of 25 or 30 members are usual, and those of 40 members or more are not uncommon), there is generally a shortage of qualified candidates for board positions, and frequent turnovers are not uncommon in smaller clubs that simply exhaust their supply of executive board candidates. Many boards meet monthly, and all board members are usually pressured to maintain a high level of participation in club affairs, and to serve on committees as well. It is not surprising that in some clubs members flee from the "honor" of serving, so as to avoid being called upon to sell journal ads, dinner tickets, raffles, etc., and being required to set up chairs, pour coffee, recruit members, and attend meetings on rainy nights, among other duties. Furthermore executive boards have been known to display controversy, and, occasionally, animosity. Many people, though they may be attracted to politics, shy away from the arguments and hostility that surround the executive board meetings of some clubs.

Along with the executive board, most clubs (as we noted above) elect a slate of officers—a president, one or more vice-presidents, one or more secretaries, and a treasurer. We found that more than 80 percent of all clubs had these officers, although we found some clubs that had fewer officers, and some that had no officers at all. It is hard to imagine a political club without officers, but there are cases, in all parties, where district leaders perform all of the official functions of the club. We also found that at least half of the clubs either elected or appointed additional officers. The following table shows the percent of clubs that elect or appoint various club officers (the "other" category includes such officers as sergeant-at-arms, chairman of the law committee, chairman of the budget committee, trustee, chairman of the executive committee, president-elect, chairman of the club (an honorary post), etc.

Office	Percent That Elect or Appoint
President	87
Vice-President	81
Treasurer	83
Secretary	86
Parliamentarian	18
Other	57

Degree of Openness

Peel found the political clubs of the thirties to be as secretive as they are today:

> Today, in New York, the inquiring stranger meets
> with a frigid reception in most of the Tammany,
> McCooey, Hague, Ward and Flynn clubs. . . .
> In the Republican and Socialist Clubs, which have
> no illegal acts to conceal, one finds this same
> reclusiveness . . . it persists, this air of
> secrecy, because it is just that—a survival
> of infantile fears and superstitions. Bosses
> are aware of the paucity of their claims to
> power; club members are painfully aware of
> the transparency of their motives. Hence, they
> hedge themselves about with all manner of symbols,
> formulas and procedures. [37]

For an institution that operates in the public arena, the political club has traditionally been secretive, if not clandestine, about much of its internal activity. The picture of smoke-filled rooms and anonymous actors that persists in American political mythology is basically a true one. Political activists have never comprised a substantial minority, much less a majority, of eligible citizens. This has come about partly because politics is neither particularly attractive as a profession nor appealing as a hobby, and partly because of the incumbent politicos who set up barriers to joining, and participating in, political organizations. The result has been that comparatively few people belong to political clubs, and little is known about the clubs. This scarceness of knowledge is often filled by myth, hearsay, speculation, and suspicion. Clubs have themselves to blame for this, since they have not been open to the public in the way that charitable groups, the YMCA, or a museum's supporting groups often are. We viewed a club's openness in two ways: the relative ease with which one may become a member of a club, and the degree to which the club is secretive about its operations, rules, and facilities.

It is difficult to compare the openness of the clubs of today with the situation that existed in the twenties and early thirties, because Peel left us only a few hints about the ways in which club affairs were conducted. Moreover, his statements on club secrecy were hardly ambivalent. He said that he found "in all political organizations, and particularly in those where clubs and clubhouses

form the base of the pattern, an incurable tendency toward secrecy. "38
There were many reasons for this secrecy. Some of the clubs
were patently dishonest, serving as screens or fronts for illegal
activities ranging from gambling to white slavery and murder.
Other clubs, while not engaged in the darker forms of criminal
activity, provided space for illegal serving of alcoholic beverages,
for dice and card games, and other such operations. Political
necessity frequently required that the clubs conceal their operations.
Some clubs, while ostensibly engaged in the service of one political
party or candidate, actually worked for the opposition. Candidates
customarily provided campaign funds to club leaders on the basis
of the number of members working in a particular campaign, and
sometimes the amounts provided were inflated. Therefore it was
in the best interest of these clubs to conceal the size of their
active membership. In addition politicians habitually raided other
clubs' membership lists, luring productive highly regarded captains
away from a certain club with promises of greater reward or prestige
with another club. Thus all political club officials were reluctant to
share their lists of members' names and addresses.

Secrecy was a tradition that originated from the days when
political clubs were fraternal lodges as well as being party organizations. In those days they adopted the secrecy of such groups as
the Masons and the Pythians, concealing from public view the
elaborate rituals and rules that made club membership desirable.
Peel noted that "there are few devices of ritual, nomenclature,
procedure and hokum which are not employed somewhere, at some
time, by the clubs of the region. In this respect, the metropolitan
party organizations are as fertile and ingenious as any group on
earth. "39

Finally political clubs have often served as extended families
for their members. Because of residential patterns and the traditional
"friends-and-neighbors" concept of membership, clubs tended to
be comprised of people from one racial or ethnic group. Most club
members either knew one another before they joined or created
mutual friendships after they joined. Cultural solidarity, suspicion
of outsiders (what Peel referred to—as noted above—as "infantile
fears and superstitions"), and a close fraternal spirit impelled
club members to keep the club to themselves, and at the same
time to wonder why others, who did not belong, would want to pry
into their affairs.

So far as access to membership is concerned, again there
is little information on past practices. A remark by Peel, however,
indicated that there was more to joining a club than walking through
the door and plunking down an initiation fee. "Initiation," Peel
noted, "is comparatively simple. Each applicant is sponsored by

a club member and voted upon. A few clubs use the formality of
the two-compartment box, with the black and white balls."[40]
Here again political clubs mirrored the behavior of fraternal
organizations in their procedures. Any emphasis on restrictive
membership procedures, while possibly serving as a lure for
some applicants, must have been for many others a discouragement.
The initiative in building membership was taken by the club, not by
the individual applicant. This was not a practice that could have led
to large numbers of voters desiring membership in political clubs.

Secrecy

To determine the degree to which clubs are secretive about
their operations, rules, and facilities, we asked our interviewers
to answer three questions, and our respondents to answer one
question. The three questions asked of our interviewers were
(1) "did you have any difficulty in gaining entrance to the clubhouse?"
(2) "were you permitted to attend a club meeting?" and (3) "what
was the disposition of the person you interviewed (friendly, helpful,
cool, evasive, openly hostile)?" The single question asked of
respondents was "may I have a copy of your club constitution?"

Getting in the Door

We cannot imagine a less open situation than one where
nonmembers are unwelcome in clubhouses and offices. Such is
the case in fraternal organizations and in some ethnic societies;
the buildings that house these secret societies are often difficult,
if not impossible, places in which to gain access. Our researchers
found no comparable situation in political clubs. However, that is
not to say that every political club willingly admits all outsiders:
our interviewers reported some difficulty in gaining entrance to the
premises of 48 clubs (18 percent of the clubs we studied). Seven
percent of the clubs had guards—usually volunteers—stationed at
the front door. In the case of one Democratic club, our researcher
was refused admission, and the police were called to escort him
away from the clubhouse. Apparently this was the first case in a
number of years in which an outsider could not get past the club's
front door. On the whole, however, political clubs in the Democratic,
Republican, and Conservative parties have eschewed the "members
only" tradition of the thirties for a more hospitable role. We found

that 209 clubhouses either had no barriers to people walking in off the street, or only employed such barriers symbolically or perfunctorily (in 11 cases [4 percent] there was no door to get in; interviews were conducted in nonclubhouse settings, either because there had never been a clubhouse, or the club was moving from one site to another, or, as in one case, there had been a fire, and the facilities were being restored).

Not only did we find clubhouse admission generally accessible, but our interviewers reported that many clubs actually encouraged visitors. Some clubs regularly hold open houses, inviting community residents in for refreshments, meetings with party dignitaries, and entertainment. Most clubs are open to the public several evenings a week, and lawyers, accountants, and other advisors are available at the clubs for consultation. Many clubs post large signs both inside and outside their meeting places announcing that everyone is welcome. In a few clubs we found that the nearby neighborhood had been blanketed with posters, placards, or leaflets giving the address of the club and urging interested or curious citizens to visit. However, several of our respondents made it clear during interviews that those visitors to their club who were not engaged in some purposeful errand were neither encouraged nor welcome.

While our researchers were readily admitted to most club-houses, club officials were less willing to permit them to attend meetings of their clubs. We cannot say whether this means that some clubs operate differently than others, and fear exposure, or they simply exhibit more paranoia about nonmembers (or observers) seeing their true face. Ninety-four clubs (36 percent of the clubs studied) refused to grant our interviewers permission to view any meetings, and with 12 other clubs (4 percent) our interviewers experienced some difficulty in gaining permission to attend a meeting. One case required a lengthy telephone conversation between one of the authors of this book and a district leader, with repeated assurances from the author that no names would find their way into our book, and a request to see our observer's notes before she left the clubhouse. But for the most part our observers were permitted to attend club meetings, with 143 clubs (53 percent) granting such permission. In some cases observers were invited not only to general membership meetings, but to executive board meetings, committee meetings, and even strategy sessions involving candidates for various offices (19 clubs [7 percent] either traditionally did not hold meetings or had none planned for the period of our research). We found no differences among the parties with respect to the willingness or reluctance of clubs to permit us to attend meetings.

While most political clubs claim to have a constitution,

and while such a document may establish the structures, procedures, and limitations under which the club is governed, the club constitution can hardly be said to be a revealing document. After reading numerous club constitutions, we concluded that the information they contain reveals little of the actual operations of the clubs. Unlike budgets, mailing lists, internal memos, newsletters, minutes of meetings, and campaign timetables, the club constitution is not an "intimate" document. Clubs tend to put their highest ideals, rather than their pragmatic political concepts into their constitution. In view of this one might expect that they would be proud to share the contents of the constitution with the inquiring researcher. Therefore we chose to ask for a copy of the constitution, believing that a reluctance to share its contents would be indicative of whether or not a club felt compelled to secrecy even in a nonstrategic situation.

We found that of the 268 clubs we studied, 131 clubs (49 percent) pointedly refused either to let us have a copy, or show us a copy, of the constitution they claimed to possess. For 37 other clubs (14 percent) a copy of the constitution was unavailable, because (1) the club claimed that it did not have a copy, (2) that it had one, somewhere, but that no one could recall having seen it in recent years, or (3) that either a single copy, or a few copies existed, but the copy or copies were in the hands of club historians, club law committee chairmen, or others who could not be reached. However, 100 clubs (37 percent) either let us have, or let us examine, a copy of their constitution.

In most cases a club's refusal to let us see its constitution was accompanied by a comment, such as "we aren't permitted to do such a thing," or "you have to be a member before you can see the constitution," or "we wouldn't want it to get into the wrong hands."

It may be that the high incidence of refusal to let us see club constitutions is not tied to the clubs' propensity for secrecy. Some clubs that claimed to have a constitution may have been embarrassed to admit that in actuality they did not have one, and so they refused to show us a nonexistent document. In addition many clubs said that, though they have drafted a constitution at some point, they do not currently make use of the document, and for this reason the document is available to no one. For the most part we discount this possibility, since we gave our respondents every opportunity to inform us of the availability of their constitution. Thus where clubs indicated to us that this was the reason why we could not see their constitution, we placed these clubs in the category of "other," rather than in the category of "refused."

Disposition of Respondents

How do club officials react to inquiries ? Are they obviously
hostile, are they cool, or are they friendly ? We ask our interviewers
to describe the overall disposition of those with whom they talked,
and 223 respondents (84 percent) were deemed friendly by our
researchers. Another 28 respondents (10 percent) were classified
as being cool while only four (2 percent) were considered hostile
(for eight clubs we have no information on this item). Since
politicians are in the business of relating to the public, the good
impression that respondents imparted to our researchers is not
surprising.

Frequently politicians are thought to be flim-flam men,
smooth but untruthful, selling a shoddy product. We asked our
interviewers to classify respondents as being either helpful or
evasive. This is a question fraught with problems: some people
are more adept at seeming earnest than others. Some politicians
are glib, while others are not. We did not ask our researchers to
note whether they believed the respondents were telling the truth
or were lying, because we were more interested in determining
whether a club official was being intentionally secretive. On the
whole respondents turned out to be helpful: 199 respondents (75
percent) were placed in this category, as opposed to the 52 (20
percent) that were placed in the "evasive" category. The remaining
5 percent fell into the category of "hostile/uncooperative" or the
category of "no response on this item." There appear to be no
differences among the parties with respect to this item.

Styles change in all fields, and politics is no exception.
Where once it was fashionable for political clubs to emulate the
secret rituals of fraternal organizations, that style is now
regarded as old-fashioned; yet secrecy lingers on. In matters
that are least important clubs eschew the appearance of being
secret organizations. Leaders seem open, friendly, and helpful
in their treatment of inquisitive visitors. Most clubs welcome
outsiders who visit their clubhouses for purposes of assistance,
or to satisfy curiosity. But when it comes to the true operations
of the political club—general business and committee and executive
board meetings—many clubs throw up barriers to observation.
Where documents, even those that serve nonessential functions,
are concerned, the majority of clubs become secretive.

How can we explain this phenomenon ? We have already
offered several explanations, but perhaps Peel was closest to
the truth when he commented (as noted above) about the

"infantile fears and superstitions" of the clubs, and observed that "bosses are aware of the paucity of their claims to power" and "club members are painfully aware of the transparency of their motives." It seems the clubs today are more open than they once were; yet at the point where nerve centers threaten to be exposed, the clubs (many of them) are playing it as close to the chest as ever.

Who May Join Clubs

We included in our interview a direct question, "May anyone join this club?" Our response was that 78 percent of all clubs indicated that they were "open to all." We found Conservatives to be the most willing to take in all applicants (88 percent of Conservative clubs follow this practice); followed by Democrats (78 percent are open to all); Republicans were the most resistant in this respect (75 percent are open to all). As we expected, reform Democrats (87 percent of these clubs) were more willing to accept members without reservation than were regular Democrats (74 percent). This is due probably to ideological factors, rather than to the fact that reform clubs tend to be the outs, and find it hard to turn away anybody. Most respondents would have agreed with the Democratic club president who commented, "You just have to come down and join."

We found that where there were restrictions on applicants for club membership, these were often very slight. Generally reform Democrats and Conservatives told us that applicants had to "subscribe to ideas of this club," as one Brooklyn Conservative club leader put it. Conservative clubs, as some observers might expect, are concerned with appearances. One Conservative club officer noted that "anyone who gives a good appearance and displays a friendly manner is welcome here." We found only one case in which prospective club members might be blackballed, although this practice was once very popular. Among clubs with specific membership restrictions, a Queens Democratic club president noted: "The prospective member must be recommended by another club member. He must be a registered Democrat. Then the Board of Governors votes him in." Another club reported it had developed a procedure that is slightly more restrictive, describing the procedure as follows: "Each person requesting membership must file an application. We want to know something about him. The application is then reviewed by the membership committee. The final process is the voting of each member on the application for membership." Most club officials agreed that although the

application process was simple, and that everyone had an equal
chance of being accepted, members were expected to do more
for the club than just pay their annual dues. As the president of
one Bronx Republican club put it, "There are no requirements
[for membership]—only dues; and there is no pressure there,
either. However, as a member, you may be called upon to
render services, such as in campaign periods."

We posed several questions concerning the 22 percent of
clubs that deviated from the general pattern of openness. Were
these clubs, for example, located in areas where the dominant
membership group in the club differed from the dominant ethnic
group in the community? We found that 42 percent of the closed
clubs are located in areas where the racial/ethnic composition
of their membership is almost identical to that of the electorate.
Among the other clubs that were closed we found less ethnic
congruence. We wondered too whether closed clubs would be
more successful electorally than open clubs, measuring this
success in terms of their having important public and party
officials in their ranks. On the one hand it seemed that more
selective clubs might have a more closely knit, highly organized
membership; on the other hand it seemed that clubs that turned
prospective members away might not be popular with the community.
It appears that there is little difference in this regard between
clubs that are open and clubs that are closed.

Closed clubs seem to hold out the promise for greater
membership stability. After all, if a club takes the time to screen
and restrict its prospective members, will it not be able to hold
its membership longer than a club that accepts anyone? We classified
each club according to the duration of membership of a majority
of its members: where the majority had belonged to the club for
less than a year we called the club "unstable," while clubs with
a majority of members of longer standing were called "very stable."
We found little difference in terms of club stability as it related
to club openness: 77 percent of the very stable clubs, 83 percent
of the stable clubs, and 80 percent of the unstable clubs we also
found to be open clubs.

Who may join a political club today?—almost anybody. We
found that the overwhelming majority of clubs habitually allow
anyone to apply for membership, and even those clubs that have
restrictions rarely apply them. We found very few club officers
who could recall the last time they turned away an applicant.
The problem in the clubs today is recruiting members, not
restricting membership. Does it make a difference to a club if it
is open or closed in its admission practices? Indications are
that this factor makes no difference to the electoral success of

clubs, to their ethnic composition, or to the stability of their membership. However, old habits die hard. Clubs may continue to follow certain restrictive rituals for some time to come, but the number of clubs using these restrictions is steadily diminishing.

Notes

1. Roy V. Peel, The Political Clubs of New York, rev. ed. (New York: Ira S. Friedman, 1968), p. 20.

2. Ibid., p. 19.

3. Edward Costikyan, Behind Closed Doors (New York: Harcourt, Brace and World, 1966), p. 85.

4. Peel, op. cit., p. 63.

5. Currin V. Shields, "A Note on Party Organization: The Democrats in California," Western Political Quarterly, No. 7, (1954): 695.

6. Joseph Schlesinger, "Political Party Organization," in James G. March, Handbook of Organizations (Chicago: Rand McNally, 1965), p. 774.

7. Peel, op. cit., p. 127.

8. Samuel P. Orth, The Boss and the Machine (New Haven: Yale University Press, 1919), p. 90.

9. Stephen A. Mitchell, Elm Street Politics (New York: Oceana Publications, 1959), 30.

10. Vernon Goetcheus, "The Village Independent Democrats: A Study in the Politics of the New Reformers," (unpublished senior dissertation thesis, Honors College, Wesleyan University, 1963), p. 98.

11. Frank Sorauf, Party Politics in America (Boston: Little, Brown, 1972), p. 88.

12. James Q. Wilson, The Amateur Democrats (Chicago: University of Chicago Press, 1962), p. 165.

13. Ibid.

14. Schlesinger, op. cit., p. 774.

15. Ibid.

16. Peel, op. cit., p. 120.

17. Mitchell, op. cit., p. 19

18. Costikyan, op. cit., p. 45.

19. Interview with Peel, Northridge, California, April 3, 1973.

20. Peel, op. cit., p. 65.

21. New York State Election Law, 1973, Article 7, Section
176.

22. Ibid., Article 1, 2, Subsection 4.

23. Peel, op. cit., p. 59.

24. Costikyan, op. cit. p. 32, footnote.

25. Francis Carney, The Rise of the Democratic Clubs in California (New York: Holt, 1958), p. 114.

26. Wallace S. Sayre and Herbert Kaufman, Governing New York City (New York: Russell Sage, 1960), p. 135.

27. Martin Tolchin and Susan Tolchin, To the Victor— Political Patronage From the Clubhouse to the White House (New York: Random House, 1971), p. 135.

28. Peel, op. cit., pp. 65-66.

29. Sayre and Kaufman, op. cit., p. 136.

30. Ibid.

31. Ibid., p. 137.

32. Peel, op. cit., p. 67.

33. New York Times, Nov. 3, 1973, p. 26.

34. Peel, op. cit., p. 111.

35. Goetcheus, op. cit., p. 65.

36. Ibid., p. 61.

37. Peel, op. cit., pp. 107-108.

38. Ibid., p. 107.

39. Ibid., p. 117.

40. Ibid., p. 116.

4

WHO'S WHO IN
NEW YORK CITY'S
POLITICAL CLUBS

Peel did not specifically address himself to a demographic
description of club members in his study. Since that time, however,
data of the demographic type has occupied the attention of many
social scientists; but it has been the demography of the electorate at
large in relation to voting trends or (to a lesser degree) the party
or public leadership strata of political life that has claimed this
attention. The voting studies that have issued from the Survey
Research Center of Michigan, and from the research efforts of
Paul F. Lazarsfeld, Herbert McCloskey, and Avery Leiserson,
among others, have established the fact that sex, age, race, religion,
ethnicity, and certain other demographic factors do indeed relate
to the scope, style, and direction of people's political activities. [1]
It remains for us to view club members from the vantage point of
their demographic characteristics, and relate these factors to
the activities of political clubs.

There are no theoretical guideposts to mark out this terrain.
In general one might agree with Sorauf, who noted that parties appear
to be the independent variable, whatever the other indices. [2] The
significance of relationships (if and where any occur) is hard to
establish, but we do know something about the party identification
of the population at large, and we are always curious about the
population at hand. Indeed Americans seem to have an absolute
passion for pigeonholing each other into demographic categories,
and perhaps this habit is universal. After all, Indians use caste
marks to distinguish their people, Englishmen and Frenchmen
develop a sensitive ear for the accents of different countrymen,
and Africans have tribal markings. Despite our formal commitment
to equality, we have an overweening concern for the trappings of
inequality. Sometimes the motive for obtaining and emphasizing

data on age, race, sex, and occupation may be wholly salutory, such as a desire to establish affirmative action toward the goal of equal opportunity. At other times (and in various places) the motive may be mere curiosity or possibly a nefarious desire to keep certain people in their proper places. Whatever the motivation, the movement pushes on, and we continuously collect data (censuses, polls, surveys) along demographic lines. By now we have a literature of what groups go where, when they go, and why they go. The literature includes political parties, and often makes party membership the litmus test for certain other ideological and demographic characteristics.

From past studies, for example, it is possible to draw an interesting profile of the typical party voter. There appear to be clearly different partisan magnets at work attracting distinct types of adherents to the two major parties. The Republicans in general are found among the wealthier, slightly older, somewhat better schooled, and more Americanized of our voters. They are viewed (along with the party itself) as the more conservative group. The Democrats operate in the remaining demographic and ideological spheres. These portraits generally emerge from studies of the party presidential preferences of voters, and also from certain party leadership studies, which remind us of the fact that party activists and rank-and-file members are known to have different orientations; they have different demographic backgrounds too.[3]

In New York City the party profile appears to be somewhat different. A general population survey done by Daniel Yankelovich in 1973 found that "two of every three Republicans consider themselves conservative, but even among liberal Democrats, 36 percent characterized themselves as conservatives."[4] The conservative, as shown in the Yankelovich survey, is more likely to be older, less educated, and less affluent than the liberal. He is as likely, however, to be a white-collar worker as a blue-collar worker. This description, as well as other data from our own study, remind us that party labels are confusing clues to any particular set of demographic variables or even ideological leanings. If we think in terms of simple equations—the Conservative party must be conservative philosophically or ideologically, and more than that, must conform to the portrait of conservatives painted by Yankelovich or others in terms of age, income, occupation, etc.—we will be disappointed. Political life in New York City is far more complicated than such portraits would indicate. Certainly, there are some conventionally assumed associations confirmed by our data. Yet there are other parts of the party membership picture that are not at all obvious, as observed by Samuel Eldersveld:

> The Political party is as significant a social group
> as it is a political group. It is a social action system
> of 'interdependent activity' to use Herbert Simon's
> phrase. . . . It is not merely an individuated aggregate
> of leaders and activists, each of whom acts and thinks
> independently. Our analysis reveals that citizens join
> the party, and maintain or improve their leadership
> status in it, to fulfill basic motivational drives and
> needs. Over 50% admitted to personally instrumental
> satisfactions. They perceive the party as a group
> meaningful for personal ends. . . .[5]

Personal motivations, therefore, may make club membership in New York City less predictable than might at first be expected. In fact the study of party affiliation in the United States as a whole is at best a tricky business. Party preference in presidential voting, for example, is occasionally belied by voting behavior at other levels. Party enrollment, party membership among public officials, leaders who comprise the official local party hierarchy, and party financial contributors call forth different universes of people, even though they all may share one partisan umbrella. In this study we had still another cat by the tail: we were dealing with New York City's local club members. We followed the lead of the other group-gropers, however, in looking at those variables generally thought to be interesting in previous demographic studies: age, sex, marital status, occupation, race, and ethnicity.

There are two ways to look at these variables among New York City's political club membership. One is to note how our total universe of 112,899 club members breaks down in terms of the SES variables about which we will speak later in this chapter. The other is to describe a profile of a typical club and to report our data in terms of the percentages of clubs that have certain dominant types of people. We shall use both methods. It should be noted, however, that our data on the age, race, ethnicity, and occupation of the typical club member is based on estimates made by club leaders who consulted their membership lists at the request of our reporters. We also asked our reporters to carefully observe the portion of a membership that were present during their visits to the clubs, and to note any discrepancies; they were advised to probe these areas where necessary.

Typical Club Members

New York City's typical club members are mostly men (62 percent), mostly whites (68 percent), mostly married people (78

percent), mostly white-collar business or professional people
(90 percent), mostly Democrats (63 percent), and mostly people
over 35 years of age (75 percent). The typical member is more
likely to be Italian than any other ethnic possibility. The typical
club, however, is likely to be one in which about one-third of the
membership is Jewish. There are about 195 members in the typical
club, and while this prototype is likely to contain a preponderance
of men, it will also likely include a sizeable cadre of women
(approximately 40 percent). And among its women the single female
is likely to be a more familiar figure than the housewife.

In 1960, when Blanche D. Blank (one of the authors of this
book), Robert Hirshfield, and Bert Swanson examined a small
subset of the city's club members—the party committeemen and
committeewomen in Manhattan—their findings looked only mildly
different from the profile sketched above.[6] In the 1960 study the
typical Manhattan activist was found to be a middle-class or upper-
middle-class person, who very likely was Jewish (or at least
compared with any other single possibility), and very unlikely
black or Puerto Rican. Oddly enough there were more women
included in the 1960 activist group than in our current overall
membership figures: 44 percent of election district leaders in
the 1960 study were found to be female, but this may merely
reflect the traditional party practice of having a male and female
captain in each district. Certain other differences between the
1960 data and our current data will be noted later in this chapter
when we discuss the variables one by one.

Of course any typical club portrait washes out the interesting
deviations that will constitute an important part of this chapter.
For example, the profile that shows the most deviation is that of
the Conservative party clubs. The Conservative clubs show a
membership with a decidedly middle-aged bulge. They have
dramatically fewer members in the oldest age bracket than either
of the two major parties: only 6 percent of the Conservatives are
51 years old or over, compared to 24 percent of the Republicans
and 23 percent of the Democrats. Conservatives also show a sharp
deviation as far as race is concerned. That is, 98 percent of their
membership is white, whereas the Democrats are about 77 percent
white, and the Republicans 72 percent. Conservatives are also the
only party with an ethnically dominant group: Conservative clubs members are over 50 percent Italian (Republicans have a 47 percent Italian
membership). Conservative clubs are also a greater magnet for blue-
collar workers (17 percent of their membership are blue-collar people
as against 12 percent for Republican clubs and 10 percent for Democratic clubs). The typical Conservative club does not seem to attract
lawyers, who make up a mere one percent of their total membership,
and housewives, who make up only 10 percent of their membership.

Sex

The question of sexual equality in the political arena has occupied too little of the political scientist's time. [7] We hope that our data will help to close this gap, and that it will soften some of the impressions that are currently abroad, such as, "The most conspicious differences between men and women in the direction of their political involvement are in issue positions and candidate choices," [8] or, "Women are substantially less likely than men to engage in the whole range of activities available to the politically interested citizen," [9] or, "There is no question that in the United States women are less politically active, less participatory than men. They vote less, join fewer organizations, do less party work, read less and care less about politics." [10] Our data shows that there is less here than meets the eye. For example, club membership is generally an index of political interest and activity, and we found that 30 percent of club members in New York City are women. In general we tend to agree with Susan Borque and Jean Grossholtz, who concluded, from their analysis of political socialization and political differentiation literature, that women have "about the same level of interest and involvement in politics as most men." [11] Borque and Grossholtz also pointed out the need to allow for the years when women are kept at home by having to care for small children. These authors felt that women therefore do not willingly "opt out" of politics, but rather that they are helped out by the men who prefer to continue their dominance over them. Peel, too, noted this male dominance factor and commented on it. After citing the sociologist Moskowski, who had reported that in primitive societies the male house originated "in certain striving of the men to emancipate themselves from the tyranny of women," [12] Peel concluded that "the male (political) clubs are today havens for oppressed heads of families." [13] However one chooses to interpret the preponderance of males in American political party life—as stemming from male "tyranny" or from Moskowski's concept of female "tyranny"—it is clear that another comment by Peel is still generally accurate: "all parties maintain the illusion of equality between men and women, but only the minor parties even approach equality." [14] The female club members that Peel studied fell heir to a "general tendency to organize them (women) as auxiliary units," despite the fact that the state laws and party rules of that period made no provision for any such enclaves. [15] In 1968 Sorauf could still say, "Women have yet to achieve even a rough measure of equality of influence within the parties. The doctrine of 'separate but equal' now banned in education and public facilities still flourishes in the major American parties." [16]

TABLE 4.1

Number and Percent of Clubs That Have Various Ranges
of Female Membership, Citywide and by Party

Range of Female Membership (percent)	Citywide		Democrats		Republicans		Conservatives	
	Number	Percent	Number	Percent	Number	Percent	Number	Percent
0	8	3	7	5	0	0	1	4
1-20	34	13	23	15	5	8	5	19
21-40	64	25	41	27	9	14	10	38
41-60	111	44	66	43	33	55	9	35
61-80	19	7	7	5	9	14	2	8
81-100	6	2	1	1	5	8	0	0

Note: A total of 254 clubs are included (12 clubs reported data in unusable form); percentages are rounded off, so totals may not equal 100 percent.

In the microcosm of New York City's local party life women have made some advances. The clubs in the city seem somewhat more responsive to women's liberation, and 46 percent of the clubs have a female membership of between 41 percent and 60 percent (see Table 4. 1). In fact 53 percent of all clubs are over 40 percent female in their membership. Republican clubs reflect this characteristic even more than Democratic or Conservative clubs—78 percent of Republican clubs have at least a 40 percent female total, with 49 percent of Democratic clubs showing a 40 percent female grouping, and 43 percent of Conservative clubs showing the same figure. The fact that Republican clubs draw more women bears out an observation made by Sorauf that on a national basis women's organizations are more common to Republicans than to Democrats.[17] Indeed, despite the recent efforts of the Democratic party to balance their internal power structures along demographic lines (an effort that resulted in having women appear as 40 percent of the delegates to the 1972 Democratic National Convention), we found that in the local clubs of New York City seven of the eight clubs that have no women at all are Democratic. No Republican Clubs are in this category. Moreover 23 of the 34 clubs that have a female membership of less than 20 percent are Democratic, and this figure represents more than 70 percent of all clubs with less than 20 percent female membership and 15 percent of all Democratic clubs. Only 8 percent of the universe of Republican clubs were in this unbalanced situation. The Conservative figure in this regard matched the Democrats (15 percent).

Taking it from the opposite pole, the Republicans again demonstrate their distaff tendencies—of the six clubs that have a female membership of more than 80 percent, five are Republican. Only one is a Democratic club. In terms of each party's total membership, without regard to how it is distributed among the individual clubs, our data shows that slightly more than 50 percent of all Republican club members are women. By comparison only 39 percent of total Conservative club membership is female and only 34 percent of Democratic club membership.

Marital Status

Republicans as a group also seem to contain more married people than Democrats. Married people in fact dominate in the clubs as a whole, as we noted previously. Only 32 clubs out of our entire universe had an unmarried contingent of more than 40 percent, although 143 clubs also had a group of members (20 percent

TABLE 4.2

Number and Percent of Unmarried Male and Female Club Members,
Citywide and by Party

	Number of Unmarried Club Members Citywide	Percent of Total Members	Number of Unmarried Democratic Club Members	Percent of Total Members	Number of Unmarried Republican Club Members	Percent of Total Members	Number of Unmarried Conservative Club Members	Percent of Total Members
Female	5,518	5	4,264	6	850	3	113	4
Male	19,751	17	11,225	15	4,145	14	300	12
Total	25,269	22	15,489	21	4,995	17	413	16

TABLE 4.3

Number and Percent of Married and Unmarried Female
Club Members, Citywide and by Party

Marital Status of Females	Citywide		Democratic		Republican		Conservative	
	Number	Percent	Number	Percent	Number	Percent	Number	Percent
Married	37,162	33	20,836	28	13,906	47	893	35
Unmarried	5,518	5	4,264	6	850	3	113	4
Total	42,690	38	25,100	34	14,756	50	1,006	39

Note: Discrepancies between the citywide club membership column and the sum of the 3 party columns is due to the absence of figures for several small third-party clubs.

or less) that were unmarried but living with another person. Some political savants have pointed out that political clubs often serve as mating grounds. Peel, for example, observed that in clubs "the underlying reason for the social affairs conducted by and for young people of both sexes is matrimonial. . . . To the girls who live in the homes of their parents, the political club is one of the safest roads to a happy marriage, but not one of the surest, for apparently there are many unmarried ladies who gather at club functions without ever attracting an escort. "[18] One might wish that Peel would have reported the same fate for an equal number of young men. Our own data indicates that most single people as a whole gravitate to the Democratic clubs, which show 11,225 unmarried male members and 4,264 unmarried female members (see Table 4.2). In addition the clubs that have the heaviest percentages of single members (60 percent or more) are primarily Democratic clubs (66 percent, while only 22 percent are Republican). Moreover the singles group represents 21 percent of the total universe of Democratic clubs, but only 17 percent of the Republican club universe and 16 percent of the Conservative.

By party, the distribution of single women and single men in the clubs is rather noteworthy. The single membership among Democrats is 6 percent female; among Conservatives it is 4 percent, and among Republicans 3 percent. Overall, women represent 38 percent of the total club membership in the city (see Table 4.3), and single women represent 13 percent of the female contingent. It is interesting that single women account for 17 percent of the female membership in the Democratic party, while the comparable figure for the Conservatives is 11 percent and for the Republicans a modest 6 percent. This variation may be due to the fact that the more ubiquitous Democratic clubs are more accessible in a city where single women are not prepared to travel great distances at night to attend meetings. Moreover the Democratic party is the holding company for most of the reform clubs that may offer more of a certain cachet for young women, that may be a bit more fashionable, a bit more in. Or it may be that the Democrats come closer to the political ideology subscribed to by the type of single women who choose politics as an avocation. This is clearly an area that deserves further probing.

Age

In the clubs studied by Peel young people were siphoned off into special club auxiliaries: a group of 18-to-30-year-olds and,

TABLE 4.4

Percent of Club Members in Various Age Groups,
All Clubs and by Party

Age Group	All Clubs	Democratic	Republican	Conservative
18–21	4	5	5	1
22–30	8	8	10	12
31–35	12	12	16	19
36–42	18	21	20	28
43–50	22	31	20	34
51 and over	18	23	24	6

Note: Our total universe = 112,899 members.

occasionally, a group of 10-to-17-year-olds. Today young people are integrated into most clubs (at least those who are 18 or over), but they are generally sparse in number. We found that 114 clubs, for example, had no members under 21, 161 clubs had 5 percent or less under 21, 176 had 10 percent or less, and 188 had 20 percent or less. It should be noted that for every age group designated in our survey instrument we found some clubs that had no members in a particular group. Thus 75 clubs had no members in the 22-30 age group; 51 clubs had no 31-35-year-olds; 31 clubs had no 36-42-year-olds; 25 clubs had no 43-50-year-olds; and 56 clubs had nobody over 51. Indeed the number of clubs with members in each age group was quite scattered. The most notable observation is that most clubs had their heaviest membership in the over 35-year old categories. This data is similar to findings regarding the ages of club members in St. Louis, reported by Robert H. Salisbury in 1968.[19]

We found that only 24 percent of New York City's total club membership is under 35 years of age (see Table 4.4). This figure is remarkably similar to the 25 percent of Manhattan activists found to be in the same category in the 1960 study cited previously.[20] Overall, club membership seems to attract mostly 43-to-50-year-olds. When we look at party breakdowns, however, some interesting differences occur. Republicans in New York City clubs seem to be younger than Democrats. This runs counter to both common wisdom and the national trends.

A 1974 public opinion survey, for example, reported that 50 percent of the Republican party was over 50 years of age. Indeed 25 percent were over 65, and a whopping 75 percent were over 40.[21] It should be noted, however, that this poll, like many polls, fails to specify exactly what constitutes its universe. Party membership might be assessed through voting statistics, self-designation, voter registration, or party enrollment figures; and in this poll we are not entirely certain which universe is being used. Whatever its precise basis, however, the report indicates that the typical national Republican party member is quite a bit older than both his Democratic counterpart and the New York City Republican club member.

The age profile at the 1972 Democratic National Convention, where the party was making an obvious effort to be representative, showed 24 percent of the delegates to be under 30, 50 percent to be between 31 and 50, and 26 percent over 51. New York City's Democratic club contingent on the whole is not as young as the 1972 national delegates were—not as young, for example, as the Democratic contingent of committeemen found in Pittsburgh in 1960,[22] not as young as New York City's Republican club members. Only 13 percent of the city's Democratic club members are under 30, while 64 percent are between 31 and 50; however, only 23 percent are over 51. By comparison 15 percent of the city's Republican club members are under 30, 31 percent are under 35, and 24 percent are over 51. Thus for the Republicans the center of gravity on age seems to be the group that is 36 to 42, while for both Democrats and Conservatives it is the 43-50 bracket.

The usually close relationship between conservatism and age is jolted not only by the data reported above, but also by the fact that the Conservative clubs in New York City boast a relatively youthful membership. Of course one can speculate, as we did, that the party label is not an accurate ideological tag. Moreover the confusion that prevails in assessing partisan proclivities and demographic variables is always exacerbated by the problem of which set of data to look at. In any event it is the Conservative party clubs in the city that have the largest membership in the under-35-year-old group (32 percent) and the smallest percentage by far in the over-51-year-old category (6 percent).

If we wish to compare our age data with citywide age patterns, we have to make a few adjustments because our data collection does not follow precisely the census age groupings. Yet certain categories are close enough to warrant comparison. On a citywide basis, 36 percent of the population (according to U.S. Census data for 1970) is in the 18-34 category, but only 24 percent of the 18-35 group appear in party club ranks. Even more dramatic is the disparity between the citywide figure of 25 percent found for 35-49-year-olds, and the 40 percent party membership found in the 36-50 group (a far greater disparity than might be accounted for by the category shift). Finally, party club membership shows its predilection for age in the over-51 group, which has an 18 percent membership, as against the citywide 14 percent grouping for 50-64-year-olds. In general we found that local clubs are not entirely reflective of citywide age patterns. Rather they show a tendency to underrepresent the city's youth, and to overrepresent its middle and upper age brackets.

Occupations

Our occupational data also revealed a few surprises. We singled out the following occupational categories for special attention: lawyers, real estate brokers, teachers, students, government employees, and housewives. We also tapped major class groupings—white-collar and blue-collar—but omitted the category of gambling that figured vividly in Peel's account.

It seems clear enough from our data that club members on

Number and Percent of Clubs That Have Various Percentages of
Blue-Collar Membership, by Party

Percentage of Blue-Collar Membership	Democratic		Republican		Conservative		Total	
	Number	Percent	Number	Percent	Number	Percent	Number	Percent
0	34	21	14	21	2	8	50	19
1–25	60	37	23	32	14	53	97	37
26–50	18	11	6	8	5	19	29	12
51–75	4	2	1	1	0	0	5	2
76 or over	2*	1	0	0	0	0	2	7/10

*One of these clubs claimed that its membership was 100 percent blue-collar.
Note: Percents do not add up to 100 percent because 75 clubs did not provide data on this item.

TABLE 4.7

Number and Percent of Blue-Collar and White-Collar Club Members
All Clubs and by Party

Group	Total For All Clubs	Percent of Total Club Membership	Democratic		Republican		Conservative	
			Number	Percent	Number	Percent	Number	Percent
Blue-collar	11,717	10	6,531	10	3,187	12	404	17
White-collar	15,882	14	8,987	14	5,333	21	673	29

Note: Totals include minor parties.

the whole are heavily middle class in terms of occupation. This agrees with the earlier study made of Manhattan activists, which pointed out the same middle-class phenomenon in terms of a number of SES variables. Salisbury noted the middle class dominance among activists in St. Louis,[23] and Sorauf also discussed this phenomenon with respect to party officeholders on a national basis,[24] the present New York City situation offers some interesting distinctions. Although the Democrats are thought to attract to their rank and file the so-called "lower classes,"[25] in New York City's club life there is some doubt about this matter. To the degree that we usually equate "lower class" with blue-collar workers, we should note that there are 34 Democratic clubs that have no blue-collar membership at all (see Table 4.6). Moreover the 14 Republican clubs that have no blue-collar members represent the same proportion (21 percent) of their party's total number of clubs as do the Democratic clubs. Only 3 percent of the Democratic club universe is predominantly (over 50 percent) blue-collar in membership. It is perhaps stranger that there should be any Republican clubs in this grouping, but there is one such club; there are no Conservative clubs with a predominance of blue-collar membership, hard-hat stereotypes notwithstanding. We found one Democratic club that claimed that its entire membership was blue-collar. Defining a membership of more than 25 percent as "substantial," we found that 14 percent of the Democratic clubs, 9 percent of the Republican clubs, and 19 percent of the Conservative clubs have a substantial blue-collar membership. Our figures hardly reflect the "distinct differences" Eldersveld found between Democratic and Republican leaders in Detroit, where Republicans were decidedly white-collar and Democrats blue-collar.[26]

Our overall membership figures reflect the same ambiguity we found between the occupations of Democratic and Republican club members (see Table 4.7). The Democrats have a 10 percent blue-collar group, the Republicans have a 12 percent blue-collar membership, and the Conservatives claim 17 percent. All of this may reflect the finding in the Yankelovich survey (noted before) that "persons who are conservative in their opinions are almost evenly divided between white- and blue-collar occupation."[27] Although white-collar workers should be the most ubiquitous category in terms of the general work distribution pattern in New York City—and they are a larger cadre than are the blue-collar workers—there are nonetheless 34 clubs in our total that have no members at all in the white-collar category (see Table 4.8). It should be noted in connection with this table, and with other findings in this book, that the nature of our survey instrument was such that people reporting items in the white-collar category were responding to the idea of clerical and, possibly, sales work, rather than to any more technical or inclusive meaning. This

TABLE 4.8

Number and Percent of Clubs That Have Various Percentages
of White-Collar Membership, by Party

Percentage of White-Collar Membership	Democratic		Republican		Conservative		Total	
	Number	Percent	Number	Percent	Number	Percent	Number	Percent
0	22	13	9	13	3	12	34	13
1-25	68	41	19	27	7	27	94	36
26-50	20	12	11	15	5	19	36	14
51-75	6	4	3	4	2	8	11	4
76 or over	2	1	1	1	3	11	6	2

Note: Percentages do not add to 100 percent because some club respondents did not have figures or refused to provide them for this item.

TABLE 4.9

Number and Percent of Club Members in Selected
Occupations, by Party

Occupation	Democratic		Republican		Conservative		Total	
	Number	Percent	Number	Percent	Number	Percent	Number	Percent
Lawyer	9,893	16	1,797	7	26	1	11,880	10
Real estate	1,180	2	2,059	8	28	1	3,279	3
Teacher	3,606	6	1,753	7	105	5	6,400	6
Student	7,280	11	942	4	156	7	9,838	9
Housewife	8,765	14	5,125	20	238	10	14,305	13
Government Employee	10,595	17	2,250	9	223	10	13,421	12

definitional problem probably accounts for the fact that there is only a 4 percent difference between the figures for total white-collar membership and total blue-collar membership. Of the clubs that have no white-collar membership, 22 are Democratic, nine are Republican, and three are Conservative. Curiously each set of figures in this category represents an almost identical proportion of each party's total number of clubs (13 percent for the Democrats and Republicans, and 12 percent for the Conservatives). On the other hand, 17 clubs are actually dominated by the white-collar group; in this instance again Republicans and Democrats are two peas in a pod, since 5 percent of each party's clubs are in this group. Among the Conservative clubs 19 percent have a preponderant membership (over 15 percent) that is white-collar.

In terms of numbers of members the Conservatives have the heaviest white-collar cadre—29 percent. Republicans have 21 percent of their membership in this group, and the Democrats only 14 percent. Regarding some of the white-collar workers not included in the foregoing tables—professionals, housewives, and students—we have more detailed information.

It is commonly supposed that the legal profession dominates the political scene. Indeed Sorauf noted, "In all of American politics, including political parties, the lawyers are the high priests of the cult."[28] However, this is not so in New York City's clubs: 170 of 263 clubs (65 percent) have lawyers' ranks of less than 25 percent. Lawyers comprise only 10 percent of the actual number of members; in fact lawyers rank third in our list of selected occupations in terms of group size (see Table 4.9). Less than 4 percent of the clubs have membership rolls in which 26-to-50 percent (which might be considered a dominating group) are lawyers, and only 2 percent of the clubs have lawyers as a majority of their membership. The Republican ranks have considerably fewer lawyers than the Democratic ranks (membership figures are 7 percent and 16 percent respectively), and the Conservatives show the smallest number of lawyers (1 percent) despite a common tendency to equate Conservatism with the legal profession. In fact neither the Republicans nor the Conservatives have a single club with a lawyers' group of over 25 percent. This, however, may be explained by motives of self-interest.

Aside from the well noted general affinity between law and politics commented on by Sorauf, Eulau, and Sprague,[29] and by others, lawyers often join political clubs because they want to find jobs and clients. They may, for example, want to break into politics in their quest for a judgeship. In New York the avenue to judgeships would seem to lie more with the Democratic party than with the Republicans, since in electoral terms only Democrats get elected to judgeships (civil court elections, for instance). Furthermore the mayor appoints a number of interim judges, and the mayors of New York have been almost exclusively Democrats. True the state has been controlled by Republicans, and indeed former Governor Rockefeller appointed a number of Republican judges, but he also made certain deals to appoint Democrats as well.

In terms of elected positions we also know that the bulk of legislators including congressmen, councilmen, assemblymen, and state senators are lawyers. And most of the congressmen in New York City are in districts that are safely Democratic. Therefore a young lawyer who aspires to these offices would do better joining a Democratic club rather than a Republican club. Finally, big contractors and others in New York City who employ lawyers would be more likely to be affiliated with the Democratic party, due to the Democratic nature of the city; thus lawyers who seek jobs related to these businesses also find that Democratic district leaders help them more than Republican leaders.

Although real-estate operators may also be commonly fancied as important members of a particular party's clubs, for the same obvious occupational advantages that might attract lawyers, the clubs in New York City do not include large numbers of real-estate people. Only 32 percent of the universe of clubs have over 10 percent of their members in the real-estate business, and this group constitutes only 3 percent of all club membership. Real-estate people are in fact the smallest club segment: Republicans have 8 percent of their members in this group, Democrats have only 3 percent, and Conservatives 1 percent. Perhaps this confirms the general impression that Republicans are the businessman's party.

Teachers are also scarce in political clubs, with only 6 percent of the club members employed as teachers, and the figure remaining most constant for each party. We found that 183 clubs have never had more than 25 percent of their members in the teaching profession, and that some 50 clubs have no teachers in their ranks at all, despite the much-publicized efforts of New York City's United Federation of Teachers to infiltrate New York City politics. Only 4 clubs have a majority of members who are teachers. Yet teachers supposedly have the time, the flexibility, and the interest in civic affairs that might draw them into club life.

Students are less scarce in clubs than teachers. While 62 clubs have no students at all, and 117 clubs show a student membership of less than 25 percent there are 4 clubs that claim students as their dominant group. The overall club membership figures show a 9 percent student grouping, with notably fewer students among Republicans (the group constitutes only 4 percent of Republican membership) than among Democrats (where students occupy 11 percent of the rolls).

We have now moved into an era where it is becoming fashionable (as well as accurate) to consider housewives as an occupational group, even though this group is still considered unlikely to figure largely in the ranks of party clubs. However, it turned out in our study that housewives are the single largest group in New York City's clubs. There are 12 Democratic clubs (7 percent of total Democratic clubs) and 7 Republican clubs (10 percent of Republican clubs) in which housewives provide the majority of the membership. Overall membership figures reveal that housewives occupy 20 percent of the Republican ranks, but only 14 percent of the Democratic ranks and 10 percent of the Conservative ranks. We found on the other hand that 38 clubs (14 percent of total clubs) have no housewives at all. This group includes 22 Democratic clubs, 8 Republican clubs, and 8 Conservative clubs. In addition 85 clubs (32 percent) have housewives' groups of less than 10 percent: 56 of these are Democratic clubs, 15 are Republican, and 14 Conservative.

Another occupational group that deserves mention are professional politicians. The presence of a high-ranking public or party officer in a particular club is in itself a symbol both of the club's past success and its future promise—it is clearly a prestige ornament for such a club. While the social status of cerain public officers is clearly higher than that of other officers, their actual and potential club usefulness is somewhat more complicated to assess—patronage, for example, does not always flow most freely from the top. A lesser official with access to government contracts or judicial patronage can sometimes do more for a membership group than a U.S. senator, whose access may be both more restrained and more broadly dispersed. There is also the question of the future plans and possibilities of particular elected or party officials— that is, does an official have a rising star or a setting sun? In this study we were unable to make sophisticated analysis of club success in terms of these variables, but the potential for this, and a part of the raw data, is available.

How many clubs have various public officials among their membership? Out of our universe of 268 clubs, we found 62 clubs had a current congressman in their ranks, 59 clubs had state senators, 113 had assemblymen, 75 had city councilmen (past or present), 145 had district leaders, 97 had state committeemen, 84 had state committeewomen, and 53 had assorted other office-holders.

There are two sets of political posts that require particular comment: the roster of administrative-type civil servants (the people who are recorded in our "government employee" category in Table 4.9) and the judges. Civil servants constitute New York City's second largest group of club members, yet they are a more modest number than might be expected in a city with over 300,000 government workers.[30] Part of the explanation for this might be the Hatch Act, a federal law that enjoins those government employees who receive national funding from active partisan political work. Therefore, although there are over 13,000 government workers in the city's clubs, there are still 158 clubs (or 59 percent of the membership universe) that have no such appointees among their members. In addition only 78 clubs (12 percent of the membership universe) have one or more government employees. As might be expected, the Democrats have the lion's share. They account for about 79 percent of the overall civil servants' group in clubs, and 17 percent of their own membership is composed of civil servants. Only 9 percent of the Republican membership are government workers, and 10 percent of the Conservatives. The Democratic strength in this category, one would assume, is due to their fairly constant political ascendancy in New York City. Most elections are expected to "go Democratic" and they usually do. Civil servants are sensitive to this constant in the city's political affairs.

The city's judicial arena is somewhat more complicated. There are upward of 600 state and local judges in New York City, but our club membership figures in relation to that figure are ambiguous at best. One club listed 82 judges as members, 6 clubs boasted six judges each, 5 clubs claimed five judges apiece, 10 clubs had four judges each, 13 clubs had three judges each, and 28 clubs had two judges each. What is curious about these figures is that they are either too large or too small. That is, the Canons of Judicial Ethics makes it illegal, immoral, and improper for judges to either belong to political clubs or be active in political affairs. In this light it is almost unbelievable that any of the city's clubs actually have judges on their membership roll. Perhaps a certain portion of these judges can be accounted for as being titular judges only, since it is not uncommon to use the title of judge for any person who has at any time served as a judge for two consecutive days. On the other hand, we must also consider the possibility that our figures are far too modest. Perhaps some club officers were being candid with us where others were not. In any event it is worth noting that former Mayor Lindsay told a House subcommittee on the judiciary that New York's judges had "become too insulated from the public and too lacking in accountability. It would be better if the judges went back into the clubhouses occasionally. At least then they'd have someone who'd ask them questions."[31]

As to being a party professional in terms of having a post in the party's governing structure, or in a club's governing structure, it should be pointed out that only 17 percent of the clubs

pay salaries to anyone. Not only that, but most of the clubs that do
pay salaries are clubs with over 500 members. We did not collect
data on the number of active salaried members, nor on their party
affiliation. It is important also to not be misled by the 17 percent
figure. Most of the salaries paid to club employees are nominal,
with many amounting to no more than several hundred dollars a
year. In some clubs the salaries are not paid out of club treasuries,
but rather out of the public till. These salaries are for "no show"
jobs handed out to club employees, usually by state legislators.
No work is entailed in these posts—the employees simply signing
for their pay checks. For the most part the club employees who
enjoy such sinecures are elderly club members, retired from their
previous jobs. They are often given honorary titles to go with these
club jobs, such as sergeant at arms, whose major responsibility
in the club is to lock and unlock the doors, answer the telephone,
and pick up the mail. Several clubs may also use these people as
part-time custodians. Full-time, paid secretaries and administrative
aides, once a feature of many clubs, are today virtually nonexistent.
The only exceptions are those clubs where legislators (councilmen,
assemblymen, state senators, and congressmen) use the clubhouse
itself as an office, and staff it with their own employees, who
occasionally take care of club business as well.

In many ways this entire situation is paradoxical, in that
it exemplifies the American ambivalence toward politics. Work
in the business world is expected to be paid. In politics people
are supposed to work hard and demand nothing in return. If they
do make demands, these needs are met with subterfuge and
sinecure. How much better our partisan politics might be if party
work were clearly recognized as legitimate, time-consuming, and
often high-level work, and if, in turn, it were paid for openly and
appropriately. Such a system might go a long way toward
legitimatizing politics in America.

Race and Ethnicity

Race and ethnicity are among the most persistent and
pervasive elements affecting life in New York City, particularly so
in political life. Peel remarked for example that metropolitan
politics is "Catholic-Jewish politics," and when now and then there
has been an emergent Wasp-type upper-class club, it has deserved
special attention as a deviant case.[32] The ethnic factor at the time
of Peel's study was such a strong force that there were 750 special
nationality clubs in existence, as well as 32 racial clubs (Negro,

Chinese, Filipino). At that time the largest ethnic group were Italians, with Germans and Slavs as runners-up. The Irish who were clearly in the driver's seat in New York City politics, were entrenched in the regular clubs, and only beginning to sense the dangers of the oncoming Italian encroachment. Peel devoted considerable attention to these special nationality clubs, which were not at all the same as the rest of his universe of political clubs, although from time to time they served certain political purposes. Peel classified these nationality clubs in terms of the manner in which they came to be organized. In many instances the nationality clubs were initiated by a regular party club as an appendage. In other instances a member of a distinctive ethnic group, chafed at being overlooked, would organize what was essentially a revoltist club, along nationality lines. Some of the nationality clubs sprang up from indigenous grassroots movements as new ethnic neighborhoods emerged in the city, and many were branches of national civil, fraternal, and recreational groups. In all cases one party or another derived some electoral benefits from the clubs. The Irish, Eastern Europeans and Orientals clung mainly to the Democratic party of that era;[33] Jews were divided between both major parties and were also attracted to the more ideological fringe parties, like the Socialists. Italians were also divided between Democrats and Republicans, although they soon began to move more strongly into Republican ranks. In the ensuing generations, however, the most notable occurrence was the disappearance altogether of the nationality clubs per se. The ethnic clubs were either absorbed into the mainstream regular clubs of their districts, or they ebbed away as a new generation appeared that was less ethnic and more American.

Nonetheless the habit of viewing club politics as ethnic politics did not die. Edward C. Banfield and James Q. Wilson still made much of racial and ethnic divisions as a key to urban analysis.[34] They claimed, for example, to perceive a considerable difference between Wasp politics and ethnic politics, considering the former to be moralistic and generalizing, and the latter personal and hierarchical. Other studies, also purporting to show a distinctive Wasp politics, found the Wasp group to be particularly amenable to political activity.[35] The ethnic data in our study, however, does not lend itself to this type of abstraction; thus our report on this data will be essentially a straightforward presentation of ethnic membership patterns among the clubs of New York City's parties.

The color line in the city's clubs is still quite clearly drawn. Most of the clubs—over 80 percent are predominantly white (see Table 4.10). In this category are 91 percent of the

TABLE 4.10

Percent of Clubs That Have a Predominantly
White or Black Membership, by Party

Membership	Democratic	Republican	Conservative	Total
50 percent white or more	89	91	100	80
50 percent black or more	9	9	0	20

TABLE 4.11

Number and Percent of Club Members of Different Races,
by Party and Citywide

Race	Democratic Number	Percent	Republican Number	Percent	Conservative Number	Percent	Citywide Number	Percent
Black	11,443	17	5,523	21	49	2	17,015	18
White	53,148	81	19,469	77	2,431	98	75,048	80
Oriental	878	1	384	2	1	0	1,263	1
Total	65,469		25,376		2,481		93,326	

Note: Percentages for parties do not total 100 percent because of NA's.

Republican clubs and 89 percent of the Democratic clubs. In all, 109 clubs are heavily white. What we refer to as "predominantly" white, or black, are those clubs reporting a white, or black, membership of more than 50 percent. We found four clubs with 100 percent black membership and ten other clubs with a black membership of over 80 percent. Twenty-four clubs were reported to have over 40 percent black membership. This picture is very similar to the one that existed at the time of Peel's study, when what there was of black political power was essentially represented by only two clubs, both of these being Republican.[36] Today it is the Democrats that are more likely to represent the black population rather than the Republicans, although the picture is far from clear. While 85 percent of the few nonwhite clubs are indeed Democratic, the Democrats also account for 61 percent of all those clubs where the membership is 80 percent white or more. In this sense they might be considered more segregationist in tone than the Republicans. Perhaps Republican blacks are more middle class, and are thus integrated more easily. Or perhaps it is premature to think in terms of integration when power politics is at stake. Maybe we have not yet advanced from the position that Peel posited in 1929 when he commented on the special ethnic and racial clubs as follows:

> There is much to be said in favor of nationality political clubs. Perhaps only through these and similar agencies can we effectively stamp out the social evils resulting from the conflicts among alien and American cultures. It seems, however, to be essential to the ultimate ordering of enlightened public opinion that we face resolutely the issue as to whether we wish to encourage or discourage the amalgamation of these heterogenous polyglot elements which now compose our urban population.[37]

According to the overall membership figures for each race (see Table 4.11) it is the Democrats that seem slightly less receptive to blacks than do the Republicans: 78 percent of all club members among the Democrats are white, whereas 72 percent among Republicans are white. The Conservatives are virtually an entirely white enclave (98 percent). Perhaps what is indicated by these figures is that the political clubs of New York City are essentially responsive to racial demography. There are black clubs in Harlem and in Bedford Stuyvesant and in other predominantly black areas of the city. Some of these areas, or portions of them, are occupied by middle-class homeowners, and

85

are essentially Republican in tone; thus black Republican clubs spring up. The 20 percent of Republican club membership that is black is almost identical to the proportion of blacks in the general population of the city (21 percent).

Orientals form a miniscule portion of New York City's club membership—roughly 1 percent, which is equally divided between Democrats and Republicans, although the two predominantly Oriental clubs are both Democratic. We found that 85 percent of all the city's clubs have not a single Oriental member. This is not entirely surprising, given the relatively small percentage of Orientals in the city, and their heavy concentration in relatively few neighborhoods. There is also a possibility that there are illegal aliens (products of a still somewhat racist U.S. immigration policy) harbored in some Oriental families, and that these families shy away from political registration or from club contact of any sort, being reluctant to call attention to themselves.

The most underrepresented ethnic group in the city's clubs is the Hispanic group: 61 percent of the clubs have no Hispanic members, 32 percent have less than 20 percent that are Spanish, and only two clubs have a Spanish membership of over 40 percent. The 5,058 Spanish club members constitute only 4 percent of the total club membership, and are 4 percent of the club membership of each of the two major parties, with the Spanish cohort among Conservatives being negligible.

Jews in American politics are something of an oddity. First, they generally appear as allies of the Wasp contingent in their political style. That is, they are "other regarding" in Banfield and Wilson's terminology,[38] and they are, generally speaking, oriented to liberal ideologies, despite enjoying, by and large, upper-middle-class socioeconomic status.[39] Peel described them in the New York club scene as a group that during their earlier immigration drifted into the Republican party, and that later had a type of "entente cordiale" with the then dominant Irish by virtue of their being given various judicial and legislative plums, but that finally emerged into both major parties, as well as becoming a dominant force in the ideologically liberal fringe parties, such as the Socialists.[40] Today the Jews are virtually the only supporters of the Liberal party, but they are also a very important part of the Democratic party.

Although there are 30 clubs in the city (16 percent) that have no Jews at all, there are 75 clubs (39 percent) that have a Jewish membership of over 40 percent (see Table 4.12). Of these 75 clubs, 88 percent are Democratic. Looking at it another way, among all Democratic clubs, one-half have what we would call a substantial Jewish membership. This follows a national trend among Jews to

TABLE 4.12

Number and Percent of Clubs That Have Various
Percentages of Jewish Members, by Party

Percentage of Club Members That Are Jewish	Democratic		Republican		Conservative		Total	
	Number	Percent	Number	Percent	Number	Percent	Number	Percent
0	14	11	9	20	7	30	30	15
1–20	30	24	22	49	7	30	62	31
21–40	19	15	7	16	6	26	33	17
41–60	25	20	6	13	3	14	35	18
61–80	16	13	1	2	0	0	17	9
81–100	23	18	0	0	0	0	23	12

Note: Percentages may total slightly more or less than 100 percent due to rounding; percentage of clubs refers to the universe reporting on these items.

TABLE 4.13

Number and Percent of Clubs That Have Various
Percentages of Italian Members, by Party

Percentage of Club Members That Are Italian	Democratic		Republican		Conservative		Total	
	Number	Percent	Number	Percent	Number	Percent	Number	Percent
0	25	20	3	7	1	4	29	15
1–20	51	41	13	29	3	13	70	36
21–40	25	20	7	16	9	39	42	21
41–60	15	12	16	36	7	30	39	20
61–80	5	4	3	7	2	9	10	5
81–100	2	2	3	7	1	4	6	3

Note: Percentages may total slightly more or less than 100 percent due to rounding; percentage of clubs refers to the universe reporting on these items.

affiliate with the Democratic Party.[41] Oddly enough, however, this Jewish strength in the dominant party of New York City had never helped put a Jew in the city's highest office, the mayoralty, until the election of Abraham Beame in 1973. The city's Jews had seemed content, until Beame's successful candidacy, with their place on the traditionally balanced ticket in the city, in which the usual "Jewish" spot was the comptroller's office (a post Beame held until his 1973 mayoral victory). There is some evidence, as noted above, that Jews, more than others, view politics as ideology, and that they have chosen to employ their influence behind those candidates (usually liberals) who expressed their ideological preferences, without regard to ethnic coloring. Jews were among the chief supporters of LaGuardia's Fusion candidacy and were clearly among the early enthusiasts for Lindsay, a Wasp. Thus Beame's election may be more an index of some weather changes in the liberalism of a significant portion of New York City's Jews than of any newfound enthusiasm for having one of their own in the political limelight.

For Italians politics may be more of a spectacle than it is for other groups. There is perhaps a greater desire in Italians for an ethnic visibility, which they have, on more than one occasion, achieved—not only in the LaGuardia and Impellitteri mayoralties, but also in many other prominent citywide offices, judgeships, legislative posts, and, for a long time, in the leadership of Tammany Hall by the "tiger of Tammany," Carmine DeSapio. Peel predicted this potential when he noted, "When the old leaders of the major parties relax (and if the Italians find a leader of metropolitan proportions) they will fall before the massed strength of the Italians."[42] And of course this prediction came to pass. Today, what Peel termed "the massed strength of the Italians" is centered heavily in the Republican party and in the Conservative ranks. The Italians are the largest single ethnic group in New York City's political club membership: they constitute 26 percent of all club troops (see Table 4.13). Their membership breaks down into party strengths as follows: 50 percent of Conservative ranks, 47 percent of Republican ranks, and only 25 percent of the Democratic membership. While 20 percent of Democratic clubs have no Italian membership, this happens in only 7 percent of the Republican clubs and in 4 percent of the Conservative clubs. In addition 28 percent of all clubs in the city have an Italian membership of over 40 percent, but only 18 percent of the Democratic clubs show this figure, compared to 50 percent of the Republican clubs and 43 percent of the Conservative clubs. To put it another way, 44 percent of all dominantly Italian clubs are Republican and 16 percent are Conservative.

One of the hardest findings to believe in our current study is the waning club role of the Irish. They had been the ethnic group for whom politics was a favorite game, and a game well played.

Peel described it as follows:

> The Irish have long enjoyed the reputation of being
> America's most skillful political leaders, particularly
> in the cities. With their genial ways, unscrupulous
> use of power, alertness in seizing opportunities,
> and industry in all the arduous duties of petty
> politics, they have kept their hands on the helm
> of the municipal ship of state for over a century.[43]

It is true that Tammany Hall leadership was under Irish control
from 1872 until 1949, which saw the advent of DeSapio and the
beginning of Italian primacy in New York City politics. As
Daniel P. Moynihan and Wilson put it, "The ancient Irish hegemony
was giving way (after 1954) before the pressure from Italians
within the regular organization and (Jewish) reform liberals as
yet outside it. . . . In fact the ticket on which Averell Harriman
ran for Governor that year was the first in decades that had no
Irish Catholic running for a major executive office."[44]

The declining significance of the Irish in club politics
is underscored by the fact that 30 percent of the city's clubs are
without a single Irish member, and only 1 percent have an Irish
membership of over 60 percent (see Table 4.14). (If we lower
the percentage that defines dominance to a membership figure of
40 percent or more, the percent of Irish in this dominating
category rises to 9 percent.) In this universe of Irish clubs 89
percent are Democratic. Yet the Irish contingent constitutes a
mere 9 percent of the Democratic universe. It is as though the
Irish still cling to the Democrats, but the Democrats no longer
cling to the Irish. Our overall membership figures did not alter
these conclusions, although the weightings were different. We
found that Irish membership constitutes an 18 percent slice among
the Democrats, a mere 2 percent among Republicans, but 22 percent
for the Conservative clubs. This last figure bears out the finding
of the Yankelovich survey (discussed earlier in this chapter) that
depicts the Irish in New York City as the most conservative group
ideologically speaking. In this instance perhaps political ideology
and party labels have some congruence. There has also been some
comment that the Irish may reascend to prominence in American
politics: a 1974 analysis indicated that "just as two years ago black,
Puerto Rican and youth were the 'in' group during the last
Presidential campaign, it may well be in terms of New York
gubernatorial politics that once again the Irish and Italians will
return to importance."[45]

If politically the Irish have waned, the Wasps have gone
into a total eclipse. The latter development has been a long-term

TABLE 4.14

Number and Percent of Clubs That Have Various
Percentages of Irish Members, by Party

Percentage of Club Members That Are Irish	Democratic		Republican		Conservative		Total	
	Number	Percent	Number	Percent	Number	Percent	Number	Percent
0	41	33	11	24	4	17	59	30
1-20	48	39	23	51	4	17	76	39
21-40	24	20	7	16	12	52	44	22
41-60	9	7	4	9	3	13	16	8
61-80	1	1	0	0	0	0	1	.5

Note: Percentage columns may total slightly more or less than 100 percent due to rounding; percent of clubs refers to the universe reporting on these items.

phenomenon—in New York City, as in other urban enclaves, the Wasps have retired to other power arenas, and have left politics to the "newer races."[46] The remaining Wasp members of the clubs in New York City, a mere 4 percent of total club membership, are more concentrated in the Conservative clubs (9 percent) than, as one would have expected, in the Republican clubs (3 percent). There are more Wasps even among the Democratic ranks (6 percent) than the Republicans. They certainly cannot be discounted as a political force in the city, but they can be more or less ignored as far as the clubs are concerned.

Notes

1. Bernard Berelson, Paul F. Lazarsfeld and W. N. McPhee, Voting: A Study of Opinion Formation in a Presidential Campaign (Chicago: University of Chicago Press, 1954); Herbert McClosky, "Conservatism and Personality," American Political Science Review 49 (March 1955); Avery Leiserson, Parties and Politics (New York: Alfred A. Knopf, 1958); Robert E. Lane, "Political Personality and Electoral Choice," American Political Science Review 49 (March 1955); James Q. Wilson, Negro Politics: The Search for Leadership (New York: The Free Press of Glencoe, 1969); M. Kent Jennings and I. Harmon Ziegler, eds., The Electoral Process (Englewood Cliffs, N.J.: Prentice-Hall, 1966).

2. Frank Sorauf, Political Parties in the American System (Boston: Little, Brown, 1964), pp. 1-6.

3. Herbert McClosky, Paul J. Hoffman, and Rosemary O'Hara, "Issue Conflict and Consensus Among Party Leaders and Followers," American Political Science Review 54 (June 1960).

4. New York Times, Jan. 15, 1974.

5. Samuel J. Eldersveld, Political Parties: A Behavioral Analysis (Chicago: Rand McNally, 1964), p. 52.

6. Blanche D. Blank, Robert Hirshfield and Bert Swanson, "A Profile of Political Activists in Manhattan," Western Political Quarterly, September 1962, p. 493.

7. Kent Jennings, "Men and Women in Party Elections," Midwest Journal of Political Science, November 1968.

8. Fred I. Greenstein, Children and Politics (New Haven: Yale University Press, 1965), p. 107.

9. Ibid., p. 108.

10. Dean Jaros, Socialization to Politics (New York: Praeger, 1973).

11. Susan Borque and Jean Grossholtz, "Politics as an Unnatural Practice: Political Science looks at Female Participation," (paper given at American Political Science Association, New Orleans, September 1973).

12. Roy V. Peel, The Political Clubs of New York, rev. ed. (New York: Ira S. Friedman, 1968), p. 127.

13. Ibid., p. 128.

14. Ibid., p. 62.

15. Ibid., p. 148.

16. Sorauf, op. cit., pp. 116-117.

17. Ibid., p. 72.

18. Peel, op. cit., p. 173.

19. Robert H. Salisbury, "The Urban Party Organization Member," Public Opinion Quarterly, No. 29 (Winter 1965), p. 553.

20. Blank, Hirshfield and Swanson, op. cit., p. 494.

21. New York Times, Jan. 21, 1974.

22. William Keefe and William Seyler, "Precinct Politicians in Pittsburgh," Social Sciences 35 (1960) 26, n. 2.

23. Salisbury, op. cit., p. 551.

24. Sorauf, op. cit., pp. 92-94.

25. Ralph Goldman, The Democratic Party and American Politics (New York: Macmillan, 1966), p. 23.

26. Samuel J. Eldersveld, op. cit., p. 58.

27. New York Times, Jan. 1, 1974.

28. Sorauf, op. cit., p. 95.

29. Heinz Eulau and John D. Sprague, Lawyers and Politics, (New York: Bobbs-Merrill, 1964), pp. 16-17.

30. Blanche D. Blank, "The Battle for Bureaucracy," The Nation, Dec. 12, 1966, pp. 694-698.

31. New York Times, Sept. 14, 1973, p. 40.

32. Peel, op. cit., p. 160.

33. Ibid., p. 258-259.

34. Edward C. Banfield, James Q. Wilson, eds., "Urban Cleavages," in Norman L. Zucker, ed., The American Party Process (New York: Dodd, Mead, 1968), pp. 267-71.

35. Robert Alford and Harry Scoble, "Sources of Political Involvement," American Political Science Review, December 1968, p. 1290.

36. Peel, op. cit., p. 259.

37. Ibid., p. 264.

38. Wilson and Banfield, "Public Regardingness as a Value Premise in Voting Behavior," American Political Science Review,

December 1964, pp. 871-77.

     39. Nathaniel Weyl, The Jew In American Politics (New Rochelle, New York: Arlington House, 1968), pp. 6-7.

     40. Peel, op. cit., pp. 251-59.

     41. Goldman, op. cit., p. 23.

     42. Peel, op. cit., p. 256.

     43. Ibid., pp. 252-253.

     44. Daniel P. Moynihan and Wilson, "Patronage in New York State," American Political Science Review 58 (June 1964): 286.

     45. New York Times, Jan. 21, 1974.

     46. Banfield and Wilson, "Urban Cleavages," op. cit., p. 268.

Though George Washington Plunkitt liked to think of his office as the bootblack's stand in the old county courthouse off Foley Square, he nonetheless had a somewhat more conventional office— in the clubhouse of the 15 Assembly District in Manhattan.[1] The location and decor of the office did not figure heavily in the tales told by Plunkitt, and one could hardly believe that his clubhouse quarters were in any way connected with Plunkitt's remarkable successes. Yet a politician's clubhouse, or office-with-house, is not without its importance, and that importance hangs on both our general curiosity about clubhouse decor and the premise that such decor might have some theoretical significance. Peel pursued both of these themes and gave us a clear, though impressionistic, picture of the clubhouse of his time; we will do the same.

Peel said the following about a Tammany club of the thirties: "What was once several rooms has been converted into a long assembly room filled with collapsible chairs. At the end of the room is a platform with a table, two chairs and a water pitcher. A large American flag is draped on the back wall; on the side walls are portraits of Jefferson and other Democratic presidents."[2]

By way of comparison, the following is a description of a Queens Democratic club of the seventies given by one of our reporters: "This club is situated in a large hall, which is owned by the club. There are several other people also waiting for an appointment to speak to Mr. ____. Pictures of Democratic presidents were hung on the wall, as also was the American flag. . . . Wooden folding chairs lined the room. . . . I entered a small office at the rear of the hall and started my interview."

Obviously, forty years have made little difference in the appearance of the political clubhouse. The stigmata of peeling paint and patriotic relics are still present. The clubs over time remain tenements rather than townhouses—saloons rather than salons.

The following is a sampling of the clubhouse descriptions given by our reporters (the clubs represent the Democratic, Republican, and Conservative parties, and are located in Brooklyn, Manhattan, the Bronx, and Queens).

"The ____ Democratic Club is in the lower level of a two-story building. The front room was wood-panelled, tiled floor, and divided into a large gathering area and two rear alcoves. All along the walls of the front room were posters of McGovern, Skolnick, Bloom, Lentol and Podell. One poster in particular was interesting. It showed a small boy sitting on a log and looking up at a quotation from John F. Kennedy: 'We have the power to make this the best generation in the history of mankind, or to make it the last.' Along one wall many folded bridge chairs were stacked and on both sides of the room card tables stood opened. At the rear of this room was the secretary's desk, and at the far back wall a long table at which sat the President. Left of the President's table was an American flag. The first of the two alcoves contained three desks, and five file cabinets—four drawers in each. Two of these were padlocked. There was no other office equipment—not even a typewriter. The second alcove contained a small kitchen with a refrigerator, sink, stove and typical kitchen cabinets."

"The ____ Democratic Club occupies two floors—the second and third—on a busy street in Brooklyn's Flatbush section. The sign that marks the club at street level is almost obscure. One has to know what he is looking for to find this club, although it is important in the community—the home club of the local assemblyman, state senator, female district leader, and headquarters for the tenants' council. Up a flight of stairs one comes upon a large, airy room, filled with wooden folding chairs. A desk is at the front, in front of large windows that look out on the street. A cardboard sign faces the street, saying welcome. In the back are several tables and more chairs. A small bathroom, dirty and cluttered, is in a corner, as is a pay telephone. There are no pictures on the walls, and no signs. The room is for meetings, social events and probably little else. Up another flight of stairs is another room, or rather several rooms lined up one after another. Here are the offices of the assemblyman and state senator, the tenants' council, the local senior citizens' association (some suggest this is a paper organization), and club officers. Desks, chairs, a long table filled with boxes of envelopes surrounded by wooden folding chairs, file cabinets, a flag, mailboxes for officials of the club and community. A mimeograph machine,

several typewriters, and boxes upon boxes of envelopes on shelves.
A sign asks people to petition for the abolition of vacancy decontrol,
and a small folding table holds petitions and mimeographed flyers
explaining the fight. Each public official has a part-time representative here several nights (and some days) a week. A few college-
student volunteers and several club officials are present, too.
During tax season—a sign informs us—a retired tax expert is here
to help senior citizens fill out their tax forms, for free. The place
is marked by clutter. People wait patiently to be helped. It is a
busy place."

"The ____ Reform Club is located in an old apartment
building in the Yorkville section of Manhattan. The over-all appearance is not entirely attractive. There is a sign across the front
fire escape of the building that announces the club's presence.
Inside, there are few appointments other than normal clerical
equipment, an American flag, an ecology poster, and pictures
of John F. Kennedy and other more anonymous club members.
Most of the chairs are the old fashioned folding variety. There are
two smaller offices provided for the district leader and the
secretarial staff. People do not seem to linger long here."

"The ____ Republican Club is in the West Bronx. It is
in a loft, on the second floor. The building is on a rather busy
street, on the corner. Downstairs are several stores. The clubhouse contains an enormous hall, with seating capacity for several
hundred people. At the front is a small stage on which a conference
table sits with several chairs. To the right of the stage is an old
upright piano. I play a few notes; it is badly in need of tuning.
There are folding tables and chairs close against the wall. In the
back, along the wall, is a long aluminum table on which sits a
coffee urn. There are paper cups, sugar, a dairy substitute, a
canister with a red label indicating the price is fifteen cents. To
the right, at the rear, is a partitioned area with a door. Inside is
a large mahogany desk, several chairs, a smaller desk with a
telephone and typewriter. A picture of [former] President Nixon
on one wall, a picture of the late President Eisenhower on a second,
and a picture of [former] Governor Rockefeller on a third wall. There
are several wooden file cabinets, as well. This is the leader's office,
and during the hours when he receives callers (every Wednesday from
7-10 PM) it is off-limits, according to the sign on the door. Tonight,
the only people in the place are three women, of middle-age, discussing
plans for a meeting of the Women's Auxiliary. An old man, who opens
up the clubhouse when it is needed for meetings, sits at a folding table
near the front of the room, playing solitaire and listening to the ball-
game on a small portable radio. The large empty hall, high-ceilinged

with neon lights aglow, makes the place seem especially lonely. In this very Democratic district, the chances are that it is. The old man tells me that the hall is used for meetings of many civic organizations, including the district Boy Scout commissioners, a veterans' group, and other charitable causes. "

"The ____ Conservative Club occupies a storefront in upper Manhattan. Large gold letters on the front window announce the club's name, the assembly district, and the name of the district leader. Curtains cover the windows and doors. The door is open. Inside the medium-sized store, there are metal folding chairs, a desk at the front of the room, and an enormous American Flag. A picture of the President of the United States and of Senator James Buckley, and a sticker addressed to the right of individuals to bear arms adorn the walls. The room is lit with a neon sign. Several women sit at a desk (actually a plank resting on wooden saw horses). They are folding flyers announcing a meeting, and placing them in envelopes. A variety of folders, pamphlets, magazines, and posters are on metal shelves on one wall. Old petitions sit on a folding table. In the front, at the desk, a meeting is going on. The people are discussing a fund-raising venture. There is a telephone on the desk, and it rings from time to time. A bulletin board of cork has notices, and when the phone calls bring a message for someone not in attendance, it is posted on the board. A bathroom is to one side in an alcove that contains several shelves filled with boxes of envelopes and several reams of paper. A very old typewriter sits on one shelf—it must be a genuine antique, for I have never seen anything quite like it before. The room is very warm, there is no air conditioning. The street outside is very quiet; this is a not very busy part of a generally busy thoroughfare. It is unlikely people will find their way here accidentally. "

"The ____ Democratic Club is in a loft over a Chinese restaurant on a busy business street in the North Bronx. A small sign hangs slightly askew on a wrought iron bar at the street level entrance. Other signs announce the presence (in no particular order) of a Republican club (the same room houses an insurance agency run by the Republican district leader), an insurgent Democratic club, the local offices of the International Ladies Garment Workers Union, a fraternal association of retired men (a front for a small-time card-playing operation), and the district offices of the Democratic state assemblyman. One long flight up, on the top of the stairs, the visitor is greeted by a door with the club's name lettered in gold, and a sign that indicates office hours: Mondays and Thursdays, 7:30 PM to 9:30 PM. The wall adjoining the front door bears a campaign poster of Senator George McGovern. Inside is a medium-sized room.

Ancient wooden folding chairs (can they possibly support anyone weighing over ninety pounds?) lean against the wall. A refrigerator sits in a back corner, noisily churning. The walls bear pictures of President Kennedy, Borough President Bob Abrams (a former club leader), an enormous American flag (with a tag indicating that it flew over the nation's capital and was donated by the local Congressman), and a campaign poster. A chart sets out deadlines for meetings. Another lists the members of the executive board and their attendance record for the year (some never attend, apparently). A battered desk near the front of the room holds boxes containing envelopes, pads and a pencil, some pamphlets on tenants' rights published by the city, a dog-eared copy of the list of registered voters in the Assembly District, and a can with a paper label reading: 'Campaign literature fund' (it is empty).

"An old man sits behind the desk. He is, we learn later, the sergeant-at-arms. He is in his mid-seventies, and is responsible for finding out what visitors want. Behind him is a door—open—that leads to a smaller room. Plywood dividers create two smaller offices, with doors, in the back of the second room. The second room has two more desks: one with a telephone, the other piled high with papers, petitions to put candidates on the ballot, magazines, old copies of the Congressional Record, boxes of envelopes. A bookshelf holds telephone directories, a few copies of old club journals (fundraising devices distributed at dinners and dinner/dances), and several file boxes. A coat rack holds coats. In one of the alcoves is a mimeograph machine of uncertain vintage. A teen-aged boy operates it, turning out copies of the club's newsletter. The motor wheezes and grinds. Piles of mimeo paper, old leaflets, newsletters, crumpled paper, cans of ink, two ancient typewriters, stacks of old law books, and boxes of envelopes fill the small room. It looks like a fire trap. The second room is a private office. An old desk with no drawers, a small bookshelf, and a file cabinet are in the room. A young lawyer is interviewing an elderly man who has come to receive help in fighting his landlord. There is no room for anyone else in this alcove. The back room, to which just about everyone has access, has dirty walls cluttered with assignment sheets for canvassing for petition signatures in some past race, notices to members (if you use the phone, pay for your call and no maids here/ clean up your butts and coffee cups before leaving), and lists of names (for what purpose?) and building addresses with check marks and circles next to each one.

"The main club house office [of a Queens Democratic Club] was cluttered with file cabinets, an old Xerox machine, an old wood desk, typewriter, and swirl wood chair, a phone on the desk. There were many black and white framed pictures on a wood panelled wall. Pictures in the office included:

1. Kennedy (John) with James A. Roe
2. Mayor Wagner with James A. Roe and John Roe
3. Lyndon Baines Johnson
4. (2 pictures) [former] Mayor Wagner and James A. Roe Jr.
5. (2 pictures) James A. Roe in United States Air Force Colonel uniform
6. Ethel Kennedy and Bobby Kennedy with James A. Roe
7. 1941—Jim Roe at annual Queens Democratic Dinner at Hotel Commodore.
8. Franklin D. Roosevelt and James A. Roe
9. James A. Roe
10. Harry Truman and James A. Roe

There were people and [the following] pictures in the main room:
1. Christopher Dinner: James A. Roe with Bishop McEntegart
2. Salute to Saint Pat, 1966, Judge Jim Roe Jr.
3. James A. Roe Jr. on the Court of Appeals
4. U.S.O. with Colonel James A. Roe in portrait with Air Force uniform
5. there was also a portrait of James Roe Jr. as a judge

The club meeting was a unique experience. A band from Saint Robert's church in the area opened the meeting with marching tunes. After the band's exhibit the Pledge of Allegiance was said and the Star-Spangled Banner was played by the band. The main room decor where the meeting was held included:
1. plain brown linoleum floor
2. brown wood panelling with pictures on the wall
3. American flag
4. Two large old-fashioned brown wood desks
5. Round tables and folding chairs
6. One pool table
7. Old-fashioned radiators painted brown to match panelling.
8. Rolling coat rack
9. Piano and bulletin board by the door
10. A kitchen to the left side of the door
11. Large brown rectangular table and chairs set on a platform
12. Loudspeaker system on platform; it was old but adequate.

The events of the evening continued as follows:
1. The cheerleaders were introduced by John Roe, District Leader and executive board member. The cheerleaders presented a cheer for Vinny Nicholosi who was running for

assemblyman from the district. Cheerleaders were young girls, age 10-13. They were the children of some club members. On the platform sat the General Chairman, Peter Gordan; District Leader, John Roe; and co-leader, Anne Larkin.

2. John Roe introduced Anne Larkin. Anne Larkin thanked the campaign workers for doing their part and asked for more help for their election ticket by phone calling.

3. Entrance of Vincent Nicholosi on a donkey, followed by Senator Murray Schwartz. Picture taking followed Nicholosi's entrance on the donkey. Pictures included: Nicholosi and wife; Senator Schwartz and Nicholosi.

4. After the grand entrance Nicholosi and Murray Schwartz proceeded to platform.

5. John Roe introduced candidates individually and each gave a little speech. Senator Schwartz gave a speech on his campaign and discussed his opponent. He accused Frank ____ of being allied with Mayor Lindsay. Schwartz accused ____ of mailing separate literature to different ethnic groups. There will be no decision made on ____'s association with Lindsay until after elections."

While the clubhouses described above are hardly settings for soignee sociability, they are nonetheless the focal points for developing strong political and community relationships. It is our feeling that the location and decor of a clubhouse—though not the vital center of any theory of local party organization—are not without theoretical relevance. After all, the present era is a particularly visual one, and if the media can reflect the message perhaps the political patina can reflect the political program. Furthermore the way in which a club strikes the senses must have some relationship to how it is viewed by its constituency. As Stephen Mitchell noted:

> In these days of air-conditioning and the supersell, the political headquarters may be the least inviting room in the neighborhood. As one of my outspoken friends wrote me, "Too often these old-style political party head-quarters, like old-style union headquarters turn the stomachs of the majority of the unhardened people who are not 'in'".[3]

Peel also made some attempts—unsystematic ones—at assessing the impact of a clubhouse setting and its relationship to party effectiveness. In an effort to study these questions more systematically, we relied on Murray Edelman for certain overall insights and on Theodore Caplow for a specific frame of reference. Symbols, as Murray Edelman pointed out, are "the only means by which groups not in a position to analyze a complex situation relationally may adjust themselves to it through stereotypization, oversimplification and reassurance."[4] The political clubhouse can be viewed in precisely these terms: it can be seen as a beacon for individuals who join a club to get their initial view of politics, and by the same token it can be seen as providing directional signals for individuals and groups outside the clubhouse as well. In either case a club's location, its setting, its furnishings, even its name, in large part may determine how people feel about joining the club and about participating in its activities. Superficial settings are seen by many analysts as influencing people's feelings about club legitimacy, cohesiveness, closeness, exclusiveness, and many other important elements in the socialization spectrum. Settings, these analysts feel, can increase or decrease the range of a club's audience, and can affect members' attitudes toward fellow members, adversaries, and the community in general.

Club Names

In a sense, as noted above, a club's name can be viewed as one of its superficial signaling devices. Edelman would certainly see a club's name in this light—as an integral part of the clubhouse. For example there are outside signposts and inside artifacts (matches and plaques) that remind members of who they are and where they are. At the point of a club's origin a name might even have been meaningful in expressing particular club aspirations, or at least the sense of style the club intended to adopt. Once it is chosen, however, the name sticks while its original significance probably atrophies, as current members may feel, "what's in a name?" Still, clubhouse names have a certain fascination, and we will discuss them here in terms of a seven-way classification, and a four-way subclassification that indicates the kind of overall signal a club may be sending out through its name. (An actual chart of names is presented in Appendix B.) The seven headings (in the Appendix) represent the various types of club names in order of their popularity: geographic names (159 clubs use these); personality names (53 clubs use these); symbolic-ideological names (41 clubs use these); Indian names (11 clubs); ethnic names (8 clubs); historical names (6 clubs); and demographic names (5 clubs). In addition there are 35 clubs that have tandem titles—usually demographic and containing such additional words as "reform" or "independents."

101

We found also that 29 clubs add to a demographic item, usually the assembly district involved, some other name. Moreover the personality-type club name, the second most popular name category, has a further four-way breakdown as follows: 45 of the clubs in this category have used historic names of deceased persons; 6 clubs have used the names of deceased district leaders (not usually an historic group); two clubs have chosen still-living political leaders; and one club has chosen a still-living district leader—the Rocco A. Fannelli Republican Club. One club—The United Mazzini Democratic Club—encompasses three major types of names (ethnic, personality, and ideological).

Our party breakdown of club names shows certain partisan proclivities. For example the Democrats have preempted all the Indian names. The reason for this preemption goes back to the Tammany tradition of using American Indian names, titles, and traditions in their fraternal lodge-like ceremonies and practices. At one time every Tammany club (all of Manhattan) had Indian names. Tammany Hall itself was referred to as the "Wigwam" and the leader was called the "Grand Sachem," apparently a bastardization of an Indian title. The Democrats also have preempted all but one of the ethnic club names—a matter of some curiosity since they can no longer claim to be the exclusive party of ethnic groups as far as New York City is concerned (as discussed in Chapter 4). Historic names and names with demographic references to an age group or to sex are almost equally scarce in all parties. As for the two most popular club name categories— geographic and personality—roughly there is a ratio of five Republican club names of the geographic type to one Democratic, and the Democrats have five club names of the personality type to every two for the Republicans.

In considering the physical variables that determine the actual ambiance of the city's clubs, if we use Caplow's theoretical underpinnings, these variables may be viewed in two ways: they may be seen as having a possible influence on party effectiveness; and they may be seen as explanatory in terms of party survival. Of course the former view would call for setting up an acceptable index of goal achievement, and, even more important, for a typology of what party goals actually are. Were these established, the exercise of constructing relationships between such measures and various items of club ambiance possibly could be played out. But these preconditions are not available. The party survival hypotheses, on the other hand, could be tested by correlating the physical and locational variables against the simple dichotomy of active clubs versus inactive clubs, or against a different variable, the longevity of clubs. Peel ventured a bit into the first (and more difficult) arena by speculating that clubs with central locations and other such favorable attributes might be more successful in attracting members or in winning elections. As a matter of fact, however, he found no such logical relationships. He noted: "As a rule, the club with the most imposing facade and the soundest construction would seem to be the most attractive to the citizens. But a comparison of election returns with type of clubhouse convinces the writer that the citizens are not particularly interested in this feature."[5] Our own findings concerning electoral success were too uncertain to report, but our overall impressionistic view supported Peel's opinion.

For purposes of classification, however, and against the possibility that future researchers may find, in a systematic approach, some further uses for our data, we will present our material (as noted above) in the frame of reference suggested by Theo Caplow.[6] This decision is supported by the fact that Lee Anderson views Caplow's theory as one of the most promising for use in party organizational research.[7] The Caplow theoretical framework posits four "system states," applicable to any organization,[8] as follows:

1. stability (maintenance of status differences)
2. integration (maintenance of interaction)
3. voluntarism (maintenance of valences)
4. achievement (maintenance of activities)

To understand Caplow's idea more fully, it should be pointed out that Caplow was trying to erect hypotheses for measuring (or at least comparing) organizational effectiveness. His four criteria are the necessary components. His "stability" is the ability of an organization to conserve or increase the status of its own position by maintaining and manipulating the status differences of its members. Status, in turn, refers to the ability of one member to modify the behavior of a fellow member. Thus increased stability, according to this model, can be achieved by an increase in the number of leadership and authority positions in the organization or by an increase in membership. Any such increase would in turn presumably increase the ability of the organization to carry out its mission.

"Integration" Caplow saw as a measure of the organization's ability to maintain or increase the total volume of interaction among its members. More interaction implies better adjustment, less factionalism, less conflict. The integration of an organization increases, for example, if all members are assembled in one place.

Caplow used the term "voluntarism" to measure the organization's ability to maintain the valences (affections, sentiments) among its membership. This is roughly equivalent to morale, and assesses an organization's ability to provide satisfaction for individual members and to thus insure their continued participation. Finally, "achievement" is the net result of all the organization's activities. Caplow described it as follows: "The appropriate units of measurement vary from one type of organization to another. An input-output ration is appropriate for a factory or farm. It is not applicable to a political party, for example, in which the votes obtained may be the appropriate measure."9

To use Caplow's model required that we make certain bridges between his "system states" (stability, integration, voluntarism, and achievement) and our own array of data on such items as club location, general club appearances, and club furnishings. Thus we recorded Caplow's "stability" (of an organization) in terms of items that we saw as measures of a club's accessibility; his "integration" we recorded as items measuring a club's visibility; his "voluntarism" is evidenced in a measure of what we called a club's "concern"; and finally we saw his "achievement" in terms of our measures of party functions. We will explain our measures in greater detail below.

Accessibility (a term also used by Peel)10 conveys both a sense of general availability to the public as well as internal hierarchical availability. That is, such items in the club environment as guards at the doorway, back offices, and private alcoves might be indices of extensive status differentials in the sense that Caplow conveys in his term "stability." To the degree that a club creates such barriers between a few of its leaders and its membership, or between members and the general public, such a club will be termed more or less inaccessible. On the other hand the absence of such barriers suggests accessibility. Obviously such measures leave something to be desired. The trappings of exclusiveness or status sometimes exist for traditional reasons, while the practices of particular leaders defy those same traditions. A new club president may be extremely accessible, yet he may hold office in a clubhouse where the backrooms and gates were constructed years before. Also, the need for confidence in certain conversations between club leaders and constituents, who frequently are embarrassed by the nature of a particular problem they are discussing with the club leader, requires private space. Thus such space does not necessarily imply inaccessibility. On the other hand some clubs appear accessible, but in actuality are not. Custom, informal cues, and what has been referred to as "anticipated reaction"11 create an aura of inaccessibility in some clubs where none of the physical manifestations of our classificatory scheme are present. Some political club leaders are rarely approached while engaged in conversation in some corner of the clubhouse, even though there is neither a door nor a guard to protect these officials. Some clubs are busy places that the whole community feels free to visit, while others are "off limits"except by invitation, although no formal notice or lock keeps visitors out. Despite all these qualifications, for the most part physical evidence of accessibility is a reliable measure of the openness of the overwhelming majority of political clubs.

Visibility (a virtually self-explanatory term) is shown by our data on club location and on the type of building in which clubs are housed. This might be seen as relating to Caplow's "interaction." The more visible the club, the greater the probability of interaction between club members and the public, and, possibly, the greater the attendance at club meetings, which would increase internal interaction. Originally we had a notion of "congruence" that might have been helpful in assessing visibility—"congruence" was meant to suggest the degree to which the physical ambiance of a club was in keeping with the surrounding area. In other words is a club the neighborhood showplace or the neighborhood eyesore, or just a well-integrated structure with protective coloration? Do clubs "stand out" or do they "hide"? We found that so little difference emerged among the clubs in this regard, however, that we concluded that in general all clubs are "congruent" with their environments.

Our measure of club "concern"—assessed through an item in our observation instrument on how shabby or well kept the club-houses were—might provide a clue to club morale, or what Caplow calls "voluntarism." This "concern" relates not only to the member-ship's attention to its own comfort, but also to its concern with how the outside world views the club. It may also help to understand what the club thinks is important, since club resources are usually scarce, and money spent on clubhouse maintenance is money lost to other areas of club operation. Finally, we feel that some measure of club activities can be reflected by our item on club furnishings. This in turn relates to the Caplow's "achievement," in that activities are indeed one form of club achievement.

Accessibility

Accessibility, as a variable of club quarters, might be measured by a number of items from our data collection: a club's street location (in terms of commercial business), whether a club maintains guarded doors and whether our student reporters had difficulty gaining entry. In terms of the first measure New York City clubs are very accessible. Out of the universe of 268 clubs, 68 were found to be in "very busy" locations and 123 in "moderately busy" streets. Together these clubs account for 74

TABLE 5.1

Number and Percent of Clubs That Are in Locations
Ranging from Very Busy to Secluded, by Party

Party	Very Busy Location Number	Percent	Moderately Busy Location Number	Percent	Side Street Number	Percent	Secluded Number	Percent	Other* Number	Percent
Democratic	42	26	80	49	28	17	2	1	12	7
Republican	15	22	21	46	15	22	1	1	5	7
Conservative	8	31	9	35	4	15	2	8	3	11
Total	65		120		47		5		20	

*Indicates responses that could not be coded in any of the established categories.

TABLE 5.2

Number and Percent of Clubs Housed in Various
Types of Structures, by Party

Party	Store Number	Percent	Loft Number	Percent	Apartment Number	Percent	Professional Apartment Number	Percent	Detached Building Number	Percent	Office Building Number	Percent	Other Number	Percent
Democratic	47	29	26	16	20	12	7	4	18	11	11	7	35	28
Republican	17	25	3	4	10	15	3	4	8	12	6	9	20	30
Conservative	10	38	4	15	3	11	1	4	1	4	1	4	6	23
Total	74	29	33	12	33	13	11	4	27	11	18	7	61	23

Percentages are rounded to the nearest integer.

percent of the entire universe. Democratic clubs, however, are just a bit more accessible than Republican clubs (as was true in Peel's study as well[12] and both are more accessible than Conservative clubs. Regular clubs are even more pronouncedly accesible than reform clubs (see Table 5.1).

There are several explanations to be noted here, one being the fact that, as in other things, accessibility is related to money. The more central locations are invariably the more expensive ones and clubs with such locations are usually housed in commercial properties—lofts, storefronts, halls, and the like (see Table 5.2). Therefore the wealthier clubs have an advantage at the outset. True, poorer clubs might simply be putting a larger proportion of their income into rent, and occupying sites they cannot really afford. But the better-heeled clubs, and those usually mean the regular Democratic clubs, are in the best position to gain a leading status in the community. Then too, in the wealthier communities, and the more suburban communities, it is increasingly difficult to get any space at all for renting. The competition is too great, there is a shortage of vacant stores and lofts, and rents are getting higher. This forces the "out" clubs—Republicans, Conservatives, and young reform and insurgent clubs—out of the commercial rental market, and into homes, part-time facilities and the like. Co-op City in the Bronx is an example of this in its worst form—no provision was made for the availability of properties that might be used for such purposes as clubhouses, and so the clubs in the Co-op City area are transient, rather than being based on a true rental setting. In this connection Peel's study offered some contrast. He reported:

> Of the clubs visited by our investigators, one hundred and ninety four were located at street intersections, and over four hundred were not. Corner lots are more expensive than other locations and when clubs are long established, their physical positions are really of little moment. [13]

But Peel did confirm that Democratic clubs were more accessible than Republican ones, noting that "the chances are ten to one that a stranger in any district will find a Democratic club before he finds a Republican one . . ."[14] Peel added that "the majority of all clubs prefer the busy thoroughfare to the side street . . . Democratic clubs are, on the whole, more strategically located than the Republican clubs."[15]

The second way we looked at accessibility was through the responses to the question, "Was anyone guarding the front door?"

We found that 91 percent of the clubs had no such guard, and only 7 percent had a guard (not all clubs responded to this question). As to how troublesome entry was, we found that 48 percent of our student investigators reported some degree of resistance on the part of various clubs, ranging from direct refusals to extreme coolness and uncooperativeness. We had one case where an investigator was physically thrown out of a clubhouse. The police were summoned by the sergeant at arms "to pick him (our investigator) up," and our investigator escaped arrest only because his father was a policeman known by the officer who came in response to the call. On the other hand one of our young female interviewers arrived at a clubhouse, was invited in, stayed for the meeting, paid dues, and was elected (without opposition) corresponding secretary of the club. Young people (all of our investigators were relatively young) were a novelty to some of the clubs, and many were invited to apply for membership. Our records indicated that approximately 15 of our investigators actually joined the clubs they studied. This would indicate to us that this type of accessibility is also a "status" measure in Caplow's sense, since it marks off a range of distance between members and nonmembers.

A closely related question, whether or not there was anyone guarding the door to the private offices, also measures the same variable. We found that 116 clubs had such doors but only 27 percent had guards for the doors. The presence of such special "alcoves" or private offices is an internal status indicator in the Caplow sense, as well as being an indicator of "openness" to the public, particularly since 12 percent of those clubs with private offices refused our investigators entry. However, 34 percent of our reporters entered such clubs without any difficulty.

Finally, our survey included the direct inquiry, "Were you permitted to attend a meeting?" Various degrees of difficulty were recorded for this question, but the most significant point was that 36 percent of our respondents gave a flat no as their answer. On the other hand 53 percent attended meetings without any difficulty; and once again, Democrats and reformers were far more accessible than regulars.

Visibility

Visibility is an obvious club asset, whether or not you tie it, as we did to Caplow's "integration" (or degree of interaction). About 35 percent of our universe was housed in storefronts. Such clubs have relatively high visibility; 11 percent could even boast detached buildings. This compares with the 281 clubs (out of 616) that Peel found occupied an entire building. [16] We found however that 12 percent of today's clubs are located upstairs in lofts, while another 13 percent are even more secluded, in apartments. Thus if one were to add the 4 percent that use professional apartments (usually first-floor apartments with separate entrances for use by doctors and dentists) these relatively secluded clubs would become an even larger slice. Eighteen clubs, another 7 percent, are almost as well hidden in office buildings. And better than 20 percent of our universe are in a location category we called "other," which includes garages, rented facilities in fraternal associations, funeral parlors, and night-by-night rentals in public and parochial schools, churches, settlement houses, clubrooms of civic and athletic associations and, in one case, a local tavern.

In any case what is particularly interesting in regard to club visibility is that a great deal of variation exists. The clubs can in fact be sorted out by party, with Democrats appearing to be slightly more visible than Republicans. The relative mildness of this difference betwen Democrats and Republicans might be somewhat unexpected.

In general our data on visibility does not differ greatly from Peel's report, which was as follows:

> The tendency among outlying clubs is to occupy
> detached buildings, usually converted private homes,
> while in the business districts clubs are often found
> concealed in a room in some office building. Many
> clubs, particularly those of the subsidiary or third
> party variety, lease abandoned stores (at low cost). [17]

In terms of our classification model this measure of visibility should associate with degrees of "interaction." While we obtained no special data on degrees of interaction, we did note that Conservative clubs and reform clubs appear somewhat more broadly participatory in their discussions. This can be taken as a form of interaction and, if so, it does agree with the slightly more "visible" quality of the Conservative and reform groups.

"Concern"

The club variables we put under the heading of "concern"— a possible measure of Caplow's club morale or "voluntarism"—can be assessed by the responses to our question, "What was the general

TABLE 5.3

General Appearance of Club Quarters, by Party
(number and percent of clubs)

Party	Extravagant		New and Clean		Old but Well Kept		Modern but Sloppy		Old and Sloppy		Other	
	Number	Percent	Number	Percent	Number	Percent	Number	Percent	Number	Percent	Number	Percent
Democratic	4	2	50	30	71	43	4	2	30	18	5	3
Republican	2	3	15	22	38	57	1	1	10	15	1	1
Conservative	–		6	23	14	54	2	8	2	8	2	8
Total	6	3	71	27	123	48	7	3	42	16	8	4

Note: Percentages are rounded to the nearest integer.

appearance of the club?" Approximately 75 percent of the universe gave what we considered to be a good appearance: that is, these clubs are either modern and clean or old and well kept. We found 3 percent to be modern but sloppy and 16 percent old and sloppy. The appearance of 3 percent was reported by our researchers as being "extravagant" (see Table 5.3). This contrasts with the following report given by Peel:

> . . . out of six hundred clubs visited, forty-four club-houses were in excellent condition, three hundred and twelve in good condition, and one hundred and ninety-five in bad condition and forty-nine in a dilapidated condition.
>
> The fourth class, "dilapidated," not deemed essential at first, was forced upon us as we encountered little, tumble-down shacks on the outskirts of the city or vile tenements in the blighted areas, reeked with filth, beer mash, uncleaned cuspidors and wet rubbish.[18]

It appears that, on the whole, today's clubs are in better shape than those that Peel studied, since only 59 percent of those were apparently in "good" (or better) condition.

As to party differences in connection with this item, they are slight, but interesting. It appears that in general, Republicans are a bit neater, or more caring, in this respect, than Democrats, with Conservatives ranking close to the Democrats on this matter.

We speculated that clubs, like people, move, and that they move for the same reasons people do, including a concern for the care and appearance of their property. Thus we asked how long a club had been at its present site and, if there had been a move, why it had occured. Our survey showed that 12 percent of the clubs indicated that their old place "was run down" (32 clubs), while 55 clubs (20.5 percent) said they "needed larger quarters." Nine clubs reported that "the neighborhood got bad." Other responses to these questions were not relevant to the notion of concern, but were a response to dramatic survival necessities, such as a building having been torn down, a drastic increase in carrying charges, or a change in district lines. Moreover, a number of clubs that move may be trying to get away from constituents of a predominant ethnic, or racial, group in the club. Although people who move to the suburbs may say that they are "doing it for the kids," what they may mean is that they are running away from blacks and Puerto Ricans. The reasons offered by club leaders should also be viewed in this light, against the shifting ethnic lines of New York City over the last decade.

In measuring "functional variety" in the clubs our data merely offers a limited listing of club furniture items. These items, however, offer some clues to club activities. For example, 79 percent of the clubs have office furniture, 6 percent have eating facilities, 4 percent have game facilities, and 4 percent have libraries (see Table 5.4). The scarcity of sports facilities reflects Peel's findings, which he described as follows:

> It was somewhat surprising to learn that of six hundred and sixteen clubhouses visited, only 25 were equipped with bowling alleys and that one hundred and sixty-two were provided with pool tables, the average number of tables being three. . . . The smaller clubs have recently installed bagatelle boards. . . . Gambling paraphernalia (slot machines, racing form sheets, etc.) are tucked way in the corners of the "anti-social" clubs. [19]

Although social activities are considered important in the clubs, this importance is not reflected in the furnishings. It seems that club decor is mainly business oriented.

What meanings might we attach to all of these variations in club accessibility, visibility, "concern", and functional items? Do these indices have something to do with club effectiveness? Possibly. With club survival? Probably. Could we have measured effectiveness? Possibly. The latter goal would have required us to determine such items as the percent of potential voters in each club district that are registered to vote; the percent that actually vote; the percent that are party enrollees; the number of important officeholders in each club; the number of successful and unsuccessful club insurgency fights; some method (perhaps) of assessing ombudsmen's activities; and so forth. The club survival estimate would have entailed a more manageable array of data on membership and on club longevity and stability. And while we have a few such data sets, and perhaps could have collected others, we felt their translation into actual indices of effectiveness would have been fraught with inevitable methodological and theoretical problems; we therefore did not attempt this. We felt that the verstehen of Peel, in this instance, is as much as we can get. Thus our conclusion is that club appearances are indeed

TABLE 5.4

Various Types of Furnishings and Facilities
in Clubs (number and percent of clubs)

Type of Furnishing or Facility	Number	Percent
Clerical	211	78.7
Game	11	4.1
Eating	15	5.5
Library	4	1.4
Lounge	5	1.8
Other*	4	1.4

*Responses that could not be coded in established categories.

Note: These figures are not cumulative. Because a club has clerical furniture does not mean it cannot also have game or lounge furniture.

important, but are not in themselves entirely reliable guides to political success. Their importance must be less strictly understood, as reflected in the words of Edelman: "There are no neutral scenes in the political process."[20]

Notes

1. William Riordan, Plunkitt of Tammany Hall (New York: Dutton, 1963).
2. Roy V. Peel, The Political Clubs of New York, rev. ed. (New York: Ira S. Friedman, 1968), p. 1.
3. Stephen Mitchell, Elm Street Politics (New York: Oceana Publications, 1959), p. 31.
4. Murray Edelman, The Symbolic Uses of Politics (Urbana: University of Illinois Press, 1967), p. 40.
5. Peel, op. cit., p. 89.
6. Theodore Caplow, The Principles of Organization, (New York: Harcourt, Brace and World, 1964).
7. Lee F. Anderson, "Organizational Theory and the Study of State and Local Parties," in William Crotty, ed., Approaches to the Study of Party Organization (Boston: Allyn & Bacon, 1968), pp. 383-384.

8. Caplow, op. cit., pp. 121-124.

9. Ibid., p. 124.

10. Peel, op. cit., p. 88.

11. Richard E. Neustadt, Presidential Power (New York: John Wiley, 1960), p. 65.

12. Peel, op. cit., p. 87.

13. Ibid., p. 88.

14. Ibid., p. 89.

15. Ibid., pp. 87-88.

16. Ibid., p. 88.

17. Ibid.

18. Ibid., pp. 89-90.

19. Ibid., p. 98.

20. Edelman, op. cit., p. 101.

6

As Peel pointed out, clubs are organized primarily to advance the political careers of certain leaders. Only secondarily do they promote the interests of a more general membership group. And finally, almost as an afterthought, clubs may enhance a more distant "party loyalty."

The activities of political clubs, today as in the past, are necessarily tied to these goals. For example, in the Cleveland Club described in William Foote Whyte's Streetcorner Society, there was no doubt as to why the club existed. As Joseph Maloney, the club's leader, put it, "Politics is business. You have to maintain the organization."[1] Whyte noted that "the Cleveland Club was organized primarily to provide political jobs and favors for its members," and, discussing a hypothetical club setup, Whyte added:

> In Cornerville there are a number of political clubs,
> each one started by a politician and built around him.
> Such a club is organized for the purpose of electing
> its boss (or one selected by him) to public office and
> of providing him with the voting strength necessary
> in order to make good political connections. In
> return, the boss is expected to advance the interests
> of the members.[2]

This description, however, covers only a small part of the activities of political clubs in New York City.

What is abundantly clear from our study is that the activities of each club also reflect the interests and tastes of the club's membership. Plunkitt noted, "There's only one way to hold a district; you must study human nature and act accordin[g]."[3] Illustrating his point,

115

Plunkitt added: "I hear of a young feller that's proud of his voice;
thinks he can sing fine. I go round and ask him to join our glee
club. He comes and sings and he's a follower of Plunkitt for
life."[4] What Plunkitt described holds true for clubs today. Most
club activities are maintenance or social activities—an obvious
effort to cater to the ubiquitous human need for companionship and
sociability (especially in a large and somewhat anonymous city).
But behind this is an anticipated, and generally realized, political
payoff from staging various events. Campaigns and elections are
sporadic—the clubs know this. Moreover campaigns create many
ad hoc groups outside the clubs. But clubs function the year round,
and they do so primarily on the strength of being so quintessentially
"social." It is this cement of sociability that keeps the clubs viable
for their ultimate, albeit periodic, political battles. There was a
time, however, when activities that bridged the gap between periods
of electoral activity might not have been so necessary for club
continuity. For example, as Sayre and Kaufman noted: "Until 1938
state assemblymen were elected annually. Consequently, the party
units in their districts [the clubs] were almost constantly ready for
action. They had a continuity, a cohesion, a steady state of
preparedness . . . that made them . . . natural shock troops. . . ."[5]
Yet even in such an optimum condition for survival, political clubs
relied heavily on noncampaign activities to maintain interest and
loyalty among their members and followers. The leaders realized
that permanent political organizations needed more for survival
than simply the trappings of campaigns: their members required,
and were given, the broad spectrum of events, programs, and human
interaction that Peel so clearly described in his book.

Club Activities in the Thirties

        In the thirties most political clubs catered thoroughly to the
human need for communication, participation, and contact with the
opposite sex. The clubs also appeared to cater quite explicitly to
a male need for authority. We pointed out (see Chapter 4) that Peel
speculated as to whether "one might conclude that the male clubs
[and in this instance he was referring to the then-typically dominant
male club] are today havens for oppressed heads of families." His
portrait of club activities proceeded to give flesh to this theme,
since most of the activities he described directly or indirectly
emphasized male, rather than female, participation.
        Peel classified all club activities into the following categories:
organizational, political, social, sociopolitical, civic welfare,

116

educational, political-educational, antisocial (or sociopathological), and ritualistic. The clubs in Peel's study clearly did organizational things: they formed a group (by inheritance or revolt), incorporated, got charters, held elections, read minutes, took care of their premises, and did all the housekeeping necessary for simple survival. They devoted much of their energy to purely political activities, such as working for the designation and election of party and public officials, general campaign work, and election day services (getting out the vote and manning the polling places). At the same time social activity played a dominant role and, as we mentioned before, an important feature of that role was interaction of the sexes. Toward this end there were dances, card parties, teas, charitable events, sporting events, clambakes, theatricals, bus rides, educational lectures, and the like. However, as Peel noted, "the underlying reason for the social affairs conducted by and for the young people of both sexes is matrimonial."[6] It is not surprising therefore that the single social activity most favored and most reported in the journals of that era was social dancing. In some clubs this appeared to be a nightly diversion, and all clubs staged every conceivable kind of dance: pajama dance, balloon dance, confetti dance, masquerade ball, cakewalk, shirt-waist dance, pirate dance, novelty dance, barn dance. Eating events were also in high fashion—luncheons, roasts, dinners, suppers, banquets, breakfasts. Peel viewed these events as being at least quasi-political if during the event a speaker was introduced or if various prominent politicos were suitably honored and heard from.

As to civic activities, Peel coined a curiously prophetic term in referring to these activities as constituting "affirmative action"—a sort of advance-guard type of activity that usually implied a criticism of existing governmental standards and practices.[7] Clearly this activity was more the province of Socialist and other ideological parties than of the two major parties, and when a major party did engage in this practice it was almost invariably the "out" party. The largest part of the civic parcel was the typical demands for legislatively bestowed special benefits, for capital improvements for the community, for morals enforcement (censorship, for example), and for the improvement and expansion of all the standard services of government.

The lopsided nature of the club's civic responsibilities, the heavy bias in favor of the status quo, might explain the strong involvement that was maintained by most clubs in so-called welfare activities. The irony of a political club having to engage in securing jobs for the unemployed, and hospital care and pensions for veterans, or in handing out baskets at Christmas—matters which it should have handled through effective public policy—did not appear to trouble club members at all. So too with the cheap or free legal services that clubs dispensed. Patronage posts were often the source of job placements, but the clubs also pressured local businesses to supply jobs and, in return for these jobs, club leaders exerted pressure on public officials to give welfare grants in the form of lowered tax assessments on property, and the like, to cooperative business concerns. A symbiotic relationship thus existed—clubs supported a government system that spawned the very service lacunae and social disruption which in turn became a major raison d'etre for the clubs. Peel was keenly aware of this irony.

He saw the educational function of clubs in the thirties (with the exception of Socialist, Communist and Social Labor clubs) as "ineffective and superficial"[8]—a great contrast to the European clubs of that era. He felt that it was actually impossible for a New York City club committed to a political party machine to truly educate; at best it propagandized. While Peel listed a few exceptions to this rule, most of his anecdotal material dismissed the educational work of the clubs as a chronicle of dismal, esoteric-type speeches or dulling "civil service school" efforts.

Finally, Peel noted that the clubs of the early thirties also engaged in a few patently unsavory activities, and some downright illegal ones, like gambling and boozing. A considerable number of New York City clubs at that time were hangouts for gamblers and loose women. The 1930-31 Seabury investigations of courts and politics in the city brought much of this to light. In the pursuit of vice there was considerable variation in club style. The gamut, not unlike operations outside clubhouse doors, ran from tawdry to opulent. There was, however, no particular correlation between vice and party preference. Democrats and Republicans alike were involved. A few somewhat dubious political clubs were actually no more than fronts for gang headquarters. A somewhat larger number of clubs were involved in the classical graft cycle of businessmen to politicos to police.

Unfortunately, illicit activity is not the stuff of which survey research data is made; thus our report does not cover this sort of activity, which might still be an important dimension of club life in some parts of the city. If in fact there are criminal connections among present-day clubs, our reporters remained happily unaware of them. If any club in our survey boasted a massage parlor or a numbers room we were never told of this. The report and analysis that follow are thus a testament to the relative lawfulness, sobriety, and, on the whole, dull sociability of today's clubs compared with days gone by.

Club Activities in the Seventies

In covering club activities in the 1970s despite an overall, and well-deserved, reluctance to press our data into any overarching theoretical mold, we explored some modest propositions—for instance the proposition that clubs can and should be explained functionally. This theory would lead us to conclude that since time, space, and general environment are controlled for our universe of clubs, and since the overt political function is similar in the clubs, we ought to find a great similarity in club activity programs. Should this not be true, however, we would have to conclude that either there are latent functions that are operative, or an intervening variable—that is, membership characteristics—creates differences among clubs.

It is important to note here that a club's membership characteristics are representative of the character of the community in which the club operates. Therefore it is not simply the SES variables of those who comprise the membership, but those variables seen against the backdrop of the community, that make for an understanding of the club's activities. The ethnic and residential character of a community lend themselves more to certain activities than to others. Backyard wine and cheese parties, a notable contribution of the North Bronx, Brooklyn Heights, and various sections of Queens, are not as common to the West Side of Manhattan, where there may be fewer backyards. Theatre parties are a less likely occurrence in a Puerto Rican neighborhood, bingo is not exactly "in" on the Upper East Side of Manhattan, nor is a Christmas party likely in the largely Jewish Crown Heights section of Brooklyn, nor a rock concert likely in stately Riverdale.

In order to provide some degree of clarity on club activities, and help make comparisons, we have put our data together under the following classification scheme that resembles Peel's, but not entirely:
1. specifically maintenance functions
    —— organization and renewal—club formation activities, charter rules promulgation and amending of these
    —— ritualization—parliamentary usages and formalities in business-type meetings, flag salutes, membership pledges
    —— routine meetings
    —— communication (publication of newsletters, etc.)
2. primarily social functions (also maintenance in the sense that these serve to continue a club's vitality and coherence)—held in the club and outside

—— parties (all types of dinners, dances, picnics, etc.)
—— routine games and eating or drinking (pool, cards, bar)
—— casual interaction (interaction during and after actual business)
—— ethnic activities
—— age-related social events
—— sporting events
3. primarily political functions (which again are maintenance and often overlap with social functions)
    —— fund-raising events (often the ostensible end product of social parties, card games, etc.)
    —— campaign meetings
    —— voter canvassing
    —— helping at the polls (observing, phoning, registering, escorting)
    —— providing candidate forums and speaking engagements
    —— holding meetings concerning nominations, suggesting nominees
    —— general political education in community (voter registration, programs for local schools)
4. primarily community service activities (again overlaps with maintenance and political activities)
    —— ombudsman-type activities (representing club members or others in legal actions, behind-scenes intervention, direct bureaucratic actions taken to redress grievances)
    —— education on issues of special community importance (providing meeting forums, speakers, and going out to speak)
    —— pressure-group-type actions (helping to foster or delay civic actions of one type or another)

This classification scheme reflects the idea of functional dominance as being explanatory in the realm of club activity. And that is what we generally found to be true.

Maintenance Functions

Our classification of maintenance functions covers such items as club ritual, rule formulations, and routine meetings. We emphasized the importance of maintenance activities because common sense tells us that these must take up a substantial proportion of any organization's time and efforts. Bowman and Boynton, in their 1963 study of grass-roots party officials' activities in Massachusetts and North Carolina, lend weight to our assumption. They reported that "almost thirty-six percent of the activities mentioned were of the organizational maintenance type; and forty-six percent of the party officials mentioned organizational work as part of their tasks at least once."[9] In our own interviews the "routine meeting" item emerged as singularly important among maintenance functions. We will discuss this activity in detail below.

Regarding another maintenance function, club constitutions and rules (which we examined in depth in Chapter 3), it should be noted that once a club is established, little further time seems to be spent on this function, except for an occasional spurt of amending the constitution. The pervasive ritualistic activities that routinely occur are ordinary garden-variety parliamentary procedure (for which reform Democratic clubs have been notorious in the past), and the usual trappings of conventional patriotism (flag salutes and pledges, singing of the national anthem or "God Bless America, " etc.).

Club Meetings

If club activity is centered on club meetings—as it often is—then the quality of those meetings must bear some relationship to the overall image that members have of the club. In an attempt to establish the general tone of club meetings, we asked our investigators a series of questions: whether the meeting they observed was orderly; who participated in discussions; whether the leaders were challenged by nonleaders during club debate; and what the degree of consensus was on club votes?

Of the 157 clubs where our observers were able to attend a meeting, 135 were found to conduct their meetings in an orderly, or even a strict orderly manner. Only 22 clubs were seen as disorderly or disorganized in their meetings, in some degree. Within this pattern, however, there lie some interesting deviations from the norm. For example, although 89 percent of all club meetings were reported as orderly, Democrats showed 18 percent in the disorderly category, while Republicans (7 percent) and Conservatives (6 percent) were found to be considerably less disorderly (see Table 6.1). Also, new clubs appear to be more effective than the older ones in organizing meetings and in keeping the peace. A possible explanation for this may be that Conservative party clubs, and reform clubs in general, tend to be newer than regular clubs, and these newer clubs tend to be more taken up with procedure because of their having a younger membership. In addition the older clubs

TABLE 6.1

Number and Percent of Clubs That Conduct Their Meetings
in Various Degrees of Orderliness, by Party

Degree of Orderliness	Democratic		Republican		Conservative		All Clubs	
	Number	Percent	Number	Percent	Number	Percent	Number	Percent
Strict Order	22	22	4	5	7	47	33	17
Orderly	60	60	76	93	7	47	143	72
Somewhat disorderly	13	13	1	1	0	0	14	7
Very disorganized	6	5	1	1	1	6	8	4

tend to be more informal because of the long association of their membership. Therefore at meetings of older clubs members may call out, speak without being recognized, mill about, and walk in and out of the room. On the other hand the new clubs maintain a central focus on meetings in order to cement their following and give themselves an identity. At times there is not a lot of business to be covered at these meetings, and so the members spend time dealing with parliamentary procedure and meeting processes. Old-line clubs tend to be short on meetings, usually reserving them for activities such as the handing out of election assignments. There is much running in and out, and a lot of arguing over how it was all done last year. Newer clubs do not have this particular kind of disorder because they meet more constantly.

Ethnicity also has some effect on the conduct of the meetings, and its effects, oddly enough, are not at all congruent with many commonly held nationality stereotypes. We tend to think of Wasps as essentially bloodless, cool, efficient, less ebullient than the presumably more voluble, emotional groups, the Italians and Jews. Yet 14 percent of the Wasp-dominated club meetings were found to be disorderly and disorganized, as against only a 5 percent disorderly rate for the Italian-dominated meetings and 9 percent for those meetings dominated by Jews. The Irish, with their reputation as fighters, might, at first glance, offer the biggest surprise of all—none of their meetings were reported as disorderly or dis-organized. However, this finding may be quite in keeping with their much-vaunted political professionalism. Irish clubs are never reform clubs, and rarely Conservative clubs, in New York City.

We assumed that political clubs run their meetings demo-cratically, with all members having an opportunity to participate. (After all, the clubs are the local units of political parties competing in a democratic system.) The findings of our observers indicated that our assumption was basically correct—almost all general membership meetings among the clubs we studied were marked by a decidedly democratic ambiance. Discussions were found to be more or less broadly spread over a reasonably large proportion of the membership. Of 136 clubs for which we have information, 129 held discussions involving not only club leaders but at least some of the general membership (see Table 6.2). The heaviest concentration of clubs appears in the category of broadest member-ship participation: approximately 40 percent of all clubs saw discussion involving a majority of members during their meetings. On the other hand a bare 5 percent of clubs restricted their discussions to club leaders. It should be noted that "leaders" were broadly defined by our observers to include not only club officers,

TABLE 6.2

Number and Percent of Clubs That Have Various Levels
of Participation in General Discussions, by Party

Participants in Club Discussions	Democratic		Republican		Conservative	
	Number	Percent	Number	Percent	Number	Percent
Club leaders only	6	6	1	4	0	0
Leaders and some members	35	37	9	31	4	31
Large minority of members	17	18	8	27	2	15
Large majority of members	36	38	11	38	7	54

Note: Percentages represent proportions of a particular party's universe of clubs.

but also executive board members, public and party officials and representatives of affiliated groups. In some clubs there can be as many as 35 or 40 such leaders. Under these circumstances it would not be strange to find clubs restricting debate to a large core group of leaders. Yet obviously this did not happen often.

It is noteworthy that, among the parties, the Conservative group not only showed no clubs restricting discussion to club leaders, but also showed 54 percent of their clubs as having a majority of members participating in discussion. By comparison, 38 percent of both Democratic and Republican clubs showed a majority of members participating. It also appears that the new clubs (three years old or less) spread discussion far more broadly than the older clubs.

In this regard the ethnicity variable is also revealing. As indicated in Table 6.3, clubs with large numbers of Wasps among their membership appear less hierarchical in the flow and participation in discussion than do clubs with large ranks of various other ethnic groups. 100 percent of clubs with substantial Wasp ranks showed participation on the part of either a majority of members or a large minority. The runner-up in this item was the 62 percent cadre of clubs with a heavy Jewish membership. This general participation breakdown seems quite naturally to move in tandem with the "disorderly" variable discussed above. It may well be that hierarchical influences that are said to be more pronounced among Italian and Irish family and church structures carry over into the neighborhood clubs.

TABLE 6.3

Percent of Various Ethnic Groups That Participate in General Club Discussion, According to Whether Discussion Involves Leaders and/or Membership

Participants in Club Discussions	Jews	Italians	Irish	Wasps
Leaders only	5	4	0	0
Leaders and some membership	32	39	57	0
Large minority of membership	18	22	14	25
Majority of membership	44	35	29	75

This suggestion, however, involves a degree of caution—the Irish and Italian clubs may be more professional as well. Reform clubs, and other clubs of the independent and more amateurish cast, tend to have large Jewish and Wasp ranks, and such clubs tend to

TABLE 6.4

Number and Percent of Clubs in Which Members Challenge Leadership
on Discussion Issues, by Frequency of Challenge and by Party

Frequency of Challenge	Democratic Number	Percent	Republican Number	Percent	Conservative Number	Percent
Very frequently (about 75 percent of the time)	8	9	2	7	1	7
Frequently (at least 50 percent of the time)	13	15	3	11	0	0
Quite often (25–50 percent of the time)	31	35	8	30	3	23
Rarely (less than 25 percent of the time)	23	26	6	22	4	31
Never	14	16	8	30	5	39

TABLE 6.5

Percent of Clubs in Which Members Challenge Leadership on Discussion
Issues, by Frequency of Challenge and by Dominant Ethnic Group in Clubs

Frequency of Challenge	Jews	Italians	Irish	Wasps
Very frequently	8	0	0	14
Frequently	5	5	10	14
Occasionally	18	20	20	29
Rarely	19	5	20	0
Never	5	16	20	0

be less hierarchical because their ideology is oriented toward full participation. [10]

We found the caliber of club discussions to have been generally lively and very open. That is, in 27 of the clubs holding general meetings, members freely challenged the leadership position on various issues more than 50 percent of the time; in another 42 clubs this occurred from 25-50 percent of the time (see Table 6.4). In only 27 clubs was there no such challenge reported. From the vantage point of party affiliation, it is hard to discern any consistent trend in this regard, except that Conservative party clubs seemed much less likely to challenge their leadership with any regularity than did Republicans or Democrats. Moreover, in line with the hierarchical tendency noted above, clubs with large Wasp memberships were more likely to feel free to challenge their leadership than other ethnically dominated clubs, although clubs with large Jewish ranks again show a less hierarchical tendency than clubs with heavy Italian or Irish memberships (see Table 6.5). The commonly advanced notion that Jews are closely akin to Wasps in their attitudes is again demonstrated by these findings.

"If everyone has the right to express his will," John Schaar noted, "what does this right mean if their will is merely an echo of the chorus around them?"[11] Schaar's comment is given support by our data, which reveals that, despite the ostensibly democratic character of New York City's political clubs, 61 percent of all clubs cast votes at their meetings that are always, or nearly always, unanimous (see Table 6.6). In the case of 23 clubs, every vote taken at observed meetings was found to be completely unanimous. Moreover Republican clubs seem to show a high degree of consensus more often than Conservatives or Democratic clubs. However, in all three parties more than 50 percent of the clubs showed near unanimity in all of their voting, though the Democratic clubs were the only clubs to show "barely a majority" in some of their votes. (4 percent of Democratic clubs were in this category.) Whether a club is old or new appears to have no effect at all on consensus voting.

Once again the ethnic variable makes its impact felt and lends credence to the stereotyped notion that New York City politics is ethnic politics (see Table 6.7). In addition, as we might expect, the Wasp-dominated clubs have a 14 percent group of clubs that show "barely a majority" in their voting habits, and 5 percent of clubs with large Jewish ranks vote this way whereas there are no Italian or Irish-dominated clubs that habitually vote in such an undisciplined and free-wheeling fashion. At the other extreme similar variations occur, with no Wasp-dominated clubs showing total unanimity in their voting, and clubs dominated by Jews showing only a 5 percent group with such a voting record; on the other hand 16 percent of

TABLE 6.6

Number and Percent of Clubs That Show Varying
Degrees of Voting Consensus, by Party

Degree of Voting	Democratic		Republican		Conservative	
Consensus	Number	Percent	Number	Percent	Number	Percent
Always unanimous	12	14	6	24	5	39
Generally unanimous	33	39	14	56	3	23
About 75 percent consensus	35	42	5	20	5	39
Barely a majority	4	4	0	0	0	0

TABLE 6.7

Percent of Clubs Displaying Various Voting
Habits, by Dominant Ethnic Group in Clubs

Voting Habits	Jews	Italians	Irish	Wasps
Always unanimous	5	16	20	0
Generally unanimous	23	16	20	14
75 percent consensus	14	14	20	29
Barely a majority	5	0	0	14

Italian-dominated clubs show this dimension and the Irish once again lead the pack with a 20 percent cadre of unanimous votes among their clubs.

Thus with every one of the variables that might be said to measure the style of this particular maintenance activity (club meetings), we find that the ethnicity factor goes further toward explaining the style of meetings than either the club party or age factor. In general, however, New York City clubs look alike: they are a well-disciplined group devoted to consensus, to parliamentarism, and to a fair degree of democratic participation where routine matters are concerned. At the same time this should not be interpreted by readers to mean that, on the whole, the clubs are a great arena of democratic decision making—even in the most effective clubs. Non-decision making (as discussed by Peter Bachrach and Morton Baratz)[12] is the overarching factor that delimits the nature of democratic discussion during club meetings. It should be pointed out also that a number of clubs absolutely barred access to our observers and it is probable that these clubs are the least, rather than the most, democratic.

In examining club publications—also a maintenance-type activity—we found the issuing of newsletters and journals to be common to clubs of all parties and in all sections of the city. Peel did not mention club newsletters, nor has anyone else who has written about the clubs. Although we knew that a number of clubs from time to time had issued newsletters to their membership, we did not ask about such publications during our interviews with club officials. However, dozens of clubs gave our interviewers copies of their newsletters. These ranged from mimeographed one-page notices of meetings, including a column by the club president, to elaborate 12-page printed newspapers featuring various columns, club news, and advertisements. Our impression was that most clubs do not issue newsletters regularly; rather they are likely to issue a newsletter if they can find one or more club members to edit it. Thus a turnover in membership sometimes can temporarily halt publication of a newsletter. A decline in club revenues can also force a club to suspend publication. Nonetheless, with most clubs holding fewer than half a dozen general membership meetings during the year, a newsletter is not only a valuable source of information about club affairs, but a way of calling meetings and a bond that holds club members together.

While journals are issued largely to describe and promote club fund-raising schemes, and thus might well be catalogued as a "political activity," they can also serve to hold a club together, dramatizing various club activities. We found that 128 clubs (nearly 50 percent of our universe) issue journals.

Political Activities

Club political activities include those meetings specifically devoted to nominating candidates for public or party office, or to planning campaigns, or to planning other political-type projects or events. Political activities outside the clubhouse consist of electioneering and voter registration activities, working at polling places both on primary and general election days, and in other ways working directly to influence the selection and success of a party's candidates. With this in mind it becomes quite clear that our researchers were unlikely to have seen any of these activities at first hand. What they could, and did, report on were what the clubs talked about doing, and in this sense established certain threads of political activity. What we discovered seems to be somewhat, though not entirely, at variance with Bowman and Boynton's report that "neither activity related to the ideological tasks of the party, nor those related to the nominating process, are mentioned very often."[13] The nature of the discussions that we observed in the clubs in New York City indicated that concern about money is dominant in the clubs. Since some proportion of the money raised in political clubs quite naturally goes to support campaigns, we feel this can be viewed as "political activity." We found that in 98 of the 157 club meetings reported on, members at some point were engaged in discussing club finances; 93 meetings also saw members engage in direct discussion of forthcoming or past elections; and 76 meetings included some discussion of primaries. Other discussion topics, though not so directly political in tone, were nonetheless in essence tied to the political mission. Discussions of club procedures for example (which we observed in 53 of the clubs) had a direct connection with the political ambitions of club members or with their particular orientation on political issues.

Whether we analyzed the various topics of club discussion according to the age of the clubs, or according to their parties, or their dominant ethnic group, we found the rank order of formal discussion topics to be remarkably consistent. Only with respect to the age factor did we notice any change—the newer clubs (three years old or less) seem far more likely to discuss club finances than the older ones. This is not surprising, however, since new clubs mean new meeting places, or no regular meeting places at all, only rented facilities. Therefore these clubs are busy buying equipment, raising funds for a downpayment on a clubhouse, or attending to other financial matters that have already been taken care of by the older clubs. Older clubs have regular sources of

TABLE 6.8

Percent of Clubs That Discuss Various Topics
at Club Meetings, by Party

Topic	Democratic	Republican	Conservative
Finances	37	25	50
Elections	37	22	42
Primaries	33	13	31
Social events	32	27	31
Club procedures	23	12	15

TABLE 6.9

Percent of Clubs That Discuss Various Topics at Club Meetings,
by Dominant Ethnic Group in Clubs

Topic	Jews	Italians	Irish	Wasps
Finances	35	34	60	37
Elections	38	25	40	29
Primaries	34	23	20	29
Social events	26	25	60	29
Club procedures	24	18	30	14

income, experienced fund raisers—the new clubs do not. Older clubs
are more likely to have incumbents, while newer clubs have more
challengers or recently elected officials, which means a larger pool
to draw upon in terms of dues, ad sellers for journals, fund raisers,
ticket buyers, etc. Older clubs probably maintain closer lines to
the county organization, which may be an additional source of funds.
　These factors aside, the functional order of club discussion
topics finds club finances generally at the top of the list (see Table
6.8 and Table 6.9). This is so particularly among clubs with a
dominant Irish membership, with these clubs also showing a strong
tendency to discuss social events during their meetings. The fact
that the Irish-dominated clubs are mostly old-line regular clubs
may help to explain their dual emphasis on fiscal and social affairs.
Plunkitt would probably feel comfortable with political clubs that
spend their time during meetings discussing important things, which
are social events, because all of the major club decisions are not

made by the membership at meetings, but by the leader somewhere else. "To hold your district study human nature and act accordin'," he would probably say. Discussions at meetings center on topics about which people can have diverse opinions, but which have no effect on the important business—the primaries. Also, Irish dominated clubs may not have as many primaries as other clubs. As Costikyan noted, the Irish are still the professional politicians.[14]

Whether we view it as maintenance or as a political function club meetings are clearly the outstanding activity of all political clubs. Over 35 percent of the clubs studied were engaged in a formal meeting of one sort or another at the time our observers were present. However, "rapping", game-playing, and partying also occurred. We found that meetings were the more favored activity among older clubs, as was game-playing. Game-playing seemed even more responsive to ethnicity. Italians were particularly game-prone.

The range of activities occuring at clubs reflects the combination of attractions that political clubs hold out for their members, and the other community residents who visit. Clubs are not open every night in the week, and when their doors are unlocked it is usually for some specific purposes. Some of these purposes are related to the maintenance of the club as an on-going body; others are related to the service function of the clubs; still others relate to the social, as well as political functions that the club serves for some people.

In some clubs, on some nights, constituents come to the club for assistance with tenant-landlord problems, problems dealing with social security, legal matters, jury notices and (in poorer neighborhoods) problems regarding welfare or unemployment benefits. In the larger clubs, and those where public officials and party leaders encourage this use of the clubhouse, there are many visitors seeking assistance. In smaller and less powerful clubs, especially when there is no public or party official present, no constituent services are provided. Here club activities in the clubhouse may center around a handful of old-timers, who come out of habit. Many clubhouses, whether they provide services or not, are a magnet for the lonely, for those who have nothing in particular to do, and for those who think that the pathway to glory (or club power) lies in being at the clubhouse whenever it is open. When there are no meetings, and that is most of the time, these hangers-on engage in desultory conversation, card playing, television watching, gossiping, and whatever tasks the leadership has set out for them to do.

Clubs cannot directly engage in year-round activities that are unambiguously political in character. Because nominations and elections are seasonal in character, and because clubs are playing less and less a role in campaigning, the rank and file members would have a thin diet if political clubs served only political fare. Therefore, social and service activities become the substitute binding that holds the club together.

Social Activities

The key role that political organizations play in providing social activities for their members is described by Peter R. Gluck as follows:

> The party organization must find and maintain a balance between two distinct areas of activity: one in which it operates primarily as an agent in the political process and a second in which it operates as an agent in the individual-oriented satisfaction fulfillment process. [15]

This explains why today, as in the time of Peel's study, a substantial proportion of club discussion, as well as actual club activity, is social in nature. Eighty-six clubs were reported by our researchers as discussing social events at the time of their observations. What social events were being discussed? As in Peel's study, dances are the club's most popular type of social event; dances are followed, in order of popularity, by dinner parties, card parties, picnics, participating sports, theatre parties, and spectator sports. The following table shows the percent of clubs that engage in each of these activities:

Dances	67%
Dinner parties	61
Card parties	34
Picnics	29
Participating sports	16
Theatre parties	12
Spectator sports	9

A wide variety of other social events—reported by some 37 percent of the clubs—include various fund-raising benefits, Christmas parties (for club members and for neighborhood children), get-togethers at members' homes (drinking and socializing), ladies days (held on Sundays and featuring speakers and refreshments), Las Vegas nights, raffle contests, concerts (held at Queens College) followed by cocktail receptions, auctions (of art works), a white elephant sale and box luncheon, a bus trip to Albany to observe the state legislature in session, a mah-jongg party, a bingo party, and a weekend trip to a Catskills resort.

In contrast to Peel's study, we noted a decline in the popularity of sports activities. Peel reported that, although sports had always been more prominent in European politics than in American politics, "hundreds of local clubs either maintain athletic teams or cooperate with other organizations in support of a neighborhood athletic club."[16] Peel's list of participating sports activities for many clubs included football, baseball, tennis, fencing, riding, swimming, golf, and fishing. Peel also mentioned several spectator sports events, such as boxing, but he did not note the extent to which the clubs scheduled these events. Many of today's clubs sponsor little league teams and teen-age baseball and bowling teams. In fact currently the emphasis on sports in many clubs seems to have shifted to children. Peel's remarks also indicate that there may have been more club picnics in his day than there are in the present day.

Clubs today hold their dinner parties in catering establishments, with the food, entertainment, and atmosphere at these parties being identical with the fare generally offered at weddings and bar mitzvahs. Even clergymen attend club dinners. Card parties remain sturdy club perennials, although when Peel studied them they might well have been black-tie soirees held in the clubhouses. The more casual club events of the twenties—members merely stopping by the clubhouse to chat with their peers in the rather elegant setting that some clubs boasted—seem to have died out. It is doubtful that elegant clubhouse settings can be found today despite the fact that there is clearly as much group affluence assembled in some of today's clubhouses as there was in the twenties. There has been, however, a stylistic change since that era in the way that affluence presents itself.

We found some notable differences in both the partisan and ethnic proclivities of clubs in terms of their various social activities, as shown in Table 6.10 and Table 6.11. Card parties, for example, are favored by Republican clubs to a greater degree than by Democratic clubs, while the Conservatives evidently hold card parties in relatively low esteem (only 13 percent of their clubs have card parties). While dinner parties are in great favor among both Democrats and Republicans (64 percent and 61 percent of their clubs respectively), these events, again, are not heavily favored by Conservative clubs (42 percent).

Our data on ethnic preferences among the clubs in this regard shows that the Irish, for example, seem particularly fond of card parties: 50 percent of clubs with a large Irish segment reported the

TABLE 6.10

Number of Clubs That Engage in Various
Social Activities, by Party

Social Activity	Democratic	Republican	Conservative	Total
Card parties	32	46	12	87
Dances	66	70	73	175
Theatre parties	15	7	4	31
Dinner parties	64	61	42	158
Participating sports	19	10	15	41
Spectator sports	12	6	4	24

TABLE 6.11

Percent of Clubs That Engage in Various Social Activities, by
Dominant Ethnic Group in Clubs

Social Activity	Jews	Italians	Irish	Wasps
Card parties	31	39	50	29
Dances	61	64	70	71
Theatre parties	19	11	10	0
Dinner parties	61	59	80	57
Picnics	26	27	20	43
Participating sports	29	16	10	14
Spectator sports	8	11	0	29

use of card parties, as against only 39 percent of the Italian-dominated clubs, 31 percent of the dominantly Jewish clubs, and 29 percent of the Wasp-dominated clubs. The Irish also are the strongest for dinner parties, with 80 percent of the Irish-dominated clubs reporting using this type of event, as against 61 percent of the dominantly Jewish clubs, 59 percent of the dominantly Italian clubs, and 57 percent of the dominantly Wasp clubs. The more casual eating events—for example picnics—find the great attraction among Wasp-dominated clubs (43 percent of these clubs). Finally, the dominantly Jewish clubs show the widest usage of participating sports (29 percent of these clubs).

Community Service Activities

In their community type programs—including educating the public in various key issues and ombudsman-type activity—we found that the political clubs in New York City seem to be less interested in community service than the clubs that Peel studied. While some clubs to this day remain deeply involved in offering services both to their own members and the community at large, vast numbers of other clubs have discontinued many such services.

In answer to our question, "What type of services does the club provide for members of the community?" we obtained the following responses (figures are the number of clubs that said yes, they do provide a particular service, and the number that said no, they do not):

Type of service provided	Yes	No
Educational	153	93
Legal	141	106
Contact with government	144	102
Landlord-tenant advice	114	131
Employment	107	137
Welfare	87	158

As the figures indicate, in at least four categories—landlord-tenant services, employment services, welfare help, and "other" services—the number of clubs that do not provide these types of services is larger than the number who do. It is notable that education is the leading service, while welfare, despite the large number of welfare recipients in New York City, is the least offered service.

When we looked at these services in terms of particular club variables, we found, first, that the age of a club seems to have some bearing on its propensity to offer legal-type services in particular. The old clubs and the new clubs are much more likely to offer legal-type services than those clubs that have been in operation between 7 and 15 years (65 percent of the clubs in operation under 7 years or over 15 offer their constituents legal help, as opposed to approximately 40 percent of clubs in the 7-15 range). A similar trend has developed in connection with providing contacts with government agencies and officials: 50 percent of such clubs, clubs in the 7-15 bracket, offer this service, and 58 percent and 67 percent, respectively, of clubs in the older and newer brackets offer it.

Party affiliation does not seem to greatly affect the types of community services clubs render (see Table 6.12). The fact that Conservatives offer legal services in only 23 percent of their clubs (as against 49 percent of the Republican clubs and 63 percent of the Democratic clubs) may only reflect our finding (noted in Chapter 4) that Conservatives have relatively few lawyers among their members. Conservatives also offer only infrequently landlord-tenant services and employment services. In both these categories only 8 percent of the Conservative clubs offer services, while Democrats offer landlord-tenant services in 53 percent of their clubs, and Republicans in 36 percent. The deviation between the two major parties in providing services to landlords and tenants may be explained in terms of the fact that the Democrats are more likely to attract tenant groups, and more advice seems to be handed out to tenants today than to landlords. The strong work ethic bias that Conservative clubs may harbor would help to explain the fact that half as many Conservative clubs as Republican or Democratic clubs offer any type of welfare service.

TABLE 6.12

Percent of Clubs Offering Various Types
of Community Services, by Party

Type of service offered	Democratic	Republican	Conservative
Educational	62	52	62
Legal	63	49	23
Contact with government	58	53	50
Landlord-tenant advice	53	36	8
Employment	48	40	8
Welfare	38	30	15

TABLE 6.13

Percent of Clubs Offering Various Types of Community
Services, by Dominant Ethnic Group in Clubs

Type of Service Offered	Jews	Italians	Irish	Wasps
Educational	66	61	50	43
Legal	62	57	70	29
Contact with government	51	66	50	43
Landlord-tenant advice	55	32	60	29
Employment	38	39	60	29
Welfare	38	23	70	29

Ethnicity also seems to have some effect on the types of
services the different clubs offer (see Table 6.13). It is not
surprising, in view of the generally accepted belief that Jews
tend to be education-minded, to find that 66 percent of the clubs
dominated by Jews offer educational-type services. Among the
educational services provided by these clubs, and by other clubs,
are the scheduling of lectures (given by city commissioners,
representatives of local police precincts, college professors,
public officials and representatives of foreign countries); the
showing of various films; the counseling of high school seniors
planning to attend college; the tutoring of school children; and
the supplying of pamphlets, leaflets, and manuals printed by the
government or by various interest groups. We found it somewhat
difficult to explain the breakdown of services offered by clubs with
Irish domination. It is possible that their services reflect the
occupational ranks of their membership; thus the large number of
Irish lawyers might account for the fact that 70 percent of the
Irish-dominated clubs offer legal services. But can one explain
the fact that 70 percent of these clubs also offer welfare services?
Perhaps, once again, it is the professionalism of the Irish that
leads them to emphasize welfare services for their constituents,
many of whom are poor (and few of whom are Irish).

Clubs also differ in their services over time and in terms of
ideology. For example the Village Independent Democrats, a reform
club in Manhattan's Greenwich Village area, had eight committees
in March 1961, according to Goetcheus. Of the eight at least three
were concerned with providing services: the community action
committee, the housing committee and the community service

committee.[17] But by 1966, in the Woodrow Wilson Democratic Club (also in Manhattan), Joseph Lyford had observed a fading away of service work as the club shifted from being a "social work"-type club to being a "political" type.[18]

Moreover, if one compares the percentage of clubs in New York City that say they provide a particular range of services with the percentage of political leaders in New Jersey that say they provide similar services—according to a study by Richard T. Frost—we find the current New York City clubs not only lagging behind the examples set by the city's clubs in the past, but also not measuring up to the practices of other present-day politicians. In every service category where comparisons could be made between our data and Frost's data, a greater percentage of New Jersey politicians claimed to provide services than did New York City's political clubs[19] (see Table 6.14).

TABLE 6.14

Percent of New York City Clubs and New Jersey
Politicians That Claim to Provide Various Community Services

Type of Service Provided	New York City Clubs	New Jersey Politicians
Educational	60	—a
Legal	56	79
Help Get Government Contracts	56	—a
Landlord-tenant relations	44	84
Employment	41	94-98b
Welfare assistance	33	89
Other	43	65

aNo comparable data was available.

bFrost used two categories: "Helping poorer [people] get work" and "helping deserving people get public jobs on a highway crew, in the fire department or police force, or in a state position."

Sources: New York City club data was compiled by the authors; data on New Jersey politicians comes from a study by Richard T. Frost, "Stability and Change in Local Party Politics," Public Opinion Quarterly 25 (Summer 1961): 231.

Our study confirmed the profound change that has occured in the type of welfare assistance provided by the clubs since Peel studied them in the thirties. Whereas in that era the food and coal baskets supplied by the clubs on holiday occasions was a routine activity (in fact year-round relief emanated from most of the clubhouses throughout the Depression), this sort of direct handout today has faded from the clubhouse scene, having been supplanted by welfare checks and other forms of government aid. However, in the same way that the clubs in Peel's study "took over" the distribution of emergency unemployment funds and special-work relief jobs during the Roosevelt era, the clubs today that are located in poverty areas help their constituents obtain relief provided by the government. In a city where one out of every seven persons is on welfare, and where there are special grants for veterans, dependent children, the elderly, and the disabled, it is evident that efforts to obtain these benefits and advice to eligible recipients can represent a substantial portion of club activity.

Among the many middle-class people who also receive club assistance are the large numbers of New York City residents who seek advice on how to deal with their landlords. In the New York City that Peel knew it was only the clubs of the Communist party that encouraged "renters' strikes" (the other clubs simply tried to "appeal" to landlords); but today there is a far broader club acceptance of more militant-type anti-landlord actions on the part of tenants, and there is as well a considerable amount of club expertise in guiding small-scale landlords through their legal loopholes. Naturally those clubs that are heavily middle-to-upper-middle-class-oriented are more apt to soft-pedal in tenant territory, and keep a careful eye not only on the real-estate interests of their membership but on the possibility of decontrolling certain rented apartments and on getting the best possible advantages for buyers of cooperatives.

We found that not only do many of the present-day New York City clubs fail to provide a broad range of the services already discussed, but that most of the clubs would be regarded as complete failures in fulfilling still another important function of the old-time clubs, that of providing higher-level government employment for club members. Of the clubs responding to the question, "How many members of this club hold government appointments to positions of Deputy Commissioner or above on the state or city level?", 66 percent answered "none." An additional 25 percent had less than five such members, and only 2 percent had more than ten. Since state patronage generally flows to Republicans and Conservatives and city appointments go to the Liberals and Democrats, hypothetically any club might receive such an appointment; but

apparently most clubs do not. Yet the use of a club's good offices
in finding jobs for members—both in government directly (as in
numerous noncivil-service court posts) and with contractors who
feed on the public trough—is still considered a welfare activity
in the clubs. So too with legal advice and with behind-the-scenes
negotiating in matters involving minor offenses by club members,
such as parking violations and failing to answer jury duty notices.

Ironically, these were club activities that Peel predicted
would wither away:

> The day is not far distant when police departments will
> work so efficiently and honestly that there will be nothing
> left for the clubs to do . . . . When the small claims,
> arbitration, and magistrates courts are eventually
> organized as permanent units in the metropolitan
> court system, the club "fixers" will disappear from
> the corridors of the courts as well as from the police
> station.[20]

Unfortunately that day is still far off, and many clubs still
become involved in traffic violations and other petty negotiating
activities.

Moreover the reported activities of clubs cannot be understood
without reflecting on their relationship to certain overarching party
functions. That is, parties in America are still in business for
three primary reasons: the recruitment and selection of public
leaders; the representation and integration of group interests; and
the overall control and directing of the government.[21] The specific
activities discussed in this chapter are in one sense merely functions
of political clubs that use such activities to stimulate members and
prime them for the political campaigns and policy battles that arise
at various intervals in an election-prone republic. On the other hand
many of the activities are worthwhile in themselves, and some, such
as the social events, may have important psychological benefits;
even these cannot be overlooked in a democratic polity that ultimately
rests on a sane and reasonably cohesive society.

Notes

1. William Foote Whyte, Streetcorner Society (Chicago:
University of Chicago Press, 1943) p. 201.

2. Ibid., p. 206.

3. William Riordan, Plunkitt of Tammany Hall (New York: Dutton, 1963) p. 25.

4. Ibid., p. 25.

5. Wallace Sayre and Herbert Kaufman, Governing New York City (New York: Russell Sage Foundation, 1960), p. 135.

6. Roy V. Peel, The Political Clubs of New York, rev. ed. (New York: Ira S. Friedman, 1968), p. 173.

7. Ibid., p. 192-93.

8. Ibid., pp. 217.

9. Lewis Bowman and G. R. Boynton, "Activities and Role Definition of Grassroots Party Officials," The Journal of Politics 20, p. 127.

10. James Q. Wilson, The Amateur Democrat (Chicago: University of Chicago Press, 1968), p. 19-21.

11. Quoted in David Schuman, A Preface to Politics (Lexington, Mass: D. C. Heath, 1973), p. 111.

12. Peter Bachrach and Morton Baratz, Power and Poverty: Theory and Practice (New York: Oxford University Press, 1970).

13. Bowman and Boynton, op. cit., p. 127.

14. Edward Costikyan, Behind Closed Doors (New York: Harcourt, Brace and World, 1966).

15. Peter R. Gluck, "Politics at the Grassroots: The Inducements and Rewards of Party Participation," (Doctoral dissertation, State University of New York at Buffalo, 1970), p. 21.

16. Peel, op. cit., p. 168.

17. Vernon M. Goetcheus, "The Village Independent Democrats: A study of the politics of the New Reformers," (dissertation, Honor College, Wesleyan University, 1963), p. 65, 14.

18. Joseph Lyford, The Airtight Cage (New York: Harper & Row, 1966), p. 400.

19. Richard T. Frost, "Stability and Change in Local Party Politics," Public Opinion Quarterly 25 (Summer 1961): 231.

20. Peel, op. cit., p. 206.

21. William Keefe, Parties, Politics and Public Policy in America (New York: Holt, Rinehart & Winston, 1972), pp. 19-22.

7

CLUB FINANCES:
WHO PAYS?
AND FOR WHAT?

Most club officials responded to our study of their organization's activities and operations with cooperation and openness—until,
that is, the subject of club finances was raised, at which point their
cooperation virtually ended. For certain reasons, Americans do not
like to discuss their personal finances with strangers (in our case
researchers); many do not discuss their finances with their friends
or family. And in this respect America's political leaders are no
different from its private citizens. If anything, club officials are
somewhat more taciturn in the matter of club income and expenditures than private citizens are about their own earnings and outlays.
Peel noted that "although the evidence touching on such matters is
not readily available, enough of it has been uncovered to warrant our
drawing certain conclusions."[1] We found ourselves in similar circumstances: on the one hand it was impossible to study political
clubs without saying something about club finances, and on the other
hand there were people who categorically refused to discuss the
subject. Moreover we suspect that, among those that did discuss
finances with us, many did not tell the truth. Approximately 15 percent of our respondents demurred when asked to give an itemized
account of their club's revenues and expenditures (13 percent refused
to discuss revenues and 16 percent refused to discuss expenditures).
Many others appeared perfectly willing to respond to questions dealing with broad categories, but would not talk about specific items.

Club finances is a matter of central importance to the clubs:
at the time we observed them, the members of 65 percent of the
political clubs were discussing some aspect of club finances during
the course of a meeting. Since the clubs generally are dependent on

their own financial resources (no party committees subsidize them), they spend much of their time discussing how to raise money, raising the money, and discussing how best to spend it. However, many of the clubs handle their financial affairs in a less than orderly manner. Only 46 percent of all clubs have a budget or financial plan; many club officials say that they have so little money that they do not have to plan what to do with it when they get it. Creditors' bills, apparently, are all the budget many clubs need.

Most of Peel's information about club finances came from newspaper accounts of the 1931 Hofstadter Committee hearings regarding corruption in New York City and from the records of the Seabury investigations. (The now-defunct New York World-Telegram was especially useful to Peel.) From such sources, and from information gathered by his staff, he drew certain conclusions about the ways in which money was obtained and spent by the clubs. We also relied on some information derived from newspaper reports. However, no recent major legislative investigation has delved into the matter of party finances, and where information has surfaced in the press, national and state party funding has been involved. Financial information on New York City's political clubs came to us from our respondents, who replied to questions about the proportion of funds raised through a number of traditional techniques, many of them suggested by Peel, and the proportion expended on a number of activities and facilities. What we learned led us to certain conclusions as well. However, we have no way of knowing how close we have come to the truth about club finances. We do not believe there is a single pattern with respect to finances; in many ways studying money in politics is like studying dinosaurs—it is a process of reconstructing, from partial evidence, the way the creature must have looked and behaved, without ever seeing the entire living organism, and always being suspicious about the possibility that circumstance or deception are paths leading away from actual fact.

For purposes of analysis we adopted Peel's scheme of separating the financial activities of political clubs into two major, and several subsidiary, categories. However, we used different words and phrasing to elicit responses to our questions, because we felt some of Peel's language today might be regarded as archaic or insulting. Although some of his subcategories do not reflect current finance practices in New York City's clubs, the use of these subcategories provides us with some idea of the shifting importance of funding sources and expenditures that has occurred since the period of Peel's study.

The two principal categories that Peel used are revenue-producing items and revenue-disbursing items. The revenue-producing items he broke down as (1) gifts from leaders or councilors,

(2) members' dues and fees, (3) rents or fees for the use of club quarters, (4) proceeds from the sale of tickets and goods, raffles, rake-offs, and capital stock investments, and (5) income from securities. To these we added a sixth subcategory, the sale of favors and offices. Peel's revenue-disbursing items included (1) formal expenditures/capital outlay, (2) salaries and wages of employees, (3) campaign contributions to central, subsidiary, or auxiliary organizations, (4) gifts, (5) contributions to welfare activities and charitable organizations, and (6) tribute on account of irregular and illigitimate activities.

Revenue-Producing Activities

Political clubs occupy a relatively weak competitive position in the quest for money. Almost without exception they are on their own when it comes to fund-raising. Moreover, as Key pointed out:

> The problem of raising money to support political
> activity is not entirely one of party finance but in
> large measure one of financing individual candidates.
> . . . American politics is atomized and each candi-
> date must in some way or another cover his own
> campaign expenses. [2]

For every potential donor to a political party there is a potential solicitor from among the national, state, and county committees of the party, the incumbent officeholders, the potential and active primary challengers, candidates in general elections, and those who have lost elections and are involved in retiring their debts. Certain donors gravitate to specific levels of government and office, or are attracted to certain styles of campaigning, while others are quite willing to hear the sales pitch of any finance chairman or fund-raiser who might come along. The clubs, because they are relatively low on the totem pole of power, have little opportunity to approach the big contributors; often, when they do, they are in competition with their own party's candidates. In a similar manner fund-raising events sponsored by the clubs usually tend to be "small potatoes" when compared with the activities of important candidates and committees. The contributors understand, and most clubs would acknowledge, that the principal reason for their contributing to political clubs is to gain the clubs' support for their particular candidates for office (or for themselves) at party conventions and caucuses, in the form of street campaigning and endorsements by the clubs. Sometimes contributors become involved in a negative purchase, hoping the clubs will not endorse an opponent, nor campaign against a favored candidate, nor throw their influence and votes to another ticket in party councils. At best contributors hope that, by currying favor with the clubs through gifts of money or goods, they may gain access to the decision makers who are affiliated with the clubs, or identify themselves with a cause for which the clubs claim to stand.

In order to determine the sources of club income, we asked our respondents to estimate the percentage of their total club budget raised from each of seven sources: members' dues, social affairs, the rental of club quarters to outsiders, money derived from advertisements placed in club journals, direct contributions, profits from the playing of bingo and other games of chance, and a catchall, or "other," category. In those cases where we were able to obtain copies of the club's annual budget, we compared the answers of our respondents with their written record, finding little disagreement between the written and spoken estimates. However, we were inclined to believe that this did not reflect on the truthfulness of other respondents who either refused to provide us with documentation or had no budget to give us.

We did not ask our respondents to estimate their total club revenue, although several volunteered this information. It is difficult to generalize about this matter, since the clubs can vary from being extremely wealthy to being nearly bankrupt. We estimated that few clubs raise more than seven to ten thousand dollars a year, and that quite a few clubs get along on substantially less. These budgets are often supplemented by payments from public officials and district leaders; we found clubs where a portion of the clubhouse was being used by state assemblymen, state senators, district leaders, or city councilmen who paid their share of the club's rent and other costs. Various candidates for office frequently have additional telephones installed in clubhouses during campaigns, and pay for them directly. Large campaign signs, bearing the names of all endorsed candidates, go up over clubhouses at election time—these too are often paid for directly by one or more candidates. District leaders and club officials also frequently bear sizeable out-of-pocket expenses for postage, refreshments, printing, and charity contributions, without recourse to club treasuries. We do not regard any of these payments as club income or expenditures, although the clubs certainly benefit from such payments.

On the whole the clubs derive their income today from the sources—listed above—that Peel mentioned. In fact, 77 percent of clubs have no other source of income (see Table 7.1). How dependent are they on any single source or combination of sources? The

TABLE 7.1

Percent and Number of Clubs Reporting Percentage of Income Derived from Various Sources

Source of Income	Percentage of Income											
	0	1-10	11-20	21-30	31-40	41-50	51-60	61-70	71-80	81-90	91-100	N.A.
Dues	7 (19)	11 (29)	7 (20)	12 (33)	9 (19)	17 (45)	3 (9)	1 (4)	8 (21)	7 (20)	6 (16)	12 (33)
Social Affairs	27 (73)	13 (34)	10 (28)	10 (27)	7 (18)	8 (22)	3 (7)	3 (9)	3 (8)	1 (4)	1 (4)	13 (34)
Rent	75 (201)	8 (22)	2 (5)	1 (4)	1 (1)	0 (0)	1 (1)	0 (0)	0 (0)	0 (0)	0 (0)	13 (34)
Journal ads	60 (160)	7 (18)	4 (11)	3 (7)	4 (10)	3 (9)	1 (3)	2 (6)	2 (6)	1 (1)	1 (3)	13 (34)
Direct contributions	47 (126)	19 (51)	7 (19)	4 (11)	2 (6)	5 (13)	1 (3)	0 (0)	1 (2)	0 (0)	0 (0)	13 (36)
Bingo, other games	65 (173)	13 (34)	3 (9)	3 (9)	1 (4)	1 (2)	0 (0)	0 (0)	1 (3)	0 (0)	0 (0)	13 (34)
Other	77 (207)	3 (8)	1 (3)	2 (4)	2 (5)	2 (5)	0 (0)	0 (0)	1 (1)	0 (0)	1 (1)	8 (21)

Note: Number of clubs is indicated in parentheses; N.A. indicates not available, or clubs that declined to respond on item; "other" is catchall of additional sources; percents do not total 100 percent due to rounding.

147

discussion that follows, based on our interviews, may help to answer this question.

Gifts—of money and goods—have been a source of income for political clubs throughout their history. Apparently when Peel studied the clubs such contributions did not come directly into a club's treasury, for he made no mention of such a practice. However, he did explain how clubs received support from outsiders.

> Funds may come from the bosses's pockets, but if this is the case they have merely found a temporary resting place there. When traced to their origins, funds of this nature are found to have been: gifts from friends and public-spirited citizens, anxious to contribute through the party organization to the relief of poverty and sickness; gifts from prominent party members desiring party victory at the polls; bribes, graft, and protection money. [3]

District leaders today continue to contribute to the support of clubs, and, on occasion, to act as a conduit for funds. However, funds do come directly to club treasuries as well, probably for most of the purposes for which they were designed in the twenties and thirties. The exception is contributions for charitable purposes; Peel studied the clubs during the depression when they often did double duty as welfare organizations (sans welfare regulations). Few clubs perform such functions today.

Direct contributions or gifts do not play a very large role in club income. Almost 50 percent of the city's clubs reported that not one penny of outside contributions had been made directly to them in the year prior to our study. Many of these clubs do receive money in forms other than direct gifts, which will be discussed later in this chapter. Of the 39 percent that did receive direct contributions, two-thirds reported that such gifts accounted for a fifth, or less, of their income. While Peel did not rank the income sources he identified in the order of their importance, he gave us the impression that gifts from district leaders were either at, or near, the top of the list. No such large contributions are forthcoming to today's clubs, except to a small minority. Several respondents indicated to us that contributions are as likely to come from club members as from outsiders, and often in small sums. Such contributions do not reflect, either in spirit or substance, the nature of the gifts category as Peel described it.

From time to time clubs have also been the recipients of, or conduits for, money from criminal sources. Alexander Heard reported, for instance, that "Senator Estes Kefauver's committee

investigating interstate crime demonstrated persuasively that for a
time in the 1940's the New York County Democratic organization,
Tammany Hall, lay under the influence of a leading underworld
figure, Frank Costello."[4] The notorious mobster Joe Adonis was
said to have similar ties with the Brooklyn Democratic organization.
Usually it was party leaders and officials, rather than club treasuries,
that were said to benefit from such associations. Undoubtedly clubs
benefited directly and indirectly, as well. Investigations conducted
by Special State Prosecutor Maurice Nadjari in 1973 and 1974 suggest
that gifts continue to come to political leaders from criminal figures.
However, we could not ascertain whether the practice of the twenties
through the forties of such funds coming directly into club treasuries
has continued as well.

Dues

Of the income that is reported by club officials, the overwhelming impression we were given is that most clubs depend more on dues
than on any other source of revenue. For some clubs this depend-
ence is so great that it would be hard to imagine their surviving were
dues to be eliminated. One-quarter of political clubs reported they
receive 50 percent or more of their total income from dues, and
only 7 percent of the clubs reported no income from dues. No other
club revenue source even comes close to dues in importance.
The present-day importance of dues to the fiscal survival of
the clubs is a far cry from the condition that existed when Peel was
conducting his research. He found that dues were not "systematically
collected in any save the most exclusive clubs," and, he noted:

> According to one prominent leader, the annual dues
> are nothing more than initiation fees: 'You pay your
> five dollars when you join, and then you forget it.'
> The dues are generally about five to six dollars per
> year. If all members of clubs actually paid these dues,
> the sum total would be staggering . . . as it is, prob-
> ably only a few thousands of dollars are received from
> dues.[5]

Today's political clubs make the payment of dues synonymous with
membership. Regarding this we asked two separate questions of
our respondents: how many members there are in the club, and how
many dues-paying members there are. Overall, the difference between the two responses was less than two percent. Many clubs, in

in their constitution, set the annual election of their officers, or their annual meeting, to coincide with the final date on which dues payments can be made. In this way a member may not vote or participate in club affairs unless his dues have been paid. Almost without fail, when asked about the requirements for joining their club, respondents included the payment of dues; for many this is the only important act that the prospective member must perform.

Dues are set rather low to encourage membership: if dues are important to the lifeblood of the clubs, members are even more important. There is some variation in the amount of dues levied by the clubs, but it is unusual to find dues charges of less than seven dollars per member or more than fifteen dollars. Dues reductions are granted to senior citizens, students, welfare recipients, the unemployed, and housewives, with the amounts depending on a club's neighborhood, party, and faction. But, contrary to what Peel found, hardly anyone in the clubs today is excused from paying something. In what are frequently considered helter-skelter, casual, or downright anarchic political units, the most systematic and well-organized club office usually is that of treasurer, and that officer's major responsibility is to see to it that members pay their dues.

Rent

While most clubs own or rent some sort of club quarters, we found that most of them do not use their quarters with any degree of efficiency. Many clubs make no use of their clubhouse on several days during the week, and the usual practice is for clubs to be open in the evenings or, at most, in the late afternoons and evenings, and on Saturdays. We had expected to find that the clubs rented their facilities to other individuals or groups during those hours when the club itself was not using the facilities. For example, Peel found that "certain clubs rent or lease a part of their quarters to other types of organizations—religious, fraternal, professional or civic," with those clubs that had recreational facilities setting "a small charge for the use of pool tables, billiard tables, bowling alleys, and card tables."[6]

Present-day clubs generally do not follow such practices. Three-quarters of the clubs we surveyed realize no revenue from the rental of club quarters or facilities. Of the 13 percent that do rent space, the practice results in a small profit, amounting to less than 10 percent of their annual income. Club officials provided various explanations for their failure to earn income from their property. First, political clubs have irregular schedules. During the periods prior to candidate petitioning and election day most clubs are open frequently, and for many hours on end. No prospective tenants want to be told that during certain months the club's property or facilities will be unavailable to them. Second, political clubs are smaller now than they once were. Many occupy one or two rooms. Multistory clubhouses have become increasingly rare as real estate taxes have risen, and maintenance costs along with them. Most of the available club space is taken up by club records, equipment, and furniture; vacant space is simply unavailable. Third, political clubs no longer feature the attractions of recreation and relaxation that they once emphasized. Gaming rooms, tennis courts, billiard and card tables, bowling alleys, and auditoriums are largely absent from today's clubs. Thus with few exceptions there is nothing available to rent except four walls and some folding chairs. Finally, the clubs no longer occupy a central position in the community. Where once people could find no other available space, at a reasonable rental, to hold meetings, conduct classes, or find amusement, there now are a variety of such places more luxurious and better equipped than political clubs.

It should be noted that the clubs continue to offer their facilities, without charge, for meetings to such community organizations as American Legion posts, the Boy Scouts, tenant groups, senior citizens' clubs, and consumer councils. During a spate of school strikes and boycotts that plagued New York City, clubhouses were used as temporary classrooms in some sections of the city. Why would a club that might have been unwilling in the first place to rent out its quarters allow the space to be used for such purposes? Sometimes community goodwill is the more valuable coin in politics.

Sales

American charitable, religious, and fraternal organizations traditionally raise funds by conducting various types of sales. Every household at one time or another has likely been visited by Boy Scouts selling lightbulbs, by parochial school children selling candy, or by Girl Scouts selling cookies. Fund-raising activities that include the sale of such items, and thus bring recognition, help raise money for thousands of groups—and political clubs are no exception. Peel identified five types of selling that earned money for the political clubs he studied: tickets to various events, journal ads, food, other goods, and stock in the club. Among these only club stock is not sold today by New York City's clubs.

Ticket sales were a highly lucrative source of income for the clubs that Peel studied. Many of those clubs held annual balls, with tickets selling for as high as twenty-five dollars, or as low as two, or three dollars. Peel noted that the Minqua Club in Manhattan reported a profit of four thousand dollars in 1931 from its annual ball.[7] The Great Depression gave rise to club social activities whose proceeds went, "theoretically at least,"[8] as Peel puts it, to charities. He described the types of events for which tickets were sold:

> Annual charity balls . . . a package party for the aid of the unemployed . . . a card party for the benefit of the poor . . . a card and bunco party for the same purpose . . . a social and dance for the benefit of a member injured in an automobile accident . . . card party and dance to raise funds for the purchase of Christmas baskets . . .[9]

Political clubs today continue to employ such sales of tickets as a major fund-raising vehicle. Dues aside, our respondents indicated that social affairs raised the largest percentage of club income. Approximately three-fourths of the clubs make use of some social activity during the course of the year, and slightly more than 10 percent raise at least half of their total funds by selling tickets to such functions. In some clubs, especially those that have close ties with the municipal administration or with some particularly important office or agency, "members are expected to 'take' a block of five or ten tickets, and either sell them to their friends or give them away," which is what they did in the thirties, according to Peel.[10]

We learned that although charitable functions are not nearly as important in the clubs now as they once were, several clubs have earmarked their profit from certain ticket sales for such charitable purposes as memorial scholarship funds named for departed members, the purchase of equipment for hospitals and neighborhood medical centers, and the purchase of toys to distribute to poor children at Christmas.

Among the social activities for which club members have sold tickets over the past few years are theatre parties, cocktail parties, annual dinners, picnics, holiday parties (Christmas, New Year's Eve, Halloween, St. Patrick's Day, Count Pulaski Day, Purim, Independence Day), dances, concerts, lectures, movies, wine and cheese parties, etc. The price of tickets to such activies varies by community and income group, but five-to-fifteen dollars is a usual charge for most of these events. Dinners occasionally cost more than other social activities, but few clubs (unlike candidates for office) ever charge more than twenty-five dollars a ticket.

Of all the social activities aimed at raising funds, club dinners are the most common—of those clubs responding affirmatively to the question of whether they raised funds through the sale of tickets to social affairs, most of them indicated that the club dinner was the most usual affair. Heard found that "in a majority of the states in every year the dinners provided more than half the funds used by the state organizations of both parties to meet the routine costs . . ."[11] While few New York City political clubs are so dependent on a single activity, Heard's finding is indicative of the strategic place that dinners have in American political fund-raising. Although we obtained no precise figures, we are inclined to agree with one New York City politician who told Heard that "in his experience sixty percent of all tickets sold are for entire tables [at dinners]."[12] Block purchases of dinner tickets provide an additional means of contributing substantial sums to the clubs—incumbent public officeholders, those candidates for office seeking club support, and important contributors use block purchases in lieu of, or in addition to, their regular contributions. As Key noted, "While dinners may bring in a fringe of new contributors, the chances are that in the main the same people who contribute directly buy the tickets."[13]

A club journal is frequently handed out at club dinners. Peel described the club journal as "a 'souvenir' publication consisting of names and pictures of the leaders and prominent members, the dance and entertainment program, and advertisements."[14] This description fits the club journal of today, with the exception that many clubs have done away with the frills (pictures, program, etc.), and concentrate almost exclusively on advertisements.

While in the 1930s "nearly every club deriv[ed] some profit from the sale of the annual 'journal and program,'"[15] today only half of all clubs have such a situation. Of those that do, half publish their journal annually, with the rest publishing less frequently, sometimes as little as once in three years. Usually it is the clubs with elected public officials, or with close connections with the city, state, or federal administration, that use journals as fund-raisers. Key provided an explanation for this:

A newspaper comment on advertising in the program of an athletic event sponsored by a Chicago ward club noted that most of the buyers of space were neighborhood saloons. A saloonkeeper never knows when he is violating the law but he does know, it was said, 'that violations by those who are not right-minded means license revocation.' Contributions may also

be exacted from contractors and other suppliers of
goods and services to public agencies.[16]

We examined several journals published in recent years and found
the following categories of advertisers: incumbent public officials,
incumbent party officials, candidates for office, seekers of nominations for city and state public office, wives and families of city
and state judges, locals of unions whose members work for the city
or state, locals of unions whose employees are licensed by the city
or state, locals of unions that either have a reputation for being
involved in questionable activities or have leaders with such repu-
tations, companies doing business with the city or state, other
political clubs and their leaders and officeholders, appointed heads
of city and state agencies, religious and ethnic fraternal organizations (including an unusually large number of Jewish yeshivas and
rabbis), chambers of commerce, local realty boards, local mer-
chants, and law firms with large practices before city and state
agencies. In the smaller clubs we found the bulk of the journal ads
to be taken by club members and a few officials.

How much money do sales of journals earn for the clubs that
publish them? For most clubs this amount is not very great. We
found that the largest group of clubs publishing journals earn less
than a tenth of their income through selling the journals, while an
equal number of clubs earn fifty percent, or more, of their income
through selling journal ads. Peel reported that:

A large Republican district club spent one thousand dollars
in payments for single subscriptions and advertising
fees. The Tammany Clubs often make five times as much
money on these 'journals.' Advertising costs run from
one hundred dollars a page in the elaborate journals to
twenty-five dollars a page in the cheaper thirty page
booklets.[17]

It is not uncommon for clubs today to raise between two and four
thousand dollars through publishing a journal. But printing costs
are relatively high for the slick, union-shop-printed publications,
and most clubs are said to be "partners with the printer," making
a 50, or 60, percent profit on the total moneys collected, with the
rest going into the pockets of the journal's printer. The more
powerful clubs have done much better than the four-thousand-dollar
figure, however, Several respondents reported an income of fifteen
thousand dollars from journals. One regular Democratic club in
Brooklyn was said to have netted more than forty thousand from a
recent journal, although that figure was unconfirmed. The apparent

champion of all club journals was the one published in 1971 in conjunction with the Second Annual Ball of the John V. Lindsay Independent Association of Brooklyn, held in honor of Lindsay. This mammoth seven-pound, 1,354-page volume had only five pages that were unpaid (a cover page, a page with the club's list of officers, a message from the club's journal chairman, a letter from Lindsay to the club on official stationery signed by Lindsay, and a page featuring Lindsay's picture). The journal's gold pages, silver pages, and white pages (in the form of full-, half-, and quarter-page ads) were reported to have earned (conservatively) $125,205. The journal was so successful that it embarrassed its sponsors, who did not distribute it at the ball (which was well covered by the press), but rather quietly shipped copies to central distribution points throughout the city later that year.

The club practice of selling campaign literature at one time prevailed exclusively among third-party clubs. For the most part such a practice continues to this day, and the third-party groups have been joined in this endeavor by several poorer clubs. In addition, New York City clubs follow a practice, begun elsewhere, of selling campaign buttons, car bumper strips, and other campaign memorabilia. While we could obtain no specific information, indications were that such sales account for a miniscule portion of club income.

At one time the sale of food and beverages also brought money into the clubs. Peel reported that those clubs in his study that maintained bars and restaurants derived "some profit" from such facilities, as they did from the sale of beer, candy bars, cigars, and cigarettes at parties and dances.[18] Few clubs have bars or food service today, and most clubs do not bother with the other items Peel mentioned because the profit from them is comparatively small. A few clubs reported income from the sale of club sweatshirts or T-shirts, and a few of the women's auxiliaries of the clubs print cookbooks, containing club members' recipes, to raise funds.

The club practice of selling stock in the clubs to members, followed by some clubs prior to the Second World War, has apparently died out in New York City—we found no club that reported doing this.

Bingo and Other Games

About one-fifth of the clubs reported income from the operation of bingo and other games, and about half of the clubs reporting such income raised ten percent, or less, of their revenue from such sources. We found this a bit unusual, for while bingo is legal in New York, political organizations are prohibited from operating the games. Several informants indicated that the games either were unlicensed and run at clubhouses rather than in bingo halls, or they were run in conjunction with a legitimate charity, which obtained the license for the clubs and split the profits with them. Card games and regular mahjongg parties are found in some, generally older, regular Democratic and Republican clubs. A form of fund-raising made popular by churches and synagogues (and totally illegal)—called Las Vegas nights—has found its way into several clubs. At these events, gambling equipment is employed, in casino fashion, to bring in money. Roulette, chuck-a-luck, dice, and blackjack tables are operated by club members. Equipment is leased from companies who service various charities. A number of clubs, notably in Queens, occasionally raise money in this manner; nonetheless we found that 65 percent of the clubs do not employ gaming activity to generate revenue.

Sale of Favors

We did not expect that club officials would admit to their clubs gaining income from such activities as gambling, prostitution, protection, or the sale of favors and public office, so we did not ask about these activities. However, casual observation indicated to us that there is probably substantially less illicit income of all kinds realized by political clubs in New York City today than was true when Peel studied the clubs. The only exception to this might occur in the sale of favors and public office. Peel noted that "it is impossible to say how much money is derived from the sale of favors."[19] It was probably quite a lot, and favors continue to be sold by clubs and party leaders. For example, 1973 saw the revelation of an elaborate scheme for the fixing of traffic violation tickets that involved commissioners of city agencies, state assemblymen, and club and party officials. Jury duty notices sent to club members were "taken care of," according to some of our informants, although not as easily or as frequently as in times past. As to the sale of offices, Martin Tolchin and Susan Tolchin reported:

> In New York, the party relies on judicial 'revenue' to finance its activities on the district level. Responsible for collecting the pay-offs, the district leader is then free to disburse the funds in whatever way he chooses.[20]

Twelve percent of the city's clubs reported some income from "other" sources. Informally we were told that those sources sometimes included contributions from persons who, as Sayre and Kaufman put it, "would like to be judges."[21] Sayre and Kaufman in 1960 described the judicial system as "a source of party revenue," and they noted:

Some District Leaders can apparently extract as much as a year's salary plus an additional 'campaign fund' of several thousand dollars. For elective office, the amount is frequently set on the basis of a fixed sum (from $50 to $100) for each Election District in the judicial area [which may run to several hundred in number]. This is apparently regarded in party circles as an ordinary part of the revenues of the District Leader and of the party workers in the field. . . . Most candidates for elective office, and even for appointive office . . . give money to their respective party units for putting forth their names and assisting them in their quests . . .[22]

The advertisements in club journals frequently provide a clue to this process. In the John V. Lindsay Association journal discussed above, quite a few ads carried the names of one or more judges or prospective judges. Judges are not permitted to purchase such ads, but their families, former law associates, friends, and relatives can, and often do, purchase these ads. Section 454, Article 16, of the New York State Election Law provides:

No candidate for judicial office shall, directly or indirectly, make any contribution of money or other thing of value, nor shall any contribution be solicited of him; but a candidate for a judicial office may make such legal expenditures other than contributions as are authorized by section 439 of this article.

Among the expenditures permitted by section 439 are payments to a candidate's staff, outlays for campaign posters and literature, payments for radio, television, and newspaper advertising, and payments for the rental of space and equipment for purposes of conducting a campaign. No other expenditures are permitted. Yet in late September 1973, the New York Times ran a front-page story that noted, in part, as follows:

Democratic nominees for the State Supreme Court in Manhattan, Queens and Brooklyn have been asked to contribute to the party by taking tables at county

organization dinners, by direct personal contributions
or through their own sponsoring committees, county
leaders and some of the candidates said during a series
of interviews. . . . Two former Civil Court judges in
Brooklyn told the New York Times 'the suggestion' had
been made to them through their district leaders that
$10,000 would be an appropriate amount for each to
raise for the party and to help defray their campaign
costs. [23]

According to Matthew J. Troy, Jr., leader of the Queens County
Democratic Committee, "The tables cost $1,000 and . . . half the
money for each candidate's purchase of a table went to the local
political club of the candidate's district."[24] While different figures
have been put forth as to what might be an acceptable amount for a
prospective judge to pay for a judgeship, five-to-ten thousand dollars
seems to be the range. City commissionerships and public office
have had comparable price tags attached to them.

We are not suggesting that every nominee or appointee actually
pays to secure his office. Obviously some are rewarded for faithful
service and others are moved upstairs to make room for newcomers.
In addition there is a great difference among clubs, leaders, and
parties, although the subject is too sensitive to gain any insight into
such relative differences. However, no account of the sources of a
club's revenue would be complete without some mention of this practice and its impressive potential for raising funds among established
clubs that have ties to appointing officials or a history of success at
the polls.

Revenue-Disbursing Activities

Very little is known about the ways in which party organizations
spend their money. It may indeed be argued that less is known about
party expenditure than about party income. Even the publicity generated by the fund-raising scandals of the 1972 Nixon presidential campaign has placed a disproportionate amount of attention on who gave
what funds to whom—and how—rather than on what happened to the
money once it was received. True, there are campaign expenditure
laws, but these laws tend to require the attention of candidates and
ad hoc campaign committees, rather than established party organizations. Until recently the clubs have felt an obligation to file financial statements with the government. But as the control of campaigns
has shifted from clubs and other organizations into the hands of

professional campaign managers and temporary campaign committees, the disbursement of party funds has become more and more a
mystery, with the clubs at the very center of the enigma.

Peel's list of club disbursements (formal expenditures/capital
outlay, salaries and wages, campaign contributions, gifts, contributions to welfare activities and charitable organizations, and tribute)
relected an age in which local clubs played a central role in campaigns at all levels of government. At that time clubhouses were in
a constant state of campaign readiness. Whatever professional personnel campaigns might have employed probably received some, or
all, of their salary from club treasuries. In addition a complex
organization of auxiliary and subsidiary organizations required financial support so that they could efficiently do their job in delivering
the vote of special subgroups (women, young people, ethnics, racial
blocs, professional and interest groups) on election day.

Our interviewers questioned respondents on the percentage of
their clubs' expenditures that go to a variety of categories paralleling
Peel's: rent and utilities, contributions to charities, the funding of
auxiliaries, contributions to campaigns, contributions to other party
functions, club communications, and a catchall category, "other."
Furthermore we asked respondents whether or not there were any
salaried employees in the club that were paid directly out of the club
treasury.

The general response to these questions was that for most clubs
no single category of disbursement dominates the club budget, with
the possible exception of formal expenditures. Our respondents
seemed no more eager to talk about how they spend club money than
about how it is raised, although a slightly larger percentage of respondents refused to discuss disbursement than that which refused
to discuss income. In a few cases respondents pleaded ignorance,
claiming that only the club treasurer had such information. Again,
where we were permitted to examine budgets or books we found the
verbal responses paralleled the written record. However, there
was a much greater reluctance to go beyond the simple percentage
breakdown that we requested for disbursement categories than there
was for income categories. Apparently money is being expended in
ways that for one reason or another political leaders are embarrassed to relate. Parenthetically, and not surprisingly, we received
the most cooperation from the poorest clubs—the Conservatives.

Formal Expenditures

Peel categorized the following as formal expenditures: "Legal
fees, entailed by organization in obtaining a charter, down-payments

159

TABLE 7.2

Percent and Number of Clubs Reporting Percentage of Disbursements for Various Expense Categories

Expense Category	Percentage of Disbursements											
	0	1-10	11-20	21-30	31-40	41-50	51-60	61-70	71-80	81-90	91-100	N.A.
Rent/utilities	10 (26)	5 (14)	6 (17)	6 (16)	7 (18)	13 (34)	7 (18)	7 (18)	10 (27)	6 (16)	9 (23)	15 (40)
Contributions to charities	53 (141)	18 (50)	8 (22)	3 (7)	1 (2)	1 (2)	0 (0)	0 (0)	1 (1)	1 (1)	0 (0)	15 (42)
Funding auxiliaries	71 (189)	10 (27)	2 (5)	1 (2)	1 (2)	1 (2)	0 (0)	0 (0)	0 (0)	0 (0)	0 (0)	15 (41)
Contributions to Campaigns	35 (94)	11 (30)	10 (28)	5 (30)	6 (14)	1 (16)	1 (3)	1 (1)	1 (3)	1 (3)	1 (2)	16 (44)
Contributions to other party functions	53 (143)	15 (41)	7 (18)	4 (11)	1 (4)	1 (3)	1 (2)	1 (1)	1 (1)	0 (0)	1 (1)	16 (43)
Communications	43 (116)	18 (48)	10 (28)	4 (12)	2 (5)	3 (8)	0 (0)	1 (1)	1 (4)	0 (0)	1 (3)	16 (43)
Other	67 (179)	6 (16)	5 (13)	1 (4)	2 (5)	1 (2)	0 (0)	1 (1)	1 (1)	1 (2)	1 (2)	15 (42)

Note: Number of clubs is indicated in parentheses; N.A. indicates not available, or clubs that declined to respond on item; "other" is catchall of additional expenses; percents do not total 100 percent due to rounding.

on quarters, rent of quarters, hire of janitors and care-takers and payments for repairs and upkeep of quarters."[25] Only 10 percent of the club officials that we questioned indicated that they spent no money on this category (see Table 7.2). Most of these clubs were housed either in private homes or offices paid for by someone else (a realty firm, a law partnership, a public official, or an interest group) or, as in one case, a storefront provided free of charge by a sympathetic landlord. We found that more than half of the clubs that did have formal expenditures showed more than 50 percent of their total expenditures in the formal expense category. In fact 39 clubs spent almost all the money they raised on rent, utilities, and liability insurance. These tended to be smaller and newer clubs, Conservative party clubs, and insurgent groups. It is not difficult to understand why some clubs cannot manage to survive in New York City when they operate in such a hand-to-mouth fashion: there simply is no money left to spend on club growth, on developing candidates for office, and on building recognition if all income goes to landlords and the utility companies. Clubs that own their property usually spend less on formal expenditures, even though they must pay taxes, upkeep, and maintenance costs that sometimes exceed those of rented facilities. Since few clubs buy their clubhouses anymore, those that possess the deed to their property have held it for many years—generally prior to the time when most of their current members joined the club.

Salaries to Workers

Only a small percentage of clubs pay salaries to workers. Of 227 clubs responding to this item, 18 percent (40 clubs) indicated that salaries were paid to one or more employees. Usually these employees were engaged in janitorial or other maintenance functions. Several clubs have paid club secretaries, but most of these are part-timers. Moreover we found only Democratic and Republican clubs with paid employees, and no reform or insurgent club reported that it had salaried help. We excluded from the salaried category those custodial workers who are paid a few dollars to clean up after club meetings, or to occasionally wash floors. As we noted previously, a few clubs have employees who are paid through some source other than the club, usually through "no show" jobs in Albany or in a city agency (during political campaigns that the clubs view as important ones, additional employees are sometimes hired, and are usually paid directly by candidates rather than by club treasuries).

161

Obviously political organizations are in the business of
campaigning for public and party office; yet if our respondents
are to be believed, the clubs spend very little money on this
supposedly central political activity. Thirty-five percent of clubs
claimed they contribute no funds to compaigns even though many
of them endorse candidates for a variety of offices. Only 5 percent
said they spend half of their expense budget, or more, on campaign
contributions. This is a far cry from Peel's report, which noted:

> It is estimated that all New York City Republican clubs,
> great and small, contributed about $75,000 to the 1928
> campaign, $15,000 to the 1929 campaign, $18,000 in
> the 1930, and $50,000 in 1932. The Democratic Clubs
> for the same period turned over approximately $250,000
> to the various campaign committees.[26]

This is not to say that the clubs today are less active politically
than in the past. The method of financing campaigns seems to have
shifted its emphasis from deploying the clubs as collecting agencies
to utilizing other vehicles (professional fund-raisers, special
finance committees, county crganizations, etc.) to bring in the
money. Many clubs provide space, phones, manpower, voter lists,
equipment, and the like to various candidates; none of these is
computed as campaign contributions. Many club members continue
to make up a core of contributors for state legislative and city
council campaigns, especially for primary contests. The high cost
of campaigning has made the small amounts that clubs can raise
seem irrelevant compared to the other important services they
perform. Campaign organizations do not ask the clubs for
contributions, and the clubs do not see their political role as that
of providing financial resources. Finally, most people have no
difficulty finding ways to channel money directly to candidates,
without the need for using the club as a conduit. Most clubs that
make direct contributions of money to campaigns do so at the level
of office they view as being most important to them: district leader,
assemblyman, or, occasionally, member of the city council.

Gifts

At one time, when local political leaders were more powerful
than most of them are today, and when clubs had money to spare,

club funds were expended for lavish gifts. Peel described such "tribute to the bosses" as follows:

> Hardly a week passes that some boss is not 'honored' and presented with a gift . . . a four-carat diamond ring . . . a $2,100 sedan . . . a watch . . . a gift of money . . . a silver table set . . . an electric clock . . . a round trip passage to Ireland to enable them to attend the Eucharistic Congress. Not only are the bosses so honored, but so also are club presidents, candidates and office-holders, councillors and county leaders. . . . The motives which inspire these gifts are various—sometimes it is pure generosity; at other times, it is desire for reciprocal favors—but always there is present in these transactions an element of group solidarity. [27]

Such gift-giving may still take place from time to time in some clubs in the city; however, it would never be so grand tóday as it was when Peel described it. Certainly such gifts today would not show up as important parts of a club's budget, or at least our respondents gave no indication that the practice was either widespread or important. The abandoning of such "tribute" is again indicative of the entire process of change that has marked the evolution of New York City's clubs. Initially the clubs tended to imitate the fraternal orders that once played an important part in city life. Immigrant groups in the clubs picked up this example, which often resulted in a burlesque of the practices and styles of private clubs and secret societies. To the many lower- and working-class people who participated in club life, expensive, flashy presents represented an assertion that "the Clinton Avenue Mohawks are as good as anybody, and not as cheap as some you could mention." Today club leaders are not as awesome to their followers, nor is there a feeling that members have to bestow gifts on their leaders (a la Father Divine) in order to achieve status in the community. Therefore, except in a few communities, gift-giving has followed such other club practices as secret oaths, Indian headresses, and lofty titles to their rightful place on the dusty shelves of memory.

Charity Contributions

Hardly a day goes by that some political leader is not asked for a contribution to charity. Approximately one-third of our respondents indicated that their clubs apportioned some funds for expenditure to local charitable groups, although half of those that give to charity said they spend 10 percent of their budget, or less, on this item. Thus it would be a gross exaggeration to report today, as Peel did forty years ago, that "vast sums have been given welfare organizations by the political clubs of the New York region"[28] On the contrary over half of today's clubs seem not to have budgeted any funds at all for such contributions.

What money is contributed by the clubs is allocated in small amounts, with charities that deal with problems in the immediate community receiving priority. A list of charities receiving funds from a club treasury might include local houses of worship, neighborhood parochial schools, teen recreation programs, religious and ethnic funds (Negro College Fund, Zionist groups, etc.), local clinics and hospitals, scholarship funds (especially those named for local residents), orphanages and homes for the aged and infirm, and local athletic and patriotic groups (little leagues, Boy Scouts, etc.). Several clubs sponsor baseball, football, and bowling teams. A few of the larger clubs continue to set aside some fund-raising activity for charitable purposes, but on the whole this practice has all but faded. As we noted previously, the clubs are seldom regarded as welfare centers anymore, and people do not expect them to provide food, clothing, lodging, employment, and money as they once did.

We made no attempt to gauge the amount of money contributed to charity by district leaders and club officials, apart from club contributions. Several of the leaders we interviewed volunteered the information that they personally contributed to charities several times the amount that the club contributed. As one leader put it, "A lot [of charities] don't ask, but when they do it isn't good politics to say no."

Funding Auxiliaries

There was a time when every political club in the city had a variety of auxiliaries. Women and young people were not welcomed as full members in all but the left-wing, third-party clubs. Many clubs tried to attract members by organizing auxiliary groups for ethnic, racial, and special-interest activities. Each auxiliary had its own officers, meeting times, stationery, activities, and, sometimes, uniforms. Clubs spent money funding these groups with the expectation that they would receive support from them at the polls on election day. Since human nature makes people heterogeneous, possibly more interested in such things as marching bands or baseball than in government, clubs figured they would organize people on the basis of their particular interest, and thereby hope to indirectly lead them into politics.

Today few clubs maintain auxiliaries. Men and women have been integrated into all but the oldest of the old-line Democratic and Republican clubs. We found only 14 percent of clubs spend any money at all on their auxiliaries, and two-thirds of these spend 10 percent or less. Most clubs have abandoned their auxiliaries because people lost interest in them, the clubs found the financial burden of auxiliaries too great, or other organizations established similar programs that proved more attractive. We found with auxiliaries as with certain other club functions, that as the clubs became no longer identified as playing a central role in the activities of many communities, they gave up once-requisite functions and stripped themselves of the structures that performed them.

Contributions to Other Party Functions

There are a number of disbursements that clubs may be obligated to make in behalf of their party. Peel noted some of these: "the purchase of forms or for the printing of petitions, posters and streamers . . . [or] for the payment of expenses of delegates to the national conventions."[29] To these might be added dues to county, city, and state political affiliates (usually paid by reform clubs); part of the cost of staging local conventions; and legal costs growing out of court challenges to nominating petitions for candidates for minor party posts (county committeemen, judicial convention delegates, and state committeemen).

More than half of our respondents denied that any expenditures were made in this category. Of those clubs that said they did spend money for other party functions, approximately two-thirds spent 20 percent or less. It is noteworthy that one club spent very heavily on this item, having been involved in a series of drawn-out court fights that arose from a split among its leaders. In years when there are hotly contested preprimary convention contests in the reform democratic movement—the New Democratic Coalition (NDC) or its county affiliates—clubs spend more money on affiliation dues. The reason for this is that delegate strength at conventions is determined by the number of members claimed by a club, for which it pays dues to its affiliate. NDC clubs pay $1 for each member they claim, for purposes of computing their delegate strength. Most clubs expand or contract their list of members depending on their eagerness to have a large delegation in attendance during conventions. Our informants indicated that candidates occasionally contribute a portion (and, in some cases, the entire cost) of the per-member fee when they are assured of a club's support. For this reason the percentage of expenditures for this category may not accurately represent its true cost to the clubs; in some cases clubs are paying out affiliation dues from funds received specifically for that purpose, rather than from monies earned from regular income sources.

Usually it is the older, larger, and better-established Democratic and Republican clubs that can afford to earmark funds for party functions such as those described above. Smaller clubs receive only enough money to pay their basic expenses. Such clubs rely on candidates for Congress, and for citywide and statewide office, to help them meet the cost of posters, affiliation dues, etc. When a smaller club finds its nominating petitions challenged it must find a volunteer lawyer who will take the case, seek help from a major candidate who is also on the petition with club candidates, or suffer the disgrace of losing a contest because of its inability to go to court. Election law is a highly technical field in which few lawyers specialize. Thus it is unlikely that smaller clubs can even obtain volunteer help. For the most part therefore, when faced with court expenses related to their political activities, the clubs that are new, smaller, and poorer either retire from the conflict or bankrupt themselves in a battle where any victory is a pyrrhic one.

Communications

Since political clubs are in the business of communicating with their constituents, with their members, with the general public, and with each other, we assumed that some portion of the income of every club would go for the publication of newsletters, newspapers, broadside sheets, leaflets, pamphlets, noncampaign advertising, postage, and, possibly, radio advertising. Peel made no mention of club communications in his book, perhaps because there were no publications or related activities among the clubs that he studied, or perhaps because he did not notice them. At one time, among New York City's many daily newspapers, each borough had more than one paper of its own, and there were hundreds of community, foreign-language, and organization newspapers published as well. Today of course the New York Times, the New York Daily News, and

the New York Post are all that remain of citywide daily press that
might cover local political news. Community papers still exist,
but with very small circulation; most of these are not newspapers
at all but so-called "shoppers," containing supermarket advertising,
inexpensive classified advertising, and a scattering of columns and
news stories. Many of these publications are distributed free of
charge through local stores.

In line with this trend, 43 percent of all clubs do not spend
any money on communications, and of the 41 percent that do, almost
70 percent spend a fifth, or less, of their funds on communications.
A number of clubs that regularly publish newsletters distribute them
to members, sympathizers, and community groups. Most of these
newsletters carry no advertising, and contain ten pages or less.
They are either mimeographed or printed by offset on standard
stock paper. Most carry a limited amount of club news, a feature
article, and a meeting notice.

The active clubs notify their members of club meetings through
the mail. Since few clubs meet more than once a month (and rarely
in summer), and most clubs meet less frequently, mailing costs
are not a large part of club expense. We found few clubs that publish
their own pamphlets or leaflets, although there were several reform
clubs that had produced propaganda pieces on a variety of issues,
some local, others national (ranging from the construction of a
highway to the peace in Vietnam). We also found several Conservative
clubs that publish informational literature and print posters relating
to such key issues as abortion, patriotism, and problems involving
police.

Summary

In summarizing his own chapter on club finances, Peel noted:

Certain features of the financial activity of clubs are
socially proper—others are bad. The whole system
is amazingly complex, and never very well comprehended
even by those who have the most intimate knowledge of
specific functions.[30]

We agree with Peel's analysis. We found in the clubs we
studied a combination of reluctance and ignorance with respect to
club finances that had no parallel in any other part of our study.
Most clubs do not handle great sums of money, and there seems
to be a feeling on the part of club leaders and members alike that

club finances can be handled in the same way that a family handles its finances. Bookkeeping in many clubs is casual; because clubs do not believe that they are required to obey laws on political finance reporting, and because they pay no taxes (except for those that have salaried employees), there is no formal obligation that club bookkeeping be anything but casual. Even where clubs try to be aboveboard and candid about their finances, frequently they are unable to do so. Some clubs, for whatever reason, have no such desire to be candid in this regard, and it is easy for them to conceal their finances from the public or even their own general membership.

Perhaps there was a time when New York City had many wealthy clubs. That time is not now. Most clubs get by in the best way they know how. Heavily dependent on dues, they look to campaign periods as an opportunity to obtain a few extra dollars from wealthy candidates who seek their support. As Sorauf noted, "it is much easier to raise political money for campaigns . . . than it is to raise it for the continuing, monthly costs of party organization."[31] While some clubs get money from questionable sources, and others draw upon well-heeled followers and friends, most regard themselves as fortunate if they balance their books at the end of the year. Moreover the average club relies on the same people to give it money over and over again. Social events and fund-raisers cater to the same clients, usually members and their families, along with officeholders and a handful of other community influentials. Every club looks forward to the time when it will win a few offices, thereby obligating the new officeholder to contribute funds on a more or less regular basis.

While illegal and immoral sources of club wealth were not in evidence through the research tools we used, other observers have claimed that there is a lot of political money around New York City obtained from questionable sources—and there has been some documentation of these claims. Our respondents, and other informants, indicated that money from mobsters, from the sale of offices and favors, and from other related sources usually flows to individual leaders, rather than to the clubs. If political clubs are making large amounts of money, they are not using such funds in ways that are visible to the clubhouse observer. No long lines of people await club membership to cash in on any "take," and no palaces of comfort and style are being constructed to house clubs, at least insofar as we could determine.

Political club finance seemed to us to be a desperate struggle on the part of the clubs to make ends meet and serve the limited goals of electing candidates and providing services to members and constituents. If someone is getting rich from local club politics, it is not the club treasuries.

Notes

1. Roy V. Peel, The Political Clubs of New York, rev. ed. (New York: Ira S. Friedman, 1968), p. 71.

2. V. O. Key, Jr., Politics, Parties and Pressure Groups, 5th ed. (New York: Thomas Y. Crowell, 1964), p. 494.

3. Peel, op. cit., p. 72.

4. Alexander Heard, The Costs of Democracy (New York: Doubleday Anchor, 1962), pp. 135-36.

5. Peel, op. cit., p. 72.

6. Ibid., p. 75.

7. Ibid., p. 72.

8. Ibid., p. 73.

9. Ibid., pp. 74-75.

10. Ibid., p. 72.

11. Heard, op. cit., p. 205.

12. Ibid., p. 207.

13. Key, op. cit., p. 499.

14. Peel, op. cit., p. 77.

15. Ibid.

16. Key, op. cit., p. 504.

17. Peel, op. cit., p. 77.

18. Peel, op. cit., p. 76.

19. Ibid., p. 77

20. Martin Tolchin and Susan Tolchin, To the Victor—Political Patronage From the Clubhouse to the White House (New York: Random House, 1971), p. 145.

21. Wallace S. Sayre and Herbert Kaufman, Governing New York City (New York: Russell Sage, 1960), p. 544.

22. Ibid., pp. 543-44.

23. New York Times, Sept. 27, 1973.

24. Ibid.

25. Peel, op. cit., p. 83.

26. Ibid.

27. Ibid., p. 85.

28. Ibid., p. 86.

29. Ibid., p. 83.

30. Ibid., p. 86.

31. Frank Sorauf, Party Politics in America (Boston: Little, Brown, 1968), p. 313.

8

"REGULARS" AND "REFORMERS": CYCLE OR STANCE

The Tradition of Reform-Regular Politics

To explain the tradition of reform-regular politics in New York City we must begin with an understanding of the deep ambivalence inherent in American thinking about politics in general. On the one hand many Americans view all politicians, and politics itself, with distaste. To be a politician (no matter what the party or stripe) is to be a conniver, a meanminded grafter, and a hypocrite. On the other hand many of these same Americans hold exalted opinions about certain present, and past, public officials. Many judges, senators, governors, mayors, and the president, as well as former holders of these offices, bask in an aura of mystical prestige. It is quite apparent that for the public the equation between high public office and low party office, between local clubhouse and national statehouse, has never been clearly drawn.

Moreover the media and other socializing agents do not help to clarify matters. We are constantly confronted with press, university, and other elite pleas to take this or that function (be it education, health, or environmental control) out of politics. This standard canon presumes to inaugurate ethical purity, and a sustaining of day-to-day administrative efficiency. In terms of democratic theory any thinking person should be able to understand that it is not only unhealthy to talk about taking things out of politics, but also impossible to do so. To further exacerbate this ambivalence, we are constantly faced with a curiously biased vocabulary. The lexicon of private business is suffused with an aura of efficiency and economy. In this arena we speak of leaders, unity of command, span of control, rational decision making, profits, and salaries. The lexicon of public business (politics) hangs in a shroud of waste, corruption, and cynicism. Here we speak of bosses, backroom intrigue, deals, patronage, and sinecures.

In general the ambivalence and confusion just described are attached to the political sphere as a whole. The political practices that elicit public cynicism are thought of as the warp and woof of regular, garden-variety party life. But in some parts of the country, particularly in large cities, there is a special use of the word "regular," and "reform"-type politics, which is meant to convey the notion of some type of purifying element—sort of "no politics, politics."

Paradoxically, however, Americans are almost as ambivalent in their attitude toward reform as they are toward politics in general. Reformers have been scorned as often as regular politicians. Reformers are frequently characterized as stuffy, narrow-minded legalists, totally bereft of any human sympathy and clearly lacking in charm. They are associated with blue laws, with hard-nosed meritocracy, with a general type of priggish elitism, perhaps even with being what Spiro Agnew, a recent American vice president, termed "effete intellectual snobs." Certainly reformers have also had their share of public opprobrium.

The Old Reform and The New

It is in the context of these opposing, confused, and self-contradictory pulls that we must place the New York City reform movements. The older reform movement, from the turn of the century to World War II, can be broadly described as being primarily a movement of "outs" seeking "in." This is the landscape that included the clubs Peel studied. In this picture the key figures were the important elected officials, primarily mayors and borough presidents, and they were always painted in tones of fiscal and moral probity. It was an era in which reform hung more on interparty politics than on intraparty politics; an era in which reform was generated by agencies outside the party system—literary muckrakers, grand juries, and upstate legislative investigators. These agents were expected to produce certain disclosures of scandal that in turn were to lead to election upsets. In these historical moments such mayors as Seth Low, John Purroy Mitchel, and LaGuardia were launched. The forces of reform rallied around a particular fusion candidate, and utilized not only whatever recent scandals were at hand, but also the internal geographic strains within the New York

City Democratic machine itself (that is, the pull of Brooklyn against Tammany), to bring about a series of temporary eclipses in the machine politics of each decade from the twenties to the fifties.

But what of the "new era" of reform, the generation that spans the fifties through the seventies? Will certain personalities or platforms, or even a more general notion of ideological liberalism, serve to distinguish the current reform era from the earlier one, or indeed from the regular politics of the current day? Unfortunately personalities, platforms, and principles refuse to be neatly compressed into either factional channels or chronological periods. There is, however, a looser cement that binds today's reform with yesterday's, while at the same time distinguishing today's reform from today's regular politics: it is simply the matter of being innovative. Theodore Lowi, for example, commenting about the "organization politician's preference for keeping the whole system as is," noted that "by contrast, the reform system is the major channel of innovation."[1]

Lowi also provided a clue to an even more critical distinction between the current reform era and the earlier one, a willingness to take on club structure as the basis for reform—both party and governmental. He pointed out, "The reform movement in New York has indeed been cyclical. Each time its onset was widespread, energetic, irresistible. But as soon as there was a partial redress of the democratic imbalance of power the components dispersed. There has been no club core and no central bureaucracy: thus the reform system has not been institutionalized."[2] We assume that Lowi was referring in these comments to neighborhood clubs, since the earlier reform movement did indeed have citywide club structures. We must also add the caveat that all regular clubs have not been entirely neighborhood setups. Yet the essence of Lowi's remark is still accurate, and it is at this juncture that our own study becomes relevant. We looked at the reform movement as a club movement, and we sought to contrast it with the picture painted by Peel, who wrote in a period when club reformers did not see themselves clearly as such. In fact Peel's study did not distinguish reform clubs in the way that we will attempt to distinguish them. Instead he included a chapter on "independent and revolt clubs," and he distinguished between these two categories as follows:

> The objectives of revolt clubs are chiefly to overthrow
> the assembly district leader and to obtain his status
> for their own marshal. In some cases all that is desired
> is attention and the satisfaction of minor grievances. . . .
> Where the objective is to "reform" the city government
> the club may have no designs on the district leadership

at all, under the present system, but may desire
independent status, so that it can participate in a
"fusion" campaign. Or a club may be merely the
vehicle whereby the marshal gives some weight
to his transfer of allegiance from one party to
the other.[3]

This is almost tantamount to saying that in the period of Peel's
study there were no reform clubs at all. Peel stated that "revolt
clubs engage in a limited way in the same range of activities as
do the regular clubs."[4] He saw revolt clubs simply as "symbols
of political instability."[5] His prophecy was:

No lasting revision of metropolitan politics will ever
come until the silent masses both within and without
the existing "regular" organizations have been inspired
with a new hope and provided with an up-to-date chart
of their course. To the writer it seems that the present
system of party organizations, leaders, and clubs is
utterly inadequate, unstable and ineffective.[6]

It is probable that a sense of passion such as Peel's infused
the originators of today's reform club movement. But the degree
to which reformers have sustained Peel's vision remains problematic.

Impressionistic Profiles of Democratic Regulars and Reformers in New York City

Despite the untidy history of New York City's earlier reform
movement and the difficulty of sorting out a coherent concept of
reform, the second half of the twentieth century has produced a
considerable impressionistic literature that influences much of the
current thinking in this domain.[7] This literature suggests the basic
idea that party regulars are somehow different from reformers in
New York City politics, that there are different magnets at work
that attract the two groups, and that they are quite clearly set apart
in ideology, demography, and style. Our own data offers less clarity,
and more complexity, in this regard. In general we suggest that there
is less, rather than more, here than meets the eye. But while our
findings did not confirm all of the common wisdom espoused on this
subject, we still concluded that there is an essential truth regarding
it: reformers somehow are different than regulars.

The style of the regulars is generally viewed as quintessentially ethnic. That is, it is the style of those immigrants in New York City whose old-country heritage made them consider personal loyalties and family ties more precious than abstract moral codes and principles of conduct. For such people there is as much merit in blood ties as in civil-service exams. Representation in terms of race and ethnicity, and public recognition along such lines, are more than acceptable to these people. These views hold not only for the older immigrants but for the newer ones, the domestic immigrants from the southern states and those from U.S. Island possessions as well.

The regulars see patronage as nothing more than well-deserved payment for services rendered, and their clubs reflect their feelings. Political clubs also represent to regulars a possible ladder for social mobility, just as honorable as any of the social ladders provided by outside occupations and competitions. The regulars are people at home with hierarchy, authority, and neighborhood focus. Their sense of style and their overall demographic roles determine to some degree the activities of the regular clubs. Roughly speaking these activities are centered around efforts to reward friends and punish enemies. The regular clubs try to win adherents through small personal favors—help for the soldier who needs a pass to visit a sick parent, help for the family with a retarded child awaiting admission to a special school, help for an immigrant citizen trying to bring over a relative, or help for less legitimate, but even more common, problems such as having a ticket "fixed" or a violation "lifted."

Certain scholars have described a prototype for a reform club in terms of a difference in basic values that set it apart from the prototypic regular club. Banfield and Wilson analyzed the reform mentality as follows:

> The Anglo Saxon middle-class style of politics, with
> its emphasis upon the obligation of the individual to
> participate in public affairs and to seek the benefit
> of the community 'as a whole' (which implies, among
> other things, the necessity of honesty, impartiality,
> and efficiency) was fundamentally incompatible with
> the immigrants' style of politics which took no account
> of the community. . . . Because of the nature of their
> political ethos, Protestants (Wasps) and Jews have been
> in the vanguard of every fight for municipal reform.[8]

The reformers themselves have a similar view. The New Chelsea Reform Democratic Club (a Manhattan group founded in

1958 by a handful of people and now boasting over 500 members)
in one of its recent (undated) club brochures answered the question,
"Just what is a Reform Democrat, anyhow?":

> A reform Democrat works in a political organization
> because he believes politics can be the most responsive
> and effective way to direct and lead a changing society.
> He works in the Democratic party because he believes
> it can be the focal point of this leadership by opening
> the doors of party politics in true grass roots fashion. . . .
> He works to become part of the community, learns of
> its needs first hand and fights to meet them with in-
> formed positions. He works to free the party from
> the corruption of patronage. The club is comprised
> of unpaid volunteers who do not depend on favors from
> party bosses.

However, the critical difference between regulars and
reformers is more often seen in quite superficial descriptions
of the style set by various clubs. As Goetcheus pointed out in
his description of Greenwich Village: "A young divorcee in blue
jeans would feel out of place among the black-dressed Italian
Catholic dowagers who lick envelopes at the regular club."[9]
Similarly, Dan Wakefield pointed out certain differences in the
material possessions of regulars and reformers. "Reformers," he
said, "have HiFi where regulars have TV's; reform women wear
toreador pants, regulars wear skirts."[10]
Of course this picture of differences between reformers and
regulars overlooks an important division in the reform movement
itself, a division that developed in the early sixties: the split between
"big R" reformers and "small r" reformers.[11] Later this same
phenomenon came to be labeled "hairshirt" reformers versus
"moderate" reformers.[12] Whatever the labels, the differences
centered around the fact that the reformers (hairshirts) made
procedural purity paramount, while the other type of reformer
remained more concerned with using practical power to achieve
effective political action. The moderate "small r" reformers are
those who have been converted to the basic idea that the only
important alternative to winning in politics is losing. A growing
number in this group is even ready to reconsider the traditional
distaste for such long-standing reform taboos as patronage.
One other overarching characteristic of the Democratic
reform movement that transcends its internal splits is the over-
weaning attachment that reformers have managed to manifest toward
certain national political figures; at times reform groups reflect

the distant shadows of such personalities. The New York Democratic Coalition (NDC), for example, which is the city's reform holding company, is a reflection of those reformers who came into the movement hanging on the shirttails of Adlai Stevenson and, later, Eugene McCarthy and McGovern. More than any other figure Stevenson stood for what NDC admired in public life. And what they admired was actually something less than a coherent ideology, something less than a set of platform planks, something less even than a thoroughgoing commitment to be unequivocally against bossism and machines (a position never entirely embraced by Stevenson himself), but rather an ingrained sense of style. It is this dimension that we will pursue below as we analyze the reform club membership of the 1970s in demographic terms.

Finally, it should be noted that there is a part of the reform ideology, emphasizing issues and positions, that often causes party conversion rather than insurgency. That is, in New York City, reform is primarily a phenomenon of the "in" party, the Democrats. When Republicans feel the urge to reform, their action often takes the form of a party change. This is how the Republicans lost, over the past few years, Lindsay, former U.S. Senator Charles Goodell, and Congressman Ogden Reid.

Peel's Study of Revolt Clubs

Peel stressed the fact that insurgency was a constant in the New York City political scene, always threatening the party status quo: "Today there are revolts, defections and insurgencies in every district, in every county and in all parties. . . . . Revolts are widespread now and apparently growing in number and vitality."[13] Peel saw these revolts as stemming from certain population and neighborhood changes, and also from the "incompatibility of leaders and marshals."[14] A majority of the revolt clubs that Peel visited "were formed by some marshal who 'could not get along with the boss.'"[15] He analyzed the perceptions of such marshals as well as the perceptions and capacities of the leaders themselves. He noted that a certain number of leaders were demonstrably incompetent—they had lost both elections and political favors. Occasionally such incompetence might have been the fault of one or more of the elected representatives chosen by the leaders, but the ultimate responsibility would still have been that of the leaders. At other times revolt was occasioned by the desire of a public official to loosen the hold of a party boss, either because the boss had been directly interfering with a political career, or perhaps because a boss's alleged corruption had prompted electoral defeat.

176

Often as not such scandals were seized upon by political aspirants as a good way to gain a foothold for themselves.

Peel pointed out another main cause of revolts: "the failure of the controlling faction to recognize, by honors or patronage, the emergence of a new bloc or clique. The Irish for decades 'ran' the East Side. . . . The ranks of the Irish voters had thinned out and the bulk of the population had become Italian. . . . Failing to obtain their just share of party power, the Italians revolted and their marshal seized the reins of party power . . ."[16]

The remainder of Peel's reasoning about the causes and distribution of revolt clubs was based on an analysis of the communities in which revolts occurred. He felt that "this is a matter which might well concern the thinking citizen: he should examine his own community critically with the view of ascertaining whether the forces making for change embody the promise of a reconstructed society on the one hand, or whether they symbolize the disintegration of command or personal values, on the other."[17]

Reform and Neighborhood Variables

As noted above, Peel hypothesized that certain critical neighborhood variables often provided the impetus for political revolts. Revolts were most likely to occur, he concluded:

. . . in new communities; in communities of fairly dense population (although this seems to be an unimportant factor); in communities of fairly low purchasing power; in communities containing large blocs of imperfectly assimilated and politically unrecognized nationality elements; and in communities where power is monopolized by one religious group to the exlusion of others. The most significant factor is apparently movement of population. Institutional organization lags behind shifts in population and when a minority cultural group increases in size and becomes aware of the disparity between its voting strength and the political rewards it receives, revolt ensues.[18]

Since the number of reform clubs in our study are considerably fewer than in Peel's study (he included 120 clubs in his "revolt" group), and since the reform clubs we studied are different from the ones he examined in terms of their self-proclaimed ideologies,

TABLE 8.1

Neighborhood Variables for Each of 24 Democratic Reform Clubs in the Bronx and Brooklyn (1974)

| | Population Density | Purchasing Power | Neighborhood Variables | | Population Shifts in past few years |
			Relative Age of Community	Dominant Ethnic Groups	
Bronx Reform Clubs					
Benjamin Franklin Reform Democratic Club	not dense	high	old	Jews, Wasps	New young married couples moving in
Bronx-Pelham Reform Democratic Club	dense	medium	old	Jews	no major changes
Eleanor Roosevelt Independent Democrats	very dense	low	old	Puerto Rican Black	Puerto Ricans and blacks moving in, Jews moving out
FDR Independent Democratic Club	dense	low	old	Jewish, Irish	blacks moving in, Jews moving out
Herbert Lehman Independent Democrats (also known as the Tom Paine Independent Democratic Club)	dense	medium	old	Jewish, Irish	no major changes
Independent Democratic Club of Co-op City	very dense	medium	new	Jewish	Jews moving in, some middle-class blacks moving in
John F. Kennedy Independent Democratic Club	very dense	low	old	Puerto Rican	no major changes
Robert F. Kennedy Independent Democrats	very dense	low	new	Puerto Rican	no major changes
Northeast Independent Democratic Club	not dense	medium	old	Italian	blacks moving in
Brooklyn Reform Clubs					
Bensonhurst Independent Democratic Club	dense	medium	old	Jewish, Italian	no major changes
Bridge Independent Democrats	not dense	medium	old	Irish, Italian	no major changes
Carl Sandburg Independent Democrats	not dense	medium	very old	Jews, Irish	no major changes
Central Brooklyn Independent Democratic Club	not dense	medium	old	no dominant group	wealthy moving in

TABLE 8.1

Neighborhood Variables for Each of 24 Democratic Reform Clubs in the Bronx and Brooklyn (1974)

Brooklyn Reform Clubs	Neighborhood Variables				
	Population Density	Purchasing Power	Relative Age of Community	Dominant Ethnic Groups	Population Shifts in past few years
Community Democrats	very dense	low	old	Jews, Blacks	Puerto Ricans and blacks moving in
Independent Democrats of Flatbush	dense	medium	old	Jewish	blacks and Chinese moving in, Jews moving out
Midbay Independent Democrats	not dense	medium	very old	Jews	no major changes
New Democratic Club	not dense	medium	old	Jews, Italians	Jews moving in
New Horizons Reform Democratic Club	not dense	medium	very old	Orthodox Jews, Italians	Jews moving in
New Leadership Independent Democrats	very dense	low	old	Jews, blacks	Jews, Puerto Ricans, blacks moving in
Roosevelt Kingsboro Independent Democrats	not dense	medium	very old	Jews	no major changes
Tom Paine Independent Democrats	not dense	medium	new	Italians, Jews	Jews moving in
Walt Whitman Reform Democratic Club	not dense	medium	old	Blacks, Jews	whites moving out, blacks moving in
West Brooklyn Independent Democrats	very dense	high	very old	WASP	Jews moving in
Williamsburg–Greenpoint Independent Democratic Club	dense	poor	old	Orthodox Jews, Blacks, Poles	blacks and Jews moving in

Source: List of Democratic reform clubs compiled by New Democratic Coalition in 1973; data on neighborhood variables is from 1972 study compiled by our research staff.

we were not surprised to learn that Peel's predictive variables on
reform politics do not hold much explanatory power in the current
era. On the contrary had we found that Peel's variables were highly
predictive of today's reform movement, we would have had some
basis for questioning the entire thrust of the impressionistic
literature that we reviewed above. A close fit between yesterday's
club revolts and today's would have led us to suspect that reform
is still, as it was, primarily a matter of "outs" wanting "in," or,
at best, a matter of "outs" rather quickly accommodating the
transient needs of temporary population shifts. Our data, however,
suggests that other forces are at work in the reform movement.

   We used two boroughs—the Bronx and Brooklyn—as the basis
for our assessment of current reform clubs in the city. We asked
our informants to delineate each individual neighborhood that houses
a reform club, in terms of the five indices suggested by Peel; and
what we found was such a mixture of responses that we were forced
to conclude that Peel's indices are not useful in understanding
why reform clubs first appeared in the various communities in which
they exist today. (See Table 8.1, which compares the varying
neighborhoods that house 9 Bronx reform clubs and 15 Brooklyn
reform clubs.)

   Taking, for example, the Benjamin Franklin Reform Democratic
Club in the wealthy Riverdale section of the Bronx, this is a reform
club in a neighborhood of relatively moderate density, high purchasing
power, a generally old and stable community, and a community with
a relatively assimilated population. It is a neighborhood in striking
contrast to the Bronx neighborhood that houses the John F. Kennedy
Independent Democratic Club. The latter district has a high population
density and low income, is new, and features a relatively unassimilated
population that is almost entirely transient. In neither case, however,
nor in the cases of the seven other Bronx clubs that fall somewhere
in between, did we find the Peel system of neighborhood variables
accurate. We found that reform throughout the Bronx remains quite
independent of population shifts, purchasing power, and the other
Peel variables. It hangs almost exclusively on the fact that pockets
of disaffected Democrats sided with former Mayor Wagner when,
in 1961, he turned "reformer," and they showed their contempt for
what they thought was a state with a boss-controlled convention by
organizing themselves under a reform banner. The most important
ingredient we found threading its way through the Bronx reform clubs
is that they are all almost exclusively composed of Jewish members,
even when they are located in districts with heavy black and Puerto
Rican constituencies, or districts with a relatively heavy Irish
constituency.

With one exception we also found the 15 reform clubs in Brooklyn to be heavily Jewish in their membership regardless of whether the neighborhoods containing these clubs are predominantly Jewish or not. The exception is the West Brooklyn Independent Democratic Club, which has a large Wasp contingent and is located in Brooklyn's oldest community—Bay Ridge (a community still dominated by Wasps). Even in this case, however, the new group moving into the community consists of Jewish people who are largely professional—a constituency made to order for the reform movement. The key point is that in all Brooklyn communities, whether Jews, or for that matter any other ethnic group are dominant, reform clubs exist.

Reform politics seems to exist regardless of variations in density, purchasing power, population movements or any other of Peel's explanatory variables. The thrust for the Democratic reformism of the sixties seems different from the revolts of Peel's era. However current reform politics might be explained, the neighborhood setting for reform clubs is not a useful part of such explanations.

Factions and Party Preference

Regarding the relationship between reform and the push for political power, Peel felt that, among the clubs he studied, power per se was responsible for the dramatic predominance of Democratic revolt clubs over Republican revolt clubs.[19] This analysis accurately characterizes the current reform movement as well. The need to gain power in the first place, and the inevitable compromises that follow in the attempts to use power, may in the end turn the current club-based reform era into simply another phase in the long-term reform cycle of American politics. At the moment, however, the power drive has worked largely to keep clubhouse reform an almost exclusively Democratic function.

As shown in Table 8.2, 30 percent of our universe of Democratic clubs counted as reform clubs, while only 8 percent of the Republican clubs are in the reform category. This same tendency is borne out in Table 8.3, which shows that club membership also measures the power principle realistically; while 17 percent of the members of the Democratic clubs are in the party's reform wing, only 4 percent of the Republican clubs members are considered reformers. Apparently Republican activists recognize that there is little to be gained from "reforming" losers. Instead Republicans in New York City keep their eye on interparty struggles. Democrats,

TABLE 8.2

Number and Percent of Clubs in Each
Major Party, by Faction

Faction	Democratic		Republican		Both Parties	
	Number	Percent	Number	Percent	Number	Percent
Regular	110	70	61	92	171	77
Reform*	46	30	5	8	51	23
Total	156	100	66	100	222	100

*In this table reform Democrats include the insurgent group, since we focused our attention on the subject of parties rather than on reform.

TABLE 8.3

Number and Percent of Club Members in Each
Major Party, by Faction

Faction	Democratic		Republican		Both Parties	
	Number	Percent	Number	Percent	Number	Percent
Regular	59,056	83	28,067	96	87,123	87
Reform	12,170	17	1,072	4	13,242	13
Total	71,226	100	29,139	100	100,365	100

Note: Membership figures are not exact, since club leaders are known to exaggerate the size of their member lists.

on the other hand, seeing the party structure itself as a prize worth winning, devote considerable energies to internal competition.

TABLE 8.4

Number and Percent of Clubs That Have More
Than 50 Percent of One Ethnic Group, by Faction

Ethnic Group	Regular		Reform	
	Number	Percent	Number	Percent
Jewish	41	46	29	74
Italian	35	39	6	15
Irish	8	9	2	5
Spanish	1	1	0	0
Wasp	4	4	2	5

Note: Universe is 89 regular clubs and 39 reform clubs.

Reform and Ethnicity

While Peel discussed revolt clubs in terms of new ethnic groups driving out older ones,[20] our data shows that in New York City in the seventies reform politics is basically Jewish politics. We found that out of a reporting universe of 39 reform clubs, 29 (or 75 percent) have a membership that is preponderantly Jewish (see Table 8.4). This confirms the impressions that most political scientists and commentators have long held regarding the ethnic factor in reform politics. Moynihan, for example, noted: "Typically the reform clubs have succeeded in districts which have a Republican (i.e. middle-class) majority or in heavily Jewish Districts which are middle class but vote Democratic."[21]

In terms of overall club membership figures (see Table 8.5), we found that Jews also comprise 49 percent of the membership in reform clubs of all parties, and 56 percent of the membership in Democratic reform clubs alone. What seems rather clear is that Jews move to the left of the political spectrum. Clearly they are more likely to be Democrats than Republicans, reformers than regulars, and as well Democratic reformers, except for the fact that they entirely dominate the city's liberal party. There is in this pattern virtually a Gutman-scale quality, in that Jewish membership figures in the clubs move downward from 56 percent of reform Democratic membership to 48 percent of all reform membership, to 24 percent of the Democratic regulars, to 13 percent of the reform Republicans, and then slightly upward to 14 percent of the Republican regulars.

TABLE 8.5

Club Membership by Ethnic Group, Faction and Party
(percent and number of members)

Ethnic Group	Regular			Reform			Overall Total
	Democratic	Republican	Total	Democratic	Republican	Total	
Jewish	24 (14,094)	14 (3,511)	21 (17,605)	56 (4,561)	13 (118)	49 (4,679)	22 (22,284)
Italians	25 (14,508)	49 (11,885)	33 (26,393)	11 (920)	24 (216)	14 (1,136)	5 (27,529)
Irish	19 (10,864)	20 (4,957)	19 (15,821)	12 (994)	14 (123)	13 (1,117)	8 (16,938)
Spanish	6 (3,217)	6 (1,370)	6 (4,587)	3 (257)	6 (54)	3 (311)	7 (4,898)
Wasp	6 (3,703)	2 (435)	5 (4,138)	7 (574)	36 (326)	10 (900)	18 (5,038)

Note: Number of members is indicated in parentheses.

On the whole these figures support the idea of Jews being continual intellectual mavericks likely to fight for their ideals, even against the very establishment that has perhaps accorded them political success. In other words Jews do not become reformers in the Democratic party because of a lack of recognition and reward from the regular Democrats, the establishment (a stance that would have confirmed Peel's ethnic theses). On the contrary strong Jewish involvement in reform seems to have stemmed from other sources: a traditional passion on the part of Jews for social justice and a predilection for being "out," rather than "in," politically. In addition there is the tradition of disputation among Jews, the taking of different sides in an argument so that all points of view are uncovered and offered as alternatives. Finally a social-generation-stylistic split occurred between immigrant and first-generation Jews and those who emulated them on one side, and the upwardly mobile, highly assimilated second- and third-generation Americans on the other. These two reform groups nonetheless have usually maintained some degree of association. Perhaps, as Moynihan noted, "unlike other ethnic groups, Jews in different factions are able to talk to each other and to respect each other."[22] This close relationship between Jews as a group and the reform movement may also be a product of the fact that Jews tend to shed their neighborhoods more easily than other ethnic groups, and are willing to set up not only new Temples of worship but new political clubs.[23]

In precisely the same dramatic way that reform seems to be a magnet for the Jews, it appears to be a repellent to other ethnic groups, notably the Italians. We found that Italian-dominated clubs comprise 39 percent of regular clubs in our universe but only 15 percent of reform clubs, and that Italian membership figures amount to 33 percent of regular club membership but only 14 percent among reformers. Italians seem to follow more closely the classic pattern proposed by Peel—that is, they tried in various ways to wrest political power from an earlier, more assimilated, ethnic group, the Irish. As Moynihan put it: "Of all the ethnic groups active at the moment in New York, the Italians have the strongest political purpose: they are fighting for social equality . . ."[24] Moynihan made this comment of course in 1961 when the Irish still dominated politics in both New York State and New York City. He pointed out that until that time rising Italians were "usually sentenced to life on the State Supreme Court bench."[25] This fate—though hardly one to be avoided—is not their only option in today's club politics. But in New York City politics this trend resulted more in Italians moving out of the party altogether and into Republican ranks, rather than in their espousal of reform. Clearly the traditions, activities, and style of regular politics more nearly conforms to the Italians' own

culture than does reform-style politics. It was not a question of
Italians wanting to do things differently (which is the dividing point
between regular and reform Democratic clubs), but just a question
of their wanting to do things. As William Whyte noted:

> From the time that the Italian immigrants got into
> street fights with their Irish predecessors, there
> was bitter feeling between the races. . . . Since
> the Irish controlled the ward politically, the Italians,
> as long as they were in the minority, had to follow
> the Cleveland Club in order to get any political
> benefits. . . . As the proportion of Italian voters
> in the ward grew steadily, it was to be expected that
> the Italians would break away from the Cleveland
> Club.[26]

Italians followed the same pattern in New York City, probably for the
same reasons. They appear to have carried on the revolt tradition
described by Peel, while the Jews have not.

The Irish are the very quintessence of the party regular.
More than any other group the Irish seem to display an almost inborn
taste and aptitude for politics: to them it is politics as a game and
an avocation as well as politics as a living. The same set of re-
inforcing values that made the Irishman almost naturally fitted for
the New York City Police Department made him a natural for New
York City club life. Peel said of the Irish: "The Irish have long
enjoyed the reputation of being America's most skillful political
leaders, particularly in the cities. With their genial ways,
scrupulous use of power, alertness in seizing opportunities, and
industry in all the arduous duties of petty politics, they have kept
their hand on the helm of the municipal ship of state for over a
century . . ."[27] Robert Considine also attempted to explain this
Irish hegemony: "They also had the singular advantages of speaking
English, being familiar with the mechanics of government, and being
here first."[28] Considine noted too that the Irish ideology was not
entirely liberal. Thus their antiabolition stance during the Civil
War found for them a natural homeland among the Democrats, and
they stayed with the Democrats, probably moored by their phenomenal
successes. Perhaps their continuing attachment to the Democrats
reflects their working-class origins, and perhaps their even stronger
attachments to "regularity" in politics reflects their hierarchical and
authoritarian qualities. Moynihan noted a "harsh streak of anti-
liberalism which is to be found on every level of Catholic society,
and which has produced a considerable body of extreme conservatives
who nonetheless remain Democrats."[29]

This Irish affinity curve is shown in part by our data: among clubs where the Irish are the dominant ethnic group, 8 out of 10 are regular clubs.

If reform is unattractive to the Irish, it is quite the reverse to their ancient rivals both in this country and abroad, the Wasps. There are only two Wasp-dominated reform clubs, but this is more a product of Wasp withdrawal from political club life in New York City (as well as from actual living in New York) than a product of Wasp style. In fact the Wasps are the second most likely ethnic group to turn to reformism. While Jews have 22 percent of their entire club membership in reform clubs, Wasps follow closely with 18 percent. In fact, among Republican reform members, 36 percent are Wasps. They are only 2 percent of the regular Republicans and 6 percent among regular Democrats.

The participation of blacks in the reform movement is of more than routine interest since it involves some anomalies. Most black party members are regulars. We found that 75 percent of the predominantly black clubs are regular clubs; and while predominantly black clubs are a very small slice in either the regular or the reform column, they are a bit more common among regular clubs than among reform. Moreover in terms of overall club membership figures only 5 percent of total black membership is in the reform group, and while black membership makes up only 8 percent of all reformers, it makes up 23 percent of all regulars (see Table 8.6). Thus the regulars are clearly more attractive to blacks than the reformers. In terms of the two major parties, the reform picture looks slightly different, with blacks constituting 23 percent of the Republican reform group, but only 6 percent of the Democratic reformers.

Perhaps all this can be explained both in terms of what blacks themselves need and want out of politics, and as a reflection of the various styles and activities of the two party groupings. For the most part the black community must confine its political energies to those arenas that can most swiftly give it what it needs at present—jobs, patronage, political office, business contracts, and an inside track to the seats of power. More than any other group blacks have a stake in "winning" politically and there are currently more "wins" available among the ranks of Democratic regulars than within any other political group or faction. Blacks have to go where the power is. As the Reverend Louis R. Gigante, a Bronx club leader who won a city council seat in 1973, described it: "Look, 95% of my club members and constituents are Puerto Ricans and Blacks. In the election I took public stand against Badillo and for Beame. [A reference to the 1973 mayoral race in which Beame represented the party regulars] They all said I was crazy. But I knew what I was doing. Badillo could never win. So I moved to the winner, and that's what gets you the power . . ."[30]

TABLE 8.6

Percent and Number of Club Members by Race,
Faction, and Party

Race	Regular			Reform			Overall Total
	Democratic	Republican	Total	Democratic	Republican	Total	
White	74	72	78	89	71	91	70,924
	(42,097)	(18,549)	(60,646)	(9,537)	(741)	(10,278)	
Black	19	21	20	6	23	8	16,772
	(10,619)	(5,260)	(15,869)	(660)	(243)	(903)	
Oriental	17	2	2	1	0	0	1,262
	(804)	(384)	(1,188)	(74)	(0)	(74)	

Note: Number of members is indicated in parentheses.

188

Father Gigante also commented on the matter of political style which is the other element involved in the black affection for regular politics. He noted that regular politics has served to elevate such black officeholders as Percy Sutton, Raymond Jones, Joseph Galiber, Sam Wright, and Shirley Chisolm. It appears than even though the ideology and broad-scale policies of the reform Democrats ought to be more congruent with the aspirations of blacks than with any other group, and even though the regulars "aren't onto the newer ethnics like Blacks and Puerto Ricans,"[31] the overall picture is still such that blacks are clinging to the regulars.

It is noteworthy that, despite these various ethnic patterns in reform and regular politics, only 10 percent of both reform and regular clubs reported using ethnic activities to attract members.

Reform Clubs and Age Groups

Not only is America a nation of ethnics, it is also a nation that pays fierce attention to the needs of its various age groups. In both social and political life America, more so than the nations of Europe, organizes its activities among groups of age-related peers. There are also certain common stereotypes about the political beliefs of the young as against those of the old. It is generally assumed, as we mentioned previously, that younger people are apt to be more liberal. Certainly there are many who feel that this same presumed correlation is also part of the dividing line between party club regulars and party reformers. Robert Lekachman, for example, described the Riverside Democrats (part of the reform movement) as being "young with an overwhelming concentration in their early and middle thirties."[32] Our data support this common wisdom, but not to a great degree. While we found reformers to be somewhat younger than regulars, the degree of difference is small: 37 percent of reform club membership is under 35 while 29 percent of the regulars are over 51, compared with 18 percent of reformers. There is little party variation either. The Republican reform clubs have a somewhat larger membership in the over-51 group (28 percent) than the Republican regulars (24 percent), and Democrats are generally more youthful than Republicans. A further similarity is that various age groups—starting from 18-to-21 and going up to 51-and-over—show a 3 percent difference, or less, between the percentage of club regulars and club reformers, with only two exceptions (see Table 8.7).

TABLE 8.7

Percent of Club Members in Various Age Groups,
by Party and Faction

Age Group	Regular	Reform
18-21	5	8
22-30	9	15
31-35	15	14
36-42	22	24
43-50	28	20
51 and over	21	18

Sex, Singles, and Political Club Factions

A certain amount of sexual inequality may be said to pervade all political club life in New York City, as we pointed out in Chapter 4. In this discussion it should be noted that perhaps sexism is more endemic to regular clubs than to reform clubs, and that women in general—single women in particular—seem to find themselves more at home in the reform clubs of the city than in the regular clubs.

As shown in Table 8.8, women comprise a larger proportion of the total membership of reform clubs than they do of the regulars (45 percent to 38 percent). However, in the Republican party there are 14,000 female regulars and only 461 female reformers. On the other hand the Democratic regulars have a 32 percent female contingent, while the Democratic reformers have a 45 percent female group. About 97 percent of Republican women belong to regular clubs, compared with 77 percent of Democratic women, indicating that women (like men although somewhat less so) are more likely to be regulars than reformers regardless of party. This is hardly surprising. In the Republican party males and females divide between regulars and reformers in almost identical proportions. What is more distinctive is that Democratic women are more likely to be reformers than either Republican women, Democratic men, or Republican men. Why? Possibly for ideological reasons. American political heroines have been almost exclusively activists and reformers. The two are almost invariably linked; thus we have Harriet Beecher Stowe, Carrie Nation, Jane Addams, Frances Perkins, Eleanor Roosevelt. The current scene would probably produce a political roster in which among women activists a greater

TABLE 8.8

Percent and Number of Club Members by Sex, Faction, and Party

	Regular			Reform		
	Democratic	Republican	Total	Democratic	Republican	Total
Female	32	50	38	45	43	45
	(18,794)	(14,129)	(32,923)	(5,456)	(461)	(5,917)
Male	68	50	62	55	57	55
	(40,262)	(13,938)	(54,200)	(6,714)	(611)	(7,325)
Total	100	100	100	100	100	100
	(59,056)	(28,067)	(87,123)	(12,170)	(1,072)	(13,242)

Note: Number of members is indicated in parentheses.

TABLE 8.9

Percent and Number of Club Members That Are Single or Married, by Faction and by Party

	Regular			Reform		
	Democratic	Republican	Total	Democratic	Republican	Total
Single	21	17	20	23	25	23
	(12,401)	(4,727)	(17,128)	(2,788)	(268)	(3,056)
Married	79	83	80	77	75	77
	(46,655)	(23,340)	(69,995)	(9,382)	(814)	(10,186)
Total	100	100	100	100	100	100
	(59,056)	(28,067)	(87,123)	(12,170)	(1,072)	(13,242)

Note: Number of members is indicated in parentheses.

TABLE 8.10

Percent and Number of Club Members That Are Single, by Sex, Faction, and Party

	Regular			Reform		
	Democratic	Republican	Total	Democratic	Republican	Total
Female	24	16	22	41	43	42
	(2,990)	(736)	(3,726)	(1,156)	(114)	(1,270)
Male	76	84	78	59	57	58
	(9,451)	(3,991)	(13,442)	(1,632)	(154)	(1,786)
Total	100	100	100		100	100
	(12,441)	(4,727)	(17,168)	(2,788)	(268)	(3,056)

Note: Number of members is indicated in parentheses.

number would appear under reform banners than under regular ones.

There are, however, two other possible explanations—one stylistic and the other demographic. The former might best be seen in the description by Wakefield of Herman Greitzer's conversion from the regular Tamawa Club in Greenwich Village to the Village Independent Democrats (VID), a reform club. Greitzer had originally joined the Tamawa club, Wakefield noted, "but when he found that his wife was relegated to a sort of bean-supper-serving status in the club along with all the other women, who (probably more from social than political reasons) are relagated to a kind of ladies auxiliary, he and his wife joined the VID."[33] His wife (Carol) subsequently became a city councilwoman. The same contrast in reform and regular club style can be seen in descriptions of the Sheldrick regular club, which has a separate women's division under a coleader, and where the officers are invariably men, and of the opposition Riverside reform club, which has been organized without male-female divisions.[34] Of course this style analysis is closely linked with political ideology. Moynihan noted that among regulars "conferences on issues are regarded as women's work."[35] This obviously meant that regulars denigrate the importance of issues. By contrast the NDC reform group holds "a large conference on state legislative issues"[36] in a manner which Moynihan believed to be symbolically important. This implies that reformers take issues to heart, and deal with them in a certain style. This in turn attracts women, who are also treated by reformers in a certain style. That style can best be described as "seriously."

Finally it is possible that some of the attraction females find in Democratic reform clubs stems from the simple facts of geography. In certain cases the areas in which reform clubs predominate (middle-class areas) are safer and more attractive to women, particularly single women who travel to and from meetings alone.

While club regulars (as might be guessed) are more likely to be married than reformers, we found this differential to be a small one (80 percent of regulars are married, compared to 77 percent of reformers). Only in Republican ranks, where 25 percent of the reformers are single, compared to 17 percent of the regulars, does a more substantial difference occur (see Table 8.9). On the whole most members of both major parties and both factions are married, but the group with the most married members is the regular Republican group. Married people constitute 83 percent of all regular Republicans. It should be noted that there are about two and a half times as many Democratic club members in New York City as Republican members. That proportion might therefore be expected to hold true in all the party comparisons that we made. In this

TABLE 8.11

Percent and Number of Club Members in Selected Occupations,
by Faction and by Party

Occupation	Regular			Reform		
	Democratic	Republican	Total	Democratic	Republican	Total
Lawyer	16 (8,376)	7 (1,768)	11 (10,144)	14 (1,424)	3 (25)	11 (1,449)
Teacher	5 (2,762)	7 (1,612)	5 (4,374)	7 (718)	14 (131)	.06 (849)
Student	12 (6,315)	3 (818)	8 (7,133)	8 (826)	13 (124)	.07 (950)
Housewife	13 (6,885)	20 (4,908)	13 (11,793)	17 (1,699)	15 (147)	14 (1,846)
Real estate	2 (1,065)	8 (2,015)	4 (3,080)	1 (110)	4 (38)	1 (148)
Government employee	18 (9,202)	9 (2,154)	13 (11,356)	13 (1,266)	6 (56)	10 (1,322)

Note: Number of members is indicated in parentheses.

particular instance, however, it turns out that only about two times as many Democrats are married as Republicans.

In examining single club members in terms of their sex (see Table 8.10), we found that among the regulars, singles in both parties are overwhelmingly male (Democrats, 76 percent and Republicans, 84 percent,) while among reformers, single males and females are much more evenly divided in both parties. In the Democratic reform camp single members are 59 percent male, and reform Republican singles are 57 percent male. In each party females show relatively greater strength in the party's reform wing than in its regular wing. And by far the largest number of singles, whether male or female, prefer to be Democratic regulars, following the trend among the city's electorate at large (over 70 percent in each case are Democratic regulars).

Party Factionalism and Members' Occupations

Reformers and regulars in New York City do not seem to be widely split along occupational lines. Whether we looked at club membership figures or at the numbers of clubs that have various degrees of strength along certain occupational lines, we did not find dramatic differences between the regular and reform factions. The only selected occupations for which we found the difference to be more than 1 percent between the number of regulars and the number of reformers are real estate, claiming 4 percent of the membership among regulars and 1 percent for reformers, and government work, showing 13 percent of regular members and 10 percent of reformers. Moreover our occupational breakdown by party did not yield any greater differences (see Table 8.11).

Our examination of more general work groups showed that the reform faction includes a smaller percentage of both white-collar and blue-collar workers than the regular faction (see Table 8.12). In the professional group, however, the reformers top the regulars by 3 percent. It is notable too that professional people account for 5 percent of the Democratic regulars, but 23 percent of the Democratic reformers. In the Republican party the professional groups are almost equal—11 percent among regulars and 13 percent among reformers. Thus the reform wing of the Democratic party attracts a somewhat larger number of professionals.

When we examined the numbers of clubs, by faction, that list various percentages of white-collar and blue-collar groups, our data revealed a few refinements. There are greater numbers of regular clubs with substantial percentages of white-collar members

TABLE 8.12

Percent and Number of Club Members in Various Occupational
Categories, by Faction and by Party

Category	Regular			Reform		
	Democratic	Republican	Total	Democratic	Republican	Total
White-collar	15 (8,047)	21 (5,098)	17 (13,145)	9 (888)	16 (155)	10 (1,043)
Blue-collar	11 (5,987)	13 (3,095)	13 (9,082)	5 (486)	8 (82)	6 (568)
Other Professional	5 (2,736)	11 (2,660)	7 (5,396)	23 (2,244)	13 (127)	20 (2,371)

Note: Number of members is indicated in parentheses.

TABLE 8.13

Percent and Number of Clubs Listing Various Percentages
of Membership in White-Collar and Blue-Collar
Occupations, by Faction

Percentage of Membership	White-Collar		Blue-Collar	
	Regular	Reform	Regular	Reform
0	11 (21)	18 (11)	15 (29)	31 (19)
1-10	19 (36)	26 (16)	21 (42)	28 (17)
11-25	18 (35)	16 (10)	16 (30)	10 (6)
26-50	15 (28)	11 (7)	15 (28)	3 (2)
51 and over	7 (14)	3 (2)	3 (5)	3 (2)

Note: Number of clubs is indicated in parentheses.

TABLE 8.14

Number and Percent of Clubs Claiming Various Percentages
of Members in Real Estate, by Faction

Percentage of Members in Real Estate	Regular		Reform	
	Number	Percent	Number	Percent
0	66	34	32	52
1-10	61	32	13	21
11-25	4	2	1	0
26-50	3	1	0	0
51 and over	1	0	0	0

TABLE 8.15

Number and Percent of Clubs Claiming Various Percentages
of Lawyers Among Their Members, by Faction

Percentage of Members Who Are Lawyers	Regular		Reform	
	Number	Percent	Number	Percent
0	27	14	11	18
1-10	76	39	23	38
11-25	20	10	5	8
26-50	6	3	4	8
51 and over	7	4	2	3

TABLE 8.16

Number and Percent of Clubs Claiming Various Percentages
of Teachers Among Their Members, by Faction

Percentage of Members Who Are Teachers	Regular		Reform	
	Number	Percent	Number	Percent
0	51	26	8	13
1-10	63	33	29	50
11-25	16	8	5	8
26-50	2	1	4	8
51 and over	1	0	1	0

TABLE 8.17

Number and Percent of Clubs Claiming Various Percentages
of Students Among Their Members, by Faction

Percentage of Members Who Are Students	Regular		Reform	
	Number	Percent	Number	Percent
0	50	26	9	13
1–10	63	33	29	50
11–25	16	8	5	8
26–50	2	1	4	8
51 and over	1	0	1	0

TABLE 8.18

Number and Percent of Clubs Claiming Various Percentages
of Government Employees Among Their Members, by Faction

Percentage of Members Who Are Government Employees	Regular		Reform	
	Number	Percent	Number	Percent
0	33	17	10	16
1–10	86	45	29	50
11–25	30	16	10	16
26–50	10	5	5	8
51 and over	6	3	1	0

TABLE 8.19

Number and Percent of Clubs Claiming Various Percentages
of Housewives Among Their Members, by Faction

| Percentage of Members | Regular | | Reform | |
Who Are Housewives	Number	Percent	Number	Percent
0	28	15	9	15
1-10	36	19	13	21
11-25	32	17	11	18
26-50	36	19	7	11
51 and over	3	1	5	8

than there are reform clubs, and there are more reform clubs
showing either no white-collar members or less than 10 percent
(see Table 8.13). Our data on blue-collar workers reveals exactly
the same tendency. The slack in the reform ranks is taken up by
professionals and, possibly, students.

We also broke down selected occupations according to the
number of regular and reform clubs that claim to have various
percentages of members in each occupation. The breakdowns showed
no striking differences in these figures except that 52 percent of
reform clubs report having no members in real estate, while 34
percent of regular clubs report no members in real estate. (The
breakdowns are given in Tables 8.14-8.19.)

Our overall findings on the distribution of occupations among
reformers and regulars somewhat dissipate that portion of the
impressionist literature that suggests there is something overwhelmingly professional, and more occupationally elevated, about reformers.
There is, however, one occupational grouping, for which we did not
collect data, that might have been important in this regard—the
communications industry (newspapers, television, radio and advertising). Goetcheus, for example, described the reform VID club as
one in which many members are in the communications field.[37]

Party Factionalism and Electoral Success

Common sense, to say nothing of the general literature on
the subject, indicates that regulars are more politically successful
than reformers. Yet our data suggests that the reform clubs of
New York City are in many cases as successful as the regular clubs
in winning certain elected and appointed posts.

First there are the generally accepted facts of political life,
such as the following data reported by Martin Tolchin: the regular
organization controls about 90 percent of the city's county committeemen, and uses its power to fill the main vacancies that occur in
various public offices (city councilmen, judges, and others)—in
1970, for example, 11 of the 37 city councilmen were first appointed
by county leaders, that is, "regular" leaders; "the regulars also
arrange for judicial patronage (guardianships, receiverships, law
secretaries, trusteeships)."[38] We asked our respondents what public
and party officials were members of their clubs; this implied the clubs
had a role in electing certain officials. We found that although the
regular organization does indeed elect or appoint most city councilmen and judges, overall, in terms of factions, the clubs' success in
helping to put candidates in office is fairly equal for the offices of
state senator, state party committeeman, and government appointees
and officials. However, reform club officials whom we interviewed
claimed that they help elect congressmen, assemblymen and state
party committeewomen at a greater rate than regulars (see Table
8.20). To confirm this claim on the part of reformers, we asked a
panel of key reform and regular activists in New York City to identify
those public officials who are considered to be reformers. Our panel
came up with the following data, which shows the number and percent
of various New York City officials identified as reformers:

Public Officials	Number	Percent
Councilmen	6	14
State senators	5	18
State assemblymen	19	29
Congressmen	6	37

How can we account for the differences between the panel's data and
our own? Our initial response is that reform club officials exaggerate
their responses because they wanted to appear more successful and
powerful in the one area that is always important to clubs: winning
office and consorting with powerful officials. Then too reform clubs
sometimes gang up on a particular candidate in a campaign; several
clubs lend their support to a single race in order to achieve at least

TABLE 8.20

Number and Percent of Clubs That Have Members in Various
Public Offices, by Faction

Office	Regular		Reform	
	Number	Percent	Number	Percent
State senator	45	23	13	21
Assemblyman	78	41	29	48
City councilman	52	27	22	36
District leader	106	55	31	51
State committeeman	69	36	22	36
State committeewoman	58	30	22	36
Government appointees	57	30	18	30
Judges	88	46	17	28
Congressman	42	22	18	30
Other	39	20	12	20

one reform victory. Furthermore, because reform clubs spring up
without any overall control, many areas of the city may have several
reform clubs, while it is rare for there to be more than one regular-
organization club in a district because of the tighter control exercised
by the regulars. In any event the data in Table 8.20 should be viewed
as representing what club leaders believe to be, or claim to be, the
truth, rather than as an accurate portrayal of the dimensions of
electoral success and failure of each of the factions.

Factions and Club Stability

Another possible measure of success in the clubs is their
stability. We attempted to find out the proportion of each club's
members that had been in the club for periods of less than one year,
one-to-three years, four-to-six, and so forth. We also inquired as
to the successive terms of office of a club's leadership group. From
our responses on these data we sorted out general and partisan
profiles of club stability, in an effort to determine whether or not,
and to what degree, "regular" clubs were more stable than reform
ones. As we might have expected, the regulars are indeed more
stable. Only 3 percent of their clubs show a majority of their members
as having been in the clubs for less than one year, while 14 percent
of the reform clubs are in this category (see Table 8.21).

TABLE 8.21

Number and Percent of Clubs That Show 50 Percent or more
of Their Members with Various Periods of Tenure, by Faction

	Regular		Reform	
Period of Tenure	Number	Percent	Number	Percent
Less than 1 year	3	3	5	14
1-3 years	30	29	13	36
4-6	24	24	8	22
7-10	17	17	5	14
11-15	10	10	3	8
16-20	3	3	1	3
20 or more	15	15	1	3

In addition the regulars show 15 percent of their clubs as having a
majority of members with 20 years' standing or longer, compared
to only 3 percent for the reform clubs. What is even more remarkable in this latter finding is that there are any reform clubs that
have members with 20 years' service, since with the exception of
two clubs the entire life-span of the contemporary reform movement
has been only about twenty years.

When we categorized the clubs under the heading "very stable,"
"stable," and "not stable" our data appeared in slightly sharper
focus. We accorded the "very stable" designation to those clubs where
50 percent or more of the members had been in the club for 10 years
or more. A club with a majority of members in the four-to-ten-year
category was labelled "stable"; the remainder (those clubs where a
majority of the members were in the club for three years or less) were
labelled "not stable." The result was that twice as many regular clubs
as reform clubs (28 percent as against 14 percent) appear in our
"very stable" category, while over 50 percent of the reform clubs are
in the "not stable" group, compared to 32 percent of the regular
clubs. However, among the middle-ranked "stable" clubs we found
virtually the same percentage of clubs for both factions, which again
is surprising in view of the twenty-year duration of the new reform
movement.

It should also be noted that reform clubs are generally viewed
as amateurish, and thus less stable, clubs, and that the traditional
glue that supposedly holds people to politics is considered to be the
tangible rewards proferred by the more "professional" regulars.
Therefore the fairly equal stability that we found among reform and
regular clubs may indicate that reformers are not so amateurish as

TABLE 8.22

Number and Percent of Clubs Whose Leaders Serve
Varying Terms of Office, by Faction

Terms of Office	Regular		Reform	
	Number	Percent	Number	Percent
One term or less	40	21	21	34
2 terms	50	26	17	28
3	19	10	4	7
4-5	23	12	6	10
6-10	15	8	2	3
11 or more	12	7	0	0

Note: Percentages do not add up to 100 percent because total club universe used for this data included some clubs that did not respond.

they are commonly thought to be, or that regulars are not that professional. Or perhaps there is more than one glue that binds people to politics. Moreover reform stability is that much more impressive since reformers are supposed to be more mobile than regulars—occupationally, residentially, and socially. Yet they seem to join clubs and remain in them with the same tenacity as regulars.

When we examined the variable of club leadership stability— that is, the number of terms of office held by various club leaders— we found that 34 percent of the reform leaders had one term of service, compared to 21 percent of the regular leaders (see Table 8.22). Leaders with two-to-five terms of service came to about the same percentage for both factions. But when we looked at leaders who had served six-to-ten terms, we found 8 percent of regular clubs and only 3 percent of reformers. A possible reason why reform leaders do not serve as long as regular leaders do is the fact that club presidents carry a heavier burden of leadership in reform clubs since they do not share responsibility so frequently with district leaders. Then too some reform clubs, but almost no regular clubs, have either a tradition or constitutional provision that limits terms of office.

Reformers, Regulars and Club Appearance

Whether for fiscal reasons or as a matter of lifestyle it seems as though the club quarters of regular clubs generally are more

TABLE 8.23

Percent and Number of Clubs with Various Types of
Club Structure, by Faction

Faction	Store	Loft	Professional Apartment	Private Apartment	Detached Building	Office
Regular	27 (52)	13 (24)	11 (22)	5 (9)	13 (25)	7 (14)
Reform	36 (22)	13 (8)	20 (12)	2 (1)	5 (3)	7 (4)

Note: Number of clubs is indicated in parentheses.

TABLE 8.24

Percent and Number of Clubs Located on Various Types of
Thoroughfares, by Faction

Faction	Very Busy Street	Moderately Busy	Side Street	Secluded
Regular	26 (49)	49 (95)	18 (34)	2 (3)
Reform	25 (15)	39 (24)	23 (14)	7 (4)

Note: Number of clubs is indicated in parentheses.

TABLE 8.25

Percent and Number of Clubs with Various Types of
General Appearance, by Faction

Faction	Old and Sloppy	Modern but Sloppy	Old but Well-kept	Modern and Clean	Extravagant
Regular	13 (24)	2 (4)	49 (95)	31 (59)	2 (4)
Reform	28 (17)	7 (4)	41 (25)	16 (10)	5 (3)

Note: Number of clubs is indicated in parentheses.

desirably situated, and have a more pleasant appearance, than their reform counterparts.

Viewing a detached building as the apex of desirability for a clubhouse, it is the regulars who lead the way, with 13 percent of their clubs located in such a facility, compared to 5 percent of reform clubs. On the other hand if a storefront is seen as the most advantageous facility, the reform clubs have the better of it—36 percent compared to 27 percent (see Table 8.23). Reform clubs are also much more likely to be housed in apartments than regular clubs: In general, however, apartments are not well thought of as a clubhouse location by either faction.

There is little argument that a clubhouse is best off if it is located in a very busy, or at least moderately busy, neighborhood. In this respect the regular clubs again enjoy an advantage: only 20 percent of regular clubs are located on side streets (with little traffic) or on secluded streets, compared to 30 percent of reform clubs; 75 percent of regular clubs and 64 percent of reform clubs are in moderately busy, or very busy, locations (see Table 8.24).

While the foregoing categories are most probably a reflection of club income, another related item we studied—general club appearance—might possibly reflect both income and taste. We found reform clubs are most likely to fall into categories of "old and sloppy" and "modern but sloppy," while the regular clubs were most often classified by our observers as being "well-kept," whether old or new. That there are, however, a number of highly comfortable, and possibly luxurious clubhouses among the reform group is indicated by the 5 percent of reform clubs which were listed as "extravagant" (see Table 8.25).

The quintessence of reform club quarters was perhaps caught by one of our observers who reported: "The clubhouse itself was the site of my interviews with Mr. T. It was a very large L-shaped room with two closets and a lavatory. It was in what appeared to be an extreme state of disorder, though the few members who were there both times I visted seemed to know where everything was. There were large freshly painted signs piled on top of rather worn-out office furniture. Literature was scattered about everywhere. The entire place was in need of a paint job and the windows were bare. The phone kept on ringing, so I knew that at least it was working. I could tell why most of the meetings were held in members' apartments. The only word for the clubhouse itself was bleak."

Reformers, Regulars, and Club Activities

The impressionist literature portrays regular politics as a set of clubhouse activities enmeshed in securing and dispensing personal favors both to clubhouse members and to potential supporters.

A regular club is viewed mainly as catering to human nature in terms
that the legendary Plunkitt of Tammany Hall suggested. This means
an emphasis on social events, and on "furnishing legal services, food,
medical services, rent, coal and clothing without charge . . . act [ing]
as employment brokers for positions in the public service and in
certain semi-public businesses . . . establishing face to face contact
with individual citizens . . . canvassing and political meetings which
are entertaining, informing and satisfying to the emotions . . ."[39]
    More specifically than this, we can rely on the activity list
that Peel used as an outline of what most regular clubs had been
thought to do: organizing-type work; political activities (work on
nominations of all sorts, primaries, and campaign and general
election preparation); social functions; civic activities (representing
the community in its contacts with agencies of government); welfare;
educational work; ritualism; and antisocial activities.[40] The lion's
share of club activities in the time of Peel's study appeared to have
been taken up by antisocial activities. It should be noted that these
activities, as described by Peel, do not account for the time and
energy spent on extortion, franchise-selling, contract manipulation,
and other such activities brought to light by the Seabury investigations
in the early thirties. Peel referred mainly to gambling, bootleg
speakeasies, and fronts for prostitution. As mentioned previously,
we obtained no data of this sort from the interview situations in which
we worked.
    In terms of the distribution of legitimate activities, however,
Peel had this to note: "Social activities (formal and informal) rank
first, followed by welfare, political and civic."[41] In describing a
typical club, moreover, he noted: A great amount of relief is dispensed
from club quarters, and various outings, celebrations and parades
are staged for the 'benefit' of the members . . .[42] It is clear from
his remarks that Peel was dissatisfied with club life as it was
practiced in his day. "It takes no more than a second glance at the
activities of New York's political clubs to see that something is
radically wrong."[43] Based on Peel's original study and on the
interview we had with him in 1973 it is fair to conclude that Peel
would give acclaim to the stated ambitions and activity preferences
of the clubs of the current era, and most particularly, one might
expect him to sympathize with present-day reform club programs.
    It is not clear how really different the two factions of clubs
are in terms of activities, although the differences continue to be
a talking point among the reformers. Here, for example, is an
excerpt from an editorial that appeared in a 1972 reform club
newsletter (printed, it should be mentioned, on recycled paper):
"A Reform Democratic Club invites members of the community to
participate in club activities with an equal voice and an equal vote—

on political and community decisions, for club official and political candidates. Evidently there are political activities involved here. Reform Democrats are willing to ring doorbells, testify at hearings, participate in discussions, organize debates and demonstrations, address envelopes, go to Washington, Albany, City Hall and even down to Mississippi. . . . What are the issues which have involved the club most? The War in Vietnam, establishing national health insurance, a guaranteed annual wage, mass transportation, better housing, protection for tenants, price controls, more jobs on the waterfront, civil rights, abortion reform, women's rights, student's rights, opposing environmental disasters such as the Lower Manhattan Expressway, supporting efforts to establish local school and health district accountability to the community. "[44]

This reform club's newsletter saw the regular club in the same district as follows: "The ____ Club talks a great deal about crime in the streets, but never gave much support for programs that would get at the root of much of this crime—medical treatment for addicts. The ____ Club has never denounced the political abuses of the past— the Tammany politics of selecting judges on the basis of party loyalty not competence, or patronage, the practice of no-show jobs. . . . The ____ Club has not taken a position yet on the American involvement in Vietnam. "[45] Clearly this view of a regular club is hardly unprejudiced.

From a study of this and other newsletter-type club publications, both regular and reform, one develops the notion that whatever it is they do, reformers talk a lot more about community and national problems and take positions mostly on those issues, whereas regulars devote themselves—at least in print—to discussing political races, candidate qualifications, and club finances. One Manhattan reform Democratic club's log for a recent year shows that out of 26 items that occupied the membership's time either at formal meetings or at associated events, 13 (exactly half) could be described as purely political—in the sense that they were candidate endorsements, candidate speeches, convention activities, and so forth. Ten items were what we would call community activist-type functions: these include conferences on a community environmental issue, a human rights march, and taking a position on school decentralization. The remaining items were either fiscal or social in nature—planning or executing fund-raising and social events.

A similar log from a comparable Democratic regular club in Queens yielded the following: of 19 items, 12 were political in nature, including talks by officeholders and, in one case, by a political columnist for a New York City newspaper. Four items were specifically community activities, including a protest meeting against publicly subsidized housing, a Christmas party for neighborhood

TABLE 8.26

Number and Percent of Clubs That Offer Various
Types of Services to Constituents, by Faction

Service	Regular		Reform	
	Number	Percent	Number	Percent
Educational	114	59	37	61
Legal	105	55	34	56
Contracts with government	109	57	33	54
Landlord-tenant advice	78	41	35	57
Employment	89	46	17	28
Welfare	64	33	22	36

TABLE 8.27

Number and Percent of Clubs Engaging in Different
Types of Social Activities, by Faction

Social Activity	Regular		Reform	
	Number	Percent	Number	Percent
Card parties	79	41	6	7
Dances	133	69	40	66
Theater parties	23	12	7	11
Dinner parties	114	59	40	66
Picnics	54	28	21	34
Participating sports	29	15	12	20
Spectator sports	22	11	2	3
Other events	70	36	24	39

children, a petition drive on a local issue, and a forum on a new senior citizen's center. The remaining three were fund-raising events (a dinner-dance, a bagels-and-lox breakfast, and a card party), although the first two were political events as well, with various officeholders and candidates speaking at these affairs.

Tables 8.26 and 8.27 show our own survey results on the various club services and activities in each faction. On the whole there are few differences, and the few that are revealed are not at all spectacular. For example our listing of club services in terms of broad general types—educational, legal, and so forth—indicates that only two categories really separate the reformers from the regulars: while 57 percent of the reform clubs reporting on this item indicate that they engage in landlord-tenant-type activities, only 41 percent of the regulars do so, and concerning employment services, 46 percent of regular clubs engage in this type of service while only 28 percent of the reformers do so.

In terms of the social activities that so many people think are predominant in club life, we found one substantial area of difference: regulars frequently go in for card parties (41 percent of their clubs report this activity) while reformers don't (only 7 percent). If one thinks of the regular clubs as being addicted to the clam-bake sort of function, one would be surprised to learn that picnics are more heavily favored by reformers than by regulars—34 percent to 28 percent. Finally, spectator sports, perhaps another more middle-class, rather than upper-middle-class, type of activity engages more regular clubs (11 percent) than reform (3 percent), but obviously are not terribly important in either sphere.

Our observers also were asked to report on what was actually going on at the time they visited a club's quarters, as a form of spot-checking the two previously mentioned reports, and, again, we found very little difference between the two factions, only that regulars seem to be more prone to game-playing (generally cards) and "rap" sessions than reformers. The following table shows the number of regular and reform clubs that were engaged in various activities at the time our interviewer was on hand:

Activity	Regular	Reform
Membership meeting	48	17
Executive meeting	13	6
Gaming	21	3
"Rap" session	37	8
Partying	2	0
Other	43	17

Among reformers, formal discussion—an activity of sorts—

indicates that they are far more concerned with political election matters than are the regulars (see Table 8.28). When our investigators were present at meetings, they noted discussion about elections and primaries in over 40 percent of the reform clubs but in less than 30 percent of the regular clubs. Other differences in topics of conversation were much smaller.

TABLE 8.28

Number and Percent of Clubs That Discuss Various
Topics at Club Meetings, by Faction

Topics of Discussion	Number	Percent	Number	Percent
Club finances	71	37	19	31
Elections	55	29	29	48
Primaries	45	23	25	41
Club procedure	41	21	11	18
Upcoming social events	59	31	23	38
Other	54	28	21	34

The old-style welfare activities in clubs are still around, but they are to be found in both arenas, reform and regular. For the benefit of observers who feel that welfare is the preserve of the regulars, and that it is the regulars' claim to both fame and favor, it should be noted that the reformers report 36 percent of their clubs offer such service, compared to the regulars' 33 percent. This substantiates the view of Jewel Bellush that both modern and historic reformers have always been interested in serving the poor.[46] While the older progressive-type reformer may have more exclusively emphasized the need for the "social service state" rather than the need for the Christmas basket, the present-day reformers seem to be operating on both levels.

So too in fact are the regulars. They operate community action projects and rent clinics along with their individualized favors. If one is still expected to believe that the regulars have a monopoly on some of the less appealing activities of traditional political club-houses, one will again be disappointed. Not only do both regulars and reformers spend time on politicking, fiscal matters, and even job getting (although these may appear more heavily in regular ranks), but one is reminded, by some observers of the contemporary reform scene, of how necessity forces these grubby chores on even the most idealistic of the reform clubs.

Among the activities that are generally viewed disdainfully by reform clubs is the issuing of fund-raising journals:

210

Traditionally, political clubs have staged annual fund raising parties in connection with which they have issued a souvenir program made up mostly of advertising purchased by well-wishers—businessmen in the district, judges both appointed and elected, holders of other city and state elective offices, party officials, and any others willing to contribute financially to the club. In most cases the space purchased carried the name of the purchasers, though some remained anonymous. In many cases it was tacitly understood that purchasers were buying more than advertising space and were expressing more than their good will. They were buying personal, sympathetic treatment from the district leader if and when they needed a favor. A shadowy line divided an honest from a corrupt relationship between the club and its paying "well-wishers."

This perversion of a legitimate fund raising device led the Reform Dems to shy away from issuing a journal until 1960, despite their constant need of funds. A modest journal was issued in connection with the 1960 spring reception. [47]

Our more recent and broad-based survey clearly supports this description. Many reform clubs now issue journals—in fact 45 percent, according to our findings. But this compares with 55 percent of regular clubs that issue journals. In terms of numbers of clubs the breakdown is 103 regular clubs that publish journals and 28 reform.

There is further evidence of this reform-regular metamorphosis in certain comments made by New York State Senator Seymour Thaler (himself an odd mixture of an activist on certain community reform-type projects and, at the same time, a leader of a Queens regular Democratic organization): "You can't get the average voter excited about who's going to be an assemblyman or state senator. I've got two dozen people who are going to work so much harder because if I lose, they lose. My best captains in the primary are the ones who are on the payroll."[48] The political reporters who quoted Thaler are themselves convinced that "today, as was the case a half century ago, patronage begins in the clubhouse or in 'neighborhood city halls,' where people with problems receive the help of the political organization."[49] And while reform rhetoric pictures the reformers as being reluctant to descend to the role of patronage seekers and dispensers, many of them have not been able to avoid doing so.

Indeed when one considers the high cost of running for office, for all political candidates, even reformers, it is clear that campaigns for local offices (not to mention citywide offices) can cost tens of thousands of dollars apiece. Taken together with the unlikelihood that every reform candidate will be personally wealthy, the notion arises that patronage will be present regardless of faction—campaign favors from wealthy donors will later be redeemed by contracts, jobs for relatives, and so forth. Then too the simple availability of judicial patronage through the Surrogates Court (which alone runs to many millions of dollars annually), and the $2 million a year in "no-show" jobs given out by the state,[50] lead to the conclusion that reformers, as well as regulars, will be tempted to bend in the same direction until the basic ground rules underlying these practices are changed. Recently the paragon of reform virtue, the Village Independent Democrats, debated the desirability of handling some forms of patronage through their district leaders. Other reform clubs have stopped debating this and started practicing it. Still, some reformers see themselves differently from regulars. Reform rhetoric continues to be loud and more persistently in favor of changing such practices as campaign expenditures, judicial appointments, surrogate dispensations and the like.[51] The reformers continue their fervent appeals to their members and to candidates alike to "eschew patronage in favor of public service as a goal."[52] If success at the polls does not spoil them, or the lure of spoils sidetrack them, the circumstances of the current era may serve as an ally to achieve these changes.

A Question of Style

The major discernible difference between regular and reform clubs in the 1970s in New York City is essentially a matter of style and tone. These are subtle matters that have to do with not only the actual conduct of club meetings (rules, openness, atmosphere), but also the style and tone of the clubs' constitutions, of their newsletters and journals (where such exist), and perhaps even of the dress and vocabulary of their members, both in political roles as well as vocational and social roles.

Our study collected information on both factions in the following categories: the openness of the club meetings, in terms of who can gain entry to meetings and who can join the club; the orderliness of meetings; the type of participation encouraged at meetings; and the voting habits of the clubs. We also tried to obtain as many club constitutions as we could. In terms of these dimensions it seems that common impressions of other observers move in one direction and our data moves in another. Various reports have made it seem that reform clubs would be more likely to have a constitution than regular clubs. Blaisdell, for example, commented on this in the sixties: "The operations of a Tammany club like____were not a matter of public record. In the first place it is regarded as____'s personal organization, more or less his property, and run without formal rules or a constitution . . . "[53] As our data indicates, however, in both factions 10 percent of the clubs operate without a constitution. The percent and number of clubs, regular and reform, that do (yes) and don't (no) have a constitution are as follows (with number of clubs given in parentheses):

	Regular	Reform
Yes	90	90
	(168)	(54)
No	10	10
	(18)	(6)
Total	100	100
	(186)	(60)

In examining a number of club constitutions we found some important sylistic differences between the two factions. Regular club constitutions appear to make membership a bit more restrictive—more likely to be open to a blackballing possibility—than appears to be the case in the ground rules of reform constitutions. Regular constitutions moreover are very unlikely to give any lip service to the high-minded prose that is found occasionally in a reform charter, such as: "Because we believe, with Adlai E. Stevenson, that the true direction of political activity is the ceaseless examination and evaluation of local and national goals in the light of our democratic faith, and because we were inspired by the principled and humane leadership . . . "[54] It is not only the appeal to large issues that are found in reformers' basic charters and newsletters, but also a presumed grassroots democratic spirit that supposedly distinguishes them from the regulars. As one reform club brochure published in 1969 put it, "Reform Clubs operate on the principle of one man one vote." There is in other words an emphasis on political egalitarianism.

We tried to test this notion of broad participation by asking our observers to report on "who did most of the talking at club meetings." The various answer choices offered were "club leaders," "leaders plus some members," a "large minority" of members, and a "large majority" of members (see Table 8.29). Our results proved to be

TABLE 8.29

Number and Percent of Clubs That Have Various Levels
of Participation in Club Discussions, by Faction

Faction	Only Club Leaders		Leaders plus Some Members		Large Minority of Members		Large Majority of Members	
	Number	Percent	Number	Percent	Number	Percent	Number	Percent
Regular	4	2	37	19	24	13	37	19
Regular	3	5	13	21	4	7	15	25

TABLE 8.30

Number and Percent of Clubs in Which Members Challenge
Leadership on Issues, by Frequency of Challenge and by Party Faction

Faction	About 75 Percent of the Time		About Half of the Time		About 25-50 Percent of the Time		Never	
	Number	Percent	Number	Percent	Number	Percent	Number	Percent
Regular	4	2	12	6	28	15	25	13
Reform	7	11	3	5	13	21	10	16

TABLE 8.31

Number and Percent of Clubs That Maintain Various Degrees of
Order at Club Meetings, by Faction

Faction	Strict Order		Orderly		Quite Disorderly		Disorganized	
	Number	Percent	Number	Percent	Number	Percent	Number	Percent
Regular	23	12	77	40	7	4	3	2
Reform	10	16	20	33	5	8	5	8

TABLE 8.32

Number and Percent of Clubs That Have
Various Voting Habits, by Faction

Faction	Always Unanimous		Generally Unanimous		Generally About 75 Percent Consensus		Generally a Bare Majority	
	Number	Percent	Number	Percent	Number	Percent	Number	Percent
Regular	18	9	38	20	30	16	2	1
Reform	7	11	11	18	15	25	1	2

somewhat bimodal. While it is true that a greater percentage of reform clubs than regular ones were reported to have shown a majority participation at meetings, it is equally true that a slightly higher percentage of reform clubs than regular clubs showed only leaders as doing the talking at meetings.

We tried to determine the same sense of broad club participation and democratization by asking our observers to report whether or not members attending club meetings indicated a willingness to challenge the leadership on various issues (see Table 8.30). In this case our response categories were "yes, about 75% of the time;" "yes, about half the time;" "yes, about 25% to 50% of the time;" and "never." Once again the reform clubs topped the regular at both ends of the spectrum: 11 percent of reform clubs saw members challenge their leadership on issues "75%" of the time, as against 2 percent showing such challenges among the regular clubs; on the other hand in 16 percent of the reform clubs the leadership was "never" challenged, whereas only 13 percent of the regular clubs landed in this category.

Our observers also evaluated the overall "degree of order" with which meetings were run; responses in this case were catalogued as "strict order," "orderly," "quite disorderly," and "disorganized" (see Table 8.31). In the same fashion as before, reformers appeared more heavily than regulars in the two opposite ends of the gamut. A larger percentage of reform clubs than regular clubs appear to be "strictly orderly" during their meetings (16 percent as against 12 percent) and a larger percentage of reform clubs appear "disorganized" (8 percent to the regulars' 2 percent).

In studying the more practical elements of club democracy, such as voting, we tried to prove whether or not a club showed a tendency to be argumentative and less disciplined in their voting habits, or, on the other hand, tended to be either entirely like-minded or, to put it more pejoratively, more "controlled." We tried to elicit this factor by recording and investigating the degree to which unanimity prevailed in club votes. We selected the following categories of voting habits to record our informants' responses: "always unanimous," "generally unanimous," "generally about a 75% consensus," and "generally a bare majority" (see Table 8.32). We found the "bare majority" to be a uniformly uncommon voting style among all political clubs. We found too that reformers are more likely than regulars to show a 75 percent voting consensus, while regulars are more likely to be "generally unanimous."

We also studied the matter of a club's relative "openness," another part of the democratic flavor that might be conveyed in party clubhouses. In this regard we measured two items: the clubs' willingness to have our investigators attend a meeting, and the clubs' responses to our question, "May anyone join this club?" Our results revealed reform clubs to be more "open" than regular clubs, but not by a large margin. In 57 percent of the reform clubs our observers easily gained entry to a club meeting; this compared with 53 percent of the regular clubs. In 39 percent of the regular clubs our investigators were actually denied entry to any meeting. This happened in only 26 percent of the reform clubs. The question of joining the clubs produced the same tendencies. In 87 percent of the reform clubs responding, the reply was "yes, anyone may join the club," while this was true in 77 percent of the regular clubs. The differences in these responses are far from substantial, but they do move consistently in the same direction, giving at least a degree of credence to the idea of differing styles in reform-regular politics.

It should be noted, however, that on the whole, members' attendance at club meetings also shows some basic similarity in the trends of reform and regular clubs. We found 22 percent of the reform clubs claim to have generally a 41-60 percent attendance record at meetings, as against 14 percent of the regulars, while 12 percent of the regulars show a 61-80 percent attendance mark, compared to 5 percent of the reformers. (This data is shown on Table 8.33.)

TABLE 8.33

Number and Percent of Clubs Reporting Various Percentages of Members That Attend Meetings, by Faction

Percentage of Members That Attend	Regular		Reform	
	Number	Percent	Number	Percent
1-20	61	34	19	32
21-40	62	34	21	35
41-60	26	14	13	22
61-80	21	12	3	5
81-100	10	6	4	7
Total	180	100	60	100

Conclusion

That the differences between regulars and reformers should be less sharp than some observers might have expected is, when

one thinks about it, not strange. The more that reformers manifest
staying power, the more they must, and do, act like regulars.
Over the past two decades of the reform movement in New York City,
what seems to have happened is that each faction has learned lessons
and techniques from the other. The regulars have learned something
about media sophistication from the reformers, just as the reformers
have learned how to do effective face-to-face canvassing from the
regulars.[55] The issue was put very pungently by Father Gigante.
He had become a city councilman, and, speaking before a group of
Harvard students, he said that the only way to bring power to the
slums was through a return to the old days of ward-heeling, "service
politics," and patronage; that the only way to fight City Hall was to
get a piece of it. He told the students that "I haven't even told my
club this, but one of the reasons I'm in politics is to become a
political boss; and I want to be a boss to get the power, and I want
the power to put good people in government."[56]

Reformers and regulars today both play at ticket balancing—
the selection of candidates with an eye to diverse racial and ethnic
groups. Both factions also work equally hard at providing service
to constituents. What differences do occur in terms of specific
services probably reflect neighborhood needs rather than factional
ideologies. The reformers have also come to understand that a
primary fight is a "struggle for power, not a contest over issues."[57]
Some are even learning that the "strain of disinterested activity is
too great for anyone to bear very long."[58] The January-February
1972 issue of the Village Independent Democrats' newsletter echoes
these strains, and admits to the club's having changed its practices
in the years since its origin.

While it is no longer absolutely necessary for the true reformer
to be distinguished by "his concern for social issues rather than
personal reward, by his willingness to take the reform vows of
abstinence (from patronage) and obedience (to the rank and file),"[59]
nonetheless each group does maintain a sufficiently distinctive flavor
so that the city's politics remains enlivened by the split. What is
surprising too of course is the degree to which they must both work
through the clubhouse system. This phenomenon seems to support the
contention of Sayre and Kaufman, who noted that "whether insurgent
or regular, however, the first objective of any faction seeking control
of a major party is to capture and retain the assembly district leadership, and the clubs are the principal instrument in this strategy."[60]
But as well, in order for the reform banner to be kept aloft, a group
of clubs will have to continue to be at least somewhat innovative, if
not pure.

Notes

1. Theodore Lowi, <u>At the Pleasure of the Mayor</u> (Glencoe:
The Free Press, 1964), p. 187.

2. Ibid., p. 186.

3. Roy V. Peel, <u>The Political Clubs of New York</u>, rev. ed.
(New York: Ira S. Friedman, 1968), pp. 292-293.

4. Ibid.

5. Ibid.

6. Ibid.

7. Among the important works that deal with New York
contemporary reformism and machine politics are James Q. Wilson,
<u>The Amateur Democrat</u> (Chicago: University of Chicago, 1966),
chap. 2; Ralph G. Martin, <u>The Bosses</u> (New York: G. P. Putnam,
1964) chaps. 1, 5; Peel, "New Machines for Old," <u>The Nation</u>,
Sept. 5, 1973, pp. 88-90; Robert Heilbruner and Carmine DeSapio,
"The Smile on the Face of the Tiger," <u>Harper's</u>, July 1954, pp.
22-23; David Hapgood, <u>The Purge that Failed: Tammany v. Powell:
Case Studies in Practical Politics</u> (New York: Henry Holt & Co.,
1959); Robert Lekachman, "How We Beat the Machine,"<u>Commentary</u>,
April 1958, pp. 290-292; Donald Blaisdell, <u>The Riverside Democrats</u>,
Eagleton Institute Cases in Practical Politics, No. 31, (New York:
McGraw-Hill, 1963); Daniel P. Moynihan, "Bosses and Reformers,"
<u>Commentary</u>,June 1961; Dan Wakefield, "Greenwich Village
Challenges Tammany," <u>Commentary</u>, October 1959; Edward
Costikyan, <u>Behind Closed Doors</u> (New York, Harcourt, Brace &
World, 1966); Blanche D. Blank, "The New Style Boss," <u>New
Republic</u>, Sept. 11, 1961; Blank, "Reform Politics: A Biopsy," <u>The
Nation</u>, Sept. 22, 1962; Vernon Goetcheus, <u>The Village Independent
Democrats: A Study of the Politics of the New Reformers</u>, (Manuscript,
1963).

8. Edward Banfield and James Q. Wilson, "Urban Cleavages"
in Norman Sacher, ed., <u>The American Party Process</u> (New York:
Dodd, Mead, 1968), p. 270.

9. Goetcheus, op. cit., p. 90.

10. Dan Wakefield, "Greenwich Village Challenges Tammany,"
<u>Commentary</u> 28 (October 1959), p. 310.

11. Blanche D. Blank, "Reform Politics: A Biopsy," op. cit.,
p. 175.

12. Goetcheus, op. cit., p. 90.

13. Peel, op. cit., pp. 271, 291.

14. Ibid., p. 276.

15. Ibid.

16. Ibid., p. 287.

17. Ibid., p. 292.

18. Ibid., p. 274

19. Ibid., p. 272.

20. Ibid., p. 289.

21. Daniel P. Moynihan, "Bosses and Reformers,"
Commentary, June 1961, 462.

22. Ibid., p. 470.

23. The mobility of Jews in regard to neighborhoods is
commented on by Marshall Sklare in "Jew, Ethnic and the American
City," Commentary, April 1972, p. 76.

24. Moynihan, op. cit., p. 469.

25. Ibid., p. 469.

26. William Whyte, Streetcorner Society, (Chicago: University
of Chicago Press, 1942), p. 195.

27. Peel, op. cit., pp. 252-53.

28. Robert Considine, It's the Irish (New York: Doubleday,
1961), p. 67.

29. Moynihan, op. cit., p. 463.

30. New York Times, Feb. 21, 1974.

31. Wakefield, op. cit., p. 310.

32. Robert Lekachman, "How We Beat The Machine,"
Commentary, March 1958, p. 292.

33. Wakefield, op. cit., p. 310.

34. Blaisdell, op. cit., p. 12.

35. Moynihan, op. cit., p. 463.

36. Ibid.

37. Goetcheus, op. cit., p. 113.

38. New York Times, June 1, 1970.

39. Harold P. Gosnell, "The Political Party versus the
Political Machine," The Annals of the American Academy, 1932,
p. 24.

40. Peel, op. cit., pp. 129-130.

41. Ibid., p. 133

42. Ibid., p. 137.

43. Ibid., p. 136.

44. The Chelsea Democrat, (undated), p. 28.

45. Ibid., p. 3.

46. Jewel Bellush, "In Defense of the Progessives," National
Civic Review, December 1973, p. 598.

47. Blaisdell, op. cit., p. 22.

48. Martin Tolchin and Susan Tolchin, To The Victor—
Political Patronage From the Clubhouse to the White House (New
York: Random House, 1971), p. 23.

49. Ibid., p. 19.

50. New York Times, March 25, 1974.

51. This type of syndrome is well described in Tolchin and Tolchin, op. cit., pp. 136-38.

52. Blaisdell, op. cit., p. 26.

53. Ibid., p. 12.

54. Village Independent Democrats' Constitution, preamble.

55. Fred Greenstein, "The Changing Pattern of Urban Party Politics," in Norman Zucker, ed, The American Party System (New York: Dodd, Mead, 1964), p. 284.

56. New York Times, Feb. 21, 1974.

57. Lekachman, op. cit., p. 294.

58. Ibid., p. 299.

59. Blank, "Politics: A Reform Biopsy," op. cit., p. 175.

60. Wallace Sayre and Herbert Kaufman, Governing New York City (New York: Russell Sage, 1960), p. 138.

9

American politics has always provided an arena open equally to the cynic and to the optimist. This is particularly true in the domain of urban politics. Although our study provided us with the raw materials from which we could adopt a negative outlook for political clubs, we have not chosen to draw any such conclusion. Although voter identification with partisan politics is currently at a long-time low (it has dropped 14 percentage points since 1940)[1], and although the club universe of New York City seems on its face to be more fragile than it was forty years ago, we still felt we were able to offer data and explanations that could leave readers with hope for the club house variant of local politics.

As we noted previously, Peel viewed political clubs at a time when the nation was tumbling headlong into economic crisis. What he saw reflected the first moves on the part of political organizations in New York City to respond to that fierce national upset. The tenor of the clubs in part reflected the tenor of the times. It still does. Following the Watergate affair, and at a time when the city's population is continuing to shift, the clubs have taken on a somewhat different cast of characters, and turned a somewhat different face to the world. How do they look in the seventies, compared to how they looked to Peel in the thirties?

The number of political clubs in New York City has diminished from a high of 1,177 in the thirties to less than 300 today. At the same time the size of the clubs probably has declined as well. However, there are fewer of the type of small, temporary revolt clubs, organized to immediately benefit one or two leaders, that thrived during the early years of the depression. The growing strength of Conservative party clubs around the city, and the appearance of new ethnically-dominated clubs in Queens, the South Bronx, and

Brooklyn, indicate that there are those for whom the organization of clubs continues to hold out promise of political opportunity.

The typical club today has 195 members, an executive board-oriented constitution, with fairly stable leadership averaging five years tenure. The clubs have eschewed the secretiveness that marked their earlier days, and have become more accessible to the community and open in their membership. Still, there is a sort of suspicion of outsiders, and a feeling that what strangers do not know about club operations and membership cannot hurt the club. We found as well that 22 percent of clubs continue to be guarded in their relations with their own membership, denying them access to club bylaws and constitutions. For the most part this does not matter to members, since they do not join the clubs because of the quality of the clubs' formal rules, but rather for other, usually personal, reasons.

A city of 8 million people should probably generate an activist partisan group numbering in the hundreds of thousands. Yet we calculated that there were 112,899 dues-paying political club members in the city's five boroughs. Typically this New York City club member is white, male, married, engaged in a white-collar or professional job, over 35 years of age, and Italian-American, and has been a member of a club for several years. More women have found their way into club politics today than ever before: approximately 40 percent of club members are women. The greatest number are in the Democratic party, but the Republicans have the highest percentage of women.

As voting tends to be the domain of the city's settled, established citizens, so too does club membership. It is the middle-aged, and older, party member who joins clubs, although the newer parties and factions draw most heavily upon younger people. The city's most established party, the Democrats, has the most established club members, who are generally older and likely to be in the most political of all occupations, law. Yet it is the Democrats who also have the fewest white-collar and professional workers, an indication that their frequently substantial electoral pluralities are reflected in their ability to attract activists from the most common groups in the city—the non-well-to-do.

Where Peel found a plethora of specifically ethnic and nationality clubs, we found almost none. The heavy immigration of pre-World War I days resulted in the heavily ethnic, foreign-speaking populations that sought help and support in places—in the club—where strange accents and foreign customs were not scorned. The largely assimilated children and grandchildren of these immigrants have little need for such places, and have found their way into the "American" clubhouses. Only the Chinese, many of whom are recent immigrants who live in their own communities, and, to a lesser extent, the Spanish, have formed clubs that are overtly built on nationality themes. However, the clubs of New York, like the city itself, are not melting pots. Heavily segregated by race, they tend to reflect the ethnic homogeneity of many of the city's communities. The overwhelming majority of clubs are lily-white, have no Hispanic members, and tend to be dominated by a single ethnic group.

Today's clubs strive to be visible to the community, even when they are not open to its participation. Storefronts seem to be the most popular club sites, because they are at street level, are less expensive than houses, apartments, or office building locations, and because they generally put clubhouses on heavily travelled thoroughfares. In contrast to the slum-type conditions in which many clubs were housed in the twenties and thirties, the majority of today's clubs are reasonably well kept. While the opulent clubhouses of past decades have vanished, for the most part there are still some comfortable old clubs that in part reflect the earlier times, with card and pool tables, bars, and the like.

As far as activities are concerned, the clubs do what they have always done: serve the welfare needs of their constituents, act as a broker between party leaders and party members, represent constituents before government agencies, and provide free assistance on important issues confronting community residents (in the present day tenant-landlord matters frequently head the list).

If people join political clubs for social reasons, the clubs respond in kind with dinners, dances, parties, and other varied social events. Today clubs must compete with television, movies, sports, and other forms of entertainment. Thus club activities that are not specifically political (petitioning, campaigning, canvassing, poll watching) continue to occupy the bulk of club members' time. A typical evening at a club centers around members talking about politics, club finances, upcoming primaries, or general elections, or members working at campaign or club maintenance-related tasks (such as envelope stuffing). Young attorneys and incumbent party and public officials often meet with community residents, frequently behind closed doors. Meetings are held by executive boards, general membership, special committees, or community leaders. Almost every club provides one or two evenings a week when the doors are thrown open to its members and community alike.

Club finances are a delicate matter for most clubs. Leaders hesitate to discuss them, and members prefer to know as little about them as possible. Clubs depend heavily on their dues, which are modest (on the average $7-$15 per year per member), on occasional contributions from officeholders who are members, and on fund-raising events, usually including an annual dinner, breakfast, or dance. Most of the money collected goes for maintenance: paying rent, utility, and liability insurance bills; mailing out club newsletters, announcements of meetings, and other information to members; and providing refreshments. While a majority of clubs expend some funds for campaign purposes, we found 35 percent spend no money at all on political campaigns, a seeming anomaly for a political organization.

The most recent phenomenon in club affairs in New York City has been the development and growth of the reform movement in the Democratic party. Much of the attention focused on clubs has been on reform clubs, where, it has been said, young, middle-class, sophisticated, and committed activists have been changing the face of local politics.

Whatever the reform movement in clubs is today, it is very similar to the way clubs have always looked. Our research could find few tangible differences between reform and regular clubs. Those differences that we did observe were in matters of style and tone, rather than substance. Reform club members in the Democratic party tends to be somewhat younger, and lean more toward the white-collar and professional groups than the blue-collar category. Many reformers are single women, and a bit more middle-class than the regulars. Dramatically, reformers tend to be Jewish. Their club quarters tend to be seedier, in less accessible locations, and less well maintained, than their regular counterparts. The activities reformers engage in are approximately similar to those of the regulars, although it was noted that reformers eschew card parties and special women's group activities, while regulars engage in both. A reform club member is more likely than a regular member to receive a club newsletter, more likely not to wear a tie at a general membership meeting, and more likely to invite a friend to join a club. On certain critical club matters such as the conduct of meetings, the tendency of members to follow the ideas and recommendations of their leaders, the providing of services to the community, the probability of key issues being discussed by members, and the presence of material rewards as incentives to membership, reformers and regulars do not appear to differ one whit.

The machine has passed, we are told; the "last hurrah" has been heard, yet in New York City the clubs go on, keeping close touch with a local citizenry on whose behalf hundreds of schemes have purportedly been hatched to bring politics closer to the people. Local city halls, urban action task forces, and community councils are proposed, are created, are occasionally corrupted, and usually die. Yet the local clubs endure, dealing with local problems, and relaying local perceptions of politics and politicians to the appropriate bent ear.

It has been suggested from time to time that the political clubs have outlived their usefulness. In an age of almost instant communication, when voluntarism has been attacked by some observers and abandoned by many, the largely voluntary association of community residents that constitutes a political club seems out of step with the times. Pathways to social change, the search for an earthly urban paradise, are proclaimed by prophets who would sweep aside clubs and parties, and substitute some supposedly finer, purer institution. Yet Robert Merton warned that "to seek social change, without due recognition of the manifest and latent functions performed by the social organization undergoing change, is to indulge in social ritual rather than social engineering."[2]

The very existence of political clubs, in a form suprisingly similar to that of its precursors, is a strong indication that club functions both manifest and latent are being performed. If every club is not the community ombudsman and political cogwheel that it ought to be, or once may have been, many are at least providing a nesting place for would-be political activists, while also serving certain community needs. The ups and downs of political clubs over the years reflect the tortoise-like pace with which they adapt to their times and constituencies, and the failure of some clubs to come to terms with the changing nature of the city and its politics. In the present day they have been characterized by some observers, such as former Tammany leader Raymond Jones, mistakenly, we believe, as failures:

> Everything has changed. The clubs don't serve the same purpose anymore. They grew on the economic and social needs of the times. They were the welfare bureaus and social service agencies of those days. But no longer [do they] have the close contact they had with the families, though many people still go to the clubs for help. The role of the political club has become one of community action—another school for neighborhood, another traffic light, and so on— not individual service. But a political organization should not be a pressure group. That's a mistake the reform people make. I don't agree. It should be responsive to community demands. Any community program is a matter of priorities. What determines these priorities? Community pressures. The council-man doesn't create these pressures, but responds to them. And it's the duty of the political unit to get the community needs moved up on the priority scale. I don't know if the local clubs have a future, but it would be tragic if they don't. The political unit has discipline. If groups without discipline take over, the result will be a demagoguery and chaos.[3]

Rather, we are inclined to belive that the shifting emphasis of club programs, and the clubs' varying relationships with the new constituencies that make up New York City, are yet another set of responses to the changing times. When political clubs are ready to die, they will so indicate. But those observers that have already set up a deathwatch should prepare themselves for a long wait.

Notes

1. New York Times, Feb. 10, 1974.
2. Robert K. Merton, "The Latent Functions of the Machine," in Bruce M. Stave, ed. Urban Bosses, Machines and Progressive Reformers (Lexington, Mass.: D. C. Heath, 1972), p. 36.
3. Alfred Connable and Edward Silberfarb, Tigers of Tammany (New York: Holt, Rinehart and Winston, 1967), p. 336.

RESEARCH INSTRUMENT

Interview number (Fill in box)

Card Number (Disregard)

Assembly District (Fill in box) (Also indicate what part of

the district it represents, i.e., southern part of district

10, only if this pertains to you.)

Part I: To Be Answered by the Student

1.   What is the party affiliation of the club you studied?

a) Democrat   b) Republican   c) Liberal

d) Conservative   c) Lindsay   f) Other

If (f) specify_____

2.   Is this club considered:

a) Regular   b) Reform   c) Insurgent

3.   Did you have any difficulty gaining entrance to the club?

a) Yes   b) No

If (b) explain_____

_____

4.   What was the club's location in terms of pedestrian flow?

a) Very busy street

b) Moderately busy

c) Side street with little traffic

d) Secluded

e) Other

If (e) specify_____

5. In what sort of structure was the club located?

   a) store front   b) loft   c) apartment

   d) professional apartment   e) detached building

   f) office building   g) other

   If (g) specify_____

6. What was the general appearance of the club?

   a) modern, but sloppy   b) modern and clean

   c) old and sloppy   d) old, but well kept

   e) extravagant

   Comments_____

   _____

7. What types of furnishings were in the club? (Answer
   a) yes or b) no for each category given.)

   Clerical (desks, files, typewriters, etc.)?

   Game (pool tables, pingpong, card tables, etc.)?

   Eating facilities (refrigerator, stove, silverware, etc.)?

   Library facilities (books, magazines, etc.)?

   Office Machines (mimeos, calculators, etc.)?

Lounge furniture (sofas, armchairs, etc.)?

American flag?

Flags other than American? If "yes," specify

other types of flags_____

Pictures? If "yes," specify_____

Other types of furniture not mentioned? If, "yes,"

specify_____

8. Were there any private offices in the club?

a) yes b) no

Describe_____

9. Were there any alcoves?

a) yes b) no

Describe_____

10. Was there anyone guarding the front door?

a) yes b) no

11. (If there were any private offices) was there anyone guarding

the front of any of them?

a) yes b) no

12. (If there were offices) were you permitted to enter at any

time?

a) Yes, without difficulty

b) yes, after clearance from the guard

c) yes, after using some persuasion

d) no

13. What was going on at the club when you arrived?

Answer a) yes, or b) no for each.

Membership meeting?

Executive board meeting?

Game playing (Cards, pool, checkers, etc.)?

Rap session?

Party?

Any activity not included above?   If "yes"

specify_____

14. What was the racial breakdown of the club? (Give % of

each racial group specified as a ratio of the total

membership.)

White

Black

Hispanic

Oriental

Other   Specify racial groups included in "Other"

category_____

15. If known, what was the ethnic breakdown of the whites?

(Give % of each ethnic group as a ratio of the total people

who were at the club.)

Jewish

Irish

Italian

Hispanic

Eastern European

Other   Specify ethnic groups included in "Other"

category_____

16. What percentage of those present were women?

17. What was the breakdown of the people present according

to age? (Give % of each age group as a ratio of the

total people who were there.)

Between the ages of:

18-21

22-30

31-35

36-42

43-50

51 and over

18. Were you permitted to attend a club meeting?

a) yes, with no difficulty

b) yes, after some persuasion

c) yes, after a great deal of persuasion

d) no

If, b), c), or d) elaborate_____

---

19. (If you attended a meeting) was the meeting orderly?

    a) yes, it was run under strict parliamentary procedure.

    b) it was generally orderly.

    c) it was somewhat disorderly.

    d) it was generally disorganized.

    Comments_____

20. (If you attended a meeting) who participated in the discussions?

    a) only the club leaders?

    b) a small minority consisting of leaders and some members?

    c) a large minority of those present?

    d) a large majority of those present?

21. (If you attended a meeting) did members challenge the recommendations of the club leader?

    a) yes, very frequently (over 75% of the time).

    b) yes, somewhat frequently (about half the time).

    c) yes, on occasion (less than half the time).

    d) yes, but rarely (less than 25% of the time).

    e) never.

22. What degree of consensus prevailed concerning motions

   brought to a vote ?

   a) always unanimous

   b) generally unanimous

   c) generally about 75% consensus

   e) generally barely a majority

23. What were the topics discussed at the meeting ?

   (answer a) yes or, b) no to each.)

   Club finances ?

   Elections ?

   Primaries ?

   Club procedure ?

   Upcoming social events ?

   Other, not specified in the above categories?

   If 'yes' for "Other," specify the topics of discussion

   _____

   Interview number (Fill in box)

   Card number (Disregard)

24. How much time elapsed between your initial contact with

   the club and the time you were granted an interview with

   a club officer ?

   a) immediately   b) 1-3 days   c) 4-7 days

   d) 8-10 days   e) 11-14 days   f) unable to secure one

If f), or g) explain_____

25. (If you were granted an interview with a club officer),

what was his or her title?

a) President   b) Vice-President   c) Treasurer

d) Secretary   e) Other

If e) give title_____

26. (If you were granted an interview), what was the dis-

position of the person you questioned?

a) friendly and helpful   b) friendly, but evasive

c) cool but helpful   d) cool and evasive

e) hostile

Part II: To be asked by the student of a club officer in a private

interview.

27. How many years has this club been in existence?

a) under a year   b) 1-3 years   c) 4-7 years

d) 8-10 years   c) 11-15 years   f) more than 15 years

If f), specify number of years_____

28. Has the club always operated under this name?

a) Yes   b) no

If b) write in previous name or names_____

29. Do you know why the current name(s) were (was) chosen?

a) yes   b) no

If a), explain_____

30. Can you give me some historical background on the club?

a) yes   b) no

If a), write in answer. Use back of sheet, if needed.

_____

31. How long has the club been at this location?

a) less than a year   b) 1-3 years   c) 4-6 years

d) 7-10 years   e) 11-15 years

If f), specify number of years_____

32. (If the club moved at any time), why did it change its

location? (Fill in a) yes, or b) no.)

Needed larger quarters?

Old place was run down?

Neighborhood got bad?

Building torn down?

District line changed?

Old place got too expensive?

Other?

If "other" category and answer is a) state reasons_____

_____

33. What is the total number of members in the club?

(Fill in number in the box to the left.)

34. How many dues-paying members are in the club? (Fill in number in the box to the left.)

35. What is the racial breakdown of the club membership? (Give % of each group as a ratio of the total membership.)

Whites

Blacks

Hispanic

Oriental

Other   Describe groups included in "Other"

category_____

36. What is the ethnic background of the whites? (Give % of each group as a ratio of the total membership.)

Jewish

Italian

Irish

Hispanic

Eastern European

White Anglo-Saxon Protestant

Other   Describe groups in "Other" category_____

_____

37. Is the ethnic composition of the club similar to that of the assembly district in which it is located?

a) yes, almost exactly

b) yes, to a great extent

c) only somewhat

d) not generally

e) not at all

38. What percentage of the members are female? (Fill in %
    in box to the left.)

39. What percentage of members are unmarried? (Fill in %
    in box to the left.)

40. What percentage of these unmarried members are women?
    (Fill in % in box to the left.)

41. Are there any auxiliaries to this club?

    a) no   b) yes, women   c) yes, youth

    d) yes, nationality, ethnic or racial

    e) yes, professional   f) yes, other

    If f), write in types. If more than one of types specified

    write in those not mentioned above._____

_____

42. What are the occupational backgrounds of the club members?
    (Fill in % for each occupational group stated as a ratio of the
    total membership.)

    Lawyer

    Real Estate Brokers or Agents

Teachers

Professionals (Other than those already mentioned)

Students

Clerical or white-collar workers

Blue-collar workers

Housewives

Other

If "Other" category is used, write in those included in

it._____

43. What percentage of the club members are government

employees ? (Fill in % in box to the left.)

44. May anyone join the club ?

a) yes   b) no

If b) explain_____

Interview number (Fill in box)

Card Number (Disregard)

45. What are the general requirements and procedures set down

for someone wishing to attain membership in the club ?

Write an answer_____

46. What is the general length of time members of the club

have been members ? (Give % of members in each time

category as a ratio of the total membership.)

Less than a year

1-3 years

4-6 years

7-10 years

11-15 years

16-20 years

20 years or more

47. Does the club have regularly scheduled meetings ?

    a) yes, once per week

    b) yes, twice per week

    c) yes, once per month

    d) yes, twice per month

    e) no

    f) other   If f) state regularity_____

48. What % of the membership usually attends the meetings ? (Fill in % in box to the left.)

49. Does the club have a journal ?

    a) yes   b) no

50. How often is it printed ?

    a) annually b) semi-annually c) other

    If c), specify_____

51. What are the primary sources of the club's funds ? (Give % of each category as a ratio of the club's total income.)

Dues

Social affairs

Club rental

Journal sales

Contributions

Bingo, Bazaars, other functions

Other sources   Specify_____

52.   What are the major expenditures of the club? (Give %

of each category of expenditures as a ratio of the total

expenses.)

Rent and utilities

Salaries

Contributions to charity

Funding to auxiliaries

Contributions to campaigns

Contributions to other party functions

Communications

Other   If "Other" explain_____

53.   Does the club have an annual budget?

a) yes   b) no

54.   (If there is a budget), is it distributed to the membership?

a) yes   b) no

Comments_____

55. (If there is a budget), may I have a copy ?

a) yes   b) no

Comments_____

56. What sort of social affairs does the club have ?

(Write a) yes or b) no for each category.)

Card Parties

Dances or other parties

Theatre parties

Dinner parties

Picnics

Participation in sports

Spectator sports

Other social events

List those types of events included in "Other"

category_____

57. Are there any social events which cater to nationality

groups ?

a) yes   b) no

Elaborate_____

58. Does the club have a constitution ?

a) yes   b) no

59. (If there is a constitution), does each member receive

a copy ?

a) yes   b) no

60. (If there is a constitution), may I have a copy ?

a) yes   b) no

61. Is there an executive board ?

a) yes   b) no

62. (If there is an executive board), how is it chosen ?

a) election by all members ?

b) election by a minority of the members ?

c) appointment by club officers ?

d) other   If d), specify_____

63. (If there is an executive board), what are the titles of the

members ? (Write a) yes or b) no for each title mentioned.)

President?

Vice-President?

Secretary?

Treasurer?

Parliamentarian?

Other ?   State "Other" titles_____

64. What are the duties of the club officers ?

Write in_____

65. Are there any members of the club, who because of personal attributes, appeal, prestige or reputation are able to exert a great deal of influence over the other members without the benefit of holding office?

a) yes   b) no   Explain_____

_____

66. What is the average tenure of executive board members?

a) less than a year   b) 1-2 years   c) 3-4 years

d) 5 years   e) over five years (Specify)_____

_____

67. Has the method of electing club officers always been the same?

a) yes   b) no

Explain if, b)_____

Interview number (Fill in)

Card Number (Disregard)

68. What types of services does the club provide for members of the community? (Write a) yes, or b) no for these services mentioned.)

Educational?

Legal Aid?

Government or bureau contacts?

Landlord services?

244

Employment ?

Welfare ?

Other ?   Specify those services included in other.

---

69.   What percentage of the potential voters in this district

        are registered to vote ? (Give % in the box to the left.)

70.   What portion of the registered voters are enrolled in

        each political party ? (Give % in each party as a ratio of

        total registered voters.)

        Democrats

        Republicans

        Liberals

        Conservatives

        Independents

71.   Have there been any major breakoffs from this club ?

        a) yes, another club formed   b) yes, no club formed

        c) no

        Elaborate_____

72.   What elected officials are currently members of this club ?

        (Write a) yes, or b) no for each office mentioned.)

        Congressman ?

        State Senator ?

        Assemblyman ?

City Councilman?

District Leader?

State Committeeman?

State Committeewoman?

Other?

Specify those included in "Other"_____

73. What is the average number of terms of these officials from the club who are now in office? (Write number in box to the left.)

74. How many judgeships have come out of this club in the last five years? (Write number in the box to the left.)

75. How many members of this club hold government appointments to positions of Deputy Commissioner or above on the state or city level? (Write in number in the box to the left.)

LIST OF NAMES OF POLITICAL CLUBS

GEOGRAPHIC CLUBS

Democratic

*Ansonia Independent Democrats (Manhattan)

*Bensonhurst Independent Democrats (Brooklyn)

*Bronx-Pelham Reform Democratic Club (Bronx)

  Chelsea Village Lane Democratic Club (Manhattan)

  Chinatown Democratic Club (Manhattan)

  Concourse Democratic Club (Bronx)

*Concourse Jefferson Reform Democratic Club (Bronx)

*Co-op City Independent Democratic Club (Bronx)

  Decatur Democratic Club (Bronx)

  Democratic Club of Glenridge (Brooklyn)

  Democratic Club of Richmond County (Staten Island)

  Democratic Club of Yorkville (Manhattan)

  Democratic Youth Club of Chinatown (Manhattan)

  Eastern Queens Democratic Club (Queens)

  East Side Democratic Club (Manhattan)

  Flatbush Democratic Club (Brooklyn)

*Independent Democrats of Flatbush (Brooklyn)

Jackson Heights Regular Democratic Club, Inc. (Queens)

Jamaica Regular Democratic Organization (Queens)

John F. Kennedy Democratic Club of the 40th AD, Inc. (Brooklyn)

Kings Highway Democratic Club & Community Center (Brooklyn)

Lenox Hill Democratic Club (Manhattan)

Lexington Democratic Club (Manhattan)

Lower East Democratic Association (Manhattan)

Manhattan Democratic Club (Manhattan)

Maspeth Democratic Club (Queens)

*Midbay Independent Club (Manhattan)

Murray Hill Democratic Club (Manhattan)

*New Chelsea Reform Democratic Club (Manhattan)

North Bronx Democratic Club (Bronx)

*Northeast Independent Democratic Club (Bronx)

Northeast Regular Democratic Club (Queens)

Northside Democratic Club (Queens)

Onondaga Regular Democratic Club of Kings County (Brooklyn)

Park Lincoln Democratic Club (Manhattan)

*Park River Independent Democrats (Manhattan)

*Queens Independent Democrats (Queens)

Queens Village Regular Democratic Club (Queens)

Rego Park Democratic Club (Queens)

Regular Rockaway Democratic Club (Queens)

Richmond Hill Regular Democratic Club (Queens)

Ridgewood Democratic Club, Inc. (Queens)

Riverdale/Kingsbridge Democratic Club (Bronx)

Riverside Democrats (Manhattan)

*Rockaway Coalition Democrats (Queens)

*Roosevelt Kingsboro Reform Democrats (Brooklyn)

St. Albans Democratic Club (Queens)

Shorefront Democratic Organization (Brooklyn)

South Beach Democratic Association (Staten Island)

South Shore Democratic Organization (Staten Island)

Staten Island Democratic Association

Stuyvesant Community Democratic Organization (Brooklyn)

Sunset Park Independent Democrats (Brooklyn)

Thomas Jefferson Democratic Club of Kings County, Inc.
(Brooklyn)

Trylon Regular Democratic Association (Queens)

*Village Independent Democrats (Manhattan)

Washington Heights Progressive Democratic Club (Manhattan)

*West Queens Independent Democrats (Queens)

Woodside Democratic Club (Queens)

Regular Democratic Club 1st AD (Queens)

20th AD Regular Democratic Club (Queens)

21st AD New Democratic Coalition (Queens)

22nd AD Democratic Club (Brooklyn)

Regular Democratic Club of the 28th AD (Queens)

Regular Democratic Club of the 33AD (Queens)

36 AD Regular Democratic Club (Brooklyn)

42 AD Democratic Organization (Brooklyn)

45 AD Democratic Club (Brooklyn)

Regular Democratic Club of the 9th AD, Inc. (Brooklyn)

51st AD Democratic Club (Brooklyn)

Democratic Club of the 52AD (Brooklyn)

United Democratic Club of Co-op City (Bronx)

Van Cortland Democratic Club (Bronx)

Broad Channel Democratic Club (Queens)

Yarmouth Regular Democratic Club (Queens)

*Bensonhurst Independent Democrats (Brooklyn)

*Bayridge Independent Democrats (Brooklyn)

Boerum Hill Independent Democrats (Brooklyn)

*West Side Free Democrats (Manhattan)

*Audubon Reform Democratic Club (Manhattan)

*Rutgers New Frontier Democratic Club (Manhattan)

Hamilton Heights Democratic Club (Manhattan)

GEOGRAPHIC CLUBS

Republican

Beechhurst Republican Club (Queens)

Bronx County Republican Club (Bronx)

Central Republican Club (Manhattan)

College Point Republican Club (Queens)

Community Republican Club of Jackson Heights (Queens)

Co-op City Republican Club (Bronx)

Crotona Republican Club (Bronx)

*Douglas MacArthur Republican Club of Lower Manhattan

East Manhattan Republican Club (Manhattan)

East Side Republican Club (Manhattan)

Elmhurst Republican Club (Queens)

Flatbush-Flatlands Republican Club (Brooklyn)

Frank Kenna Republican Club of Astoria (Queens)

Highbridge Republican Club (Bronx)

Kew-Forest Regular Republican Club (Queens)

Maspeth Republican Club (Queens)

Mid-City Republican Club (Brooklyn)

Middle Regular Republican Club (Manhattan)

Morningside Heights Republican Club (Manhattan)

North Bronx Republican Club (Bronx)

Prospect Republican Club (Bronx)

Queens Village Republican Club (Queens)

Richmond Hill Republican Club (Queens)

Riverdale Republican Club (Bronx)

Southeast Republican Club (Manhattan)

Steinway Republican Club (Queens)

Triboro Republican Club (Manhattan)

Village East Republican Club (Manhattan)

Westchester Republican Club (Bronx)

West Side Republican Club (Manhattan)

Whitestone Republican Club (Queens)

Woodhaven Republican Association (Queens)

Yale Republican Club (Queens)

21 AD Republican Club (Queens)

35th AD Republican Club (Queens)

36th AD Republican Club (Brooklyn)

38th AD Republican Club (Brooklyn)

Republican Club of the 39th AD (Brooklyn)

40th AD Regular Republican Organization (Brooklyn)

42 AD Republican Club (Brooklyn)

45th AD Republican Club (Brooklyn)

46 AD Republican Club (Brooklyn)

47 AD Republican Club of Kings County (Brooklyn)

49th Regular Republican Club (Brooklyn)

50th AD Regular Republican Organization (Brooklyn)

Regular Republican Club of the 51st AD (Brooklyn)

54 AD Republican Club (Brooklyn)

Belmont Republican Club (Bronx)

Pelham Parkway Republican Club (Bronx)

Uptown Republican Club (Manhattan)

Coliseum Republican Club (Manhattan)

GEOGRAPHIC CLUBS

Conservative

Bayside Conservative Club (Queens)

Canarsie Conservative Club (Brooklyn)

Cypress Hills Conservative Club (Queens)

Easter Richmond Conservative Club (Staten Island)

Hollis Conservative Club (Queens)

Kensington Conservative Club (Brooklyn)

Middle Richmond Conservative Club (Staten Island)

Ridge Conservative Club (Brooklyn)

Rosedale Regular Conservative Club (Queens)

Sheepshead Bay Conservatives (Brooklyn)

West Side Conservative Club (Manhattan)

36 AD Conservative Club (Brooklyn)

41 AD Conservative Club (Brooklyn)

Conservative Club of Flatbush (Brooklyn)

Conservative Party of the 52 AD, Kings County (Brooklyn)

Douglaston Little Neck Conservative Club (Queens)

West Side Conservative Party Club (Manhattan)

Conservative Party Club of Park Slope (Brooklyn)

Washington Heights-Inwood Conservative Club (Manhattan)

OTHER CLUBS

Jamaica Political Action League (Queens)

PERSONALITY CLUBS

Democratic

*Adlai Stevenson Reform Democratic Club (Queens)

Alfred E. Smith Democratic Club (Manhattan)

Alfred Issac Democratic Club (Manhattan)

Andrew Jackson Democratic Club (Brooklyn)

*Benjamin Franklin Reform Democratic Club (Bronx)

Bolivar-Douglas Democratic Club (Manhattan)

*Carl Sandburg Independent Democrats (Brooklyn)

*Concourse-Jefferson Reform Democratic Club (Bronx)

Eugene MacManus Democratic Club (Manhattan)

Franklin Delano Roosevelt Democratic Club (Queens)

*Franklin Delano Roosevelt Independent Democrats (Bronx)

*Frederick Douglas Reform Democrats (Queens)

*Herbert H. Lehman Independent Democratic Club (Bronx)

Jefferson Democratic Club (Manhattan)

Jefferson Democratic Club (Queens)

John F. Kennedy Democratic Club of the 40th AD, Inc. (Brooklyn)

John F. Kennedy Regular Democratic Club (Queens)

*John F. Kennedy Independent Democratic Club (Bronx)

The Madison Club (Democratic) (Manhattan)

Martin Luther King - Robert Kennedy Democratic Club (Brooklyn)

Robert F. Kennedy Democratic Club (Queens)

*Roosevelt Kingsboro Reform Democrats (Brooklyn)

Roosevelt Democratic Club (Brooklyn)

Stevenson Regular Democratic Club (Queens)

Thomas Jefferson Democratic Club of Kings County, Inc.
(Brooklyn)

*Walt Whitman Independent Democrats (Brooklyn)

Washington Heights Progressive Democratic Club (Manhattan)

Woodrow Wilson Democratic Club (Manhattan)

Young Democrats Affiliate of the Roosevelt Democratic Club
(Bklyn)

Monroe Democratic Club (Bronx)

John Brown Democratic Club (Queens)

*Tom Paine Reform Democratic Club (Brooklyn)

United Mazzini Democratic Club (Brooklyn)

Carver Democratic Club (Manhattan)

Samuel Tilden Democratic Club (Manhattan)

PERSONALITY CLUBS

Republican

Douglas MacArthur Republican Club of Lower Manhattan

Douglas MacArthur Republican Club (Queens)

Frank Kenna Republican Club of Astoria (Queens)

Javits Republican Club (Queens)

John Foster Dulles Republican Club (Queens)

Rocco A. Fanelli Regular Republican Organization (Manhattan)

Taft Republican Club (Bronx)

Daniel Webster Regular Republican Club (Bronx)

Harold C. Burton Republican Club (Manhattan)

Hamilton Republican Club (Manhattan)

Conservative

Del-Res De Pasquale Conservative Club (Brooklyn)

James Monroe Conservative Club (Queens)

John Paul Jones Conservative Club (Queens)

Patrick Henry Conservative (Queens) Club

Patrick Henry Conservative Club (Brooklyn)

Stephen Decatur Conservative Club (Queens)

OTHER CLUBS

B. Charney Vladeck Liberal Party Club (Brooklyn)

SYMBOLIC/IDEOLOGICAL CLUBS

Democratic

Civic Democratic Club (Bronx)

*Community Free Democrats (Manhattan)

Community Democratic Organization (Brooklyn)

Community Democratic Organizations of Inwood & Marble
                                    Hill (Bklyn)

New Democratic Club (Brooklyn)

New Democratic Club (Manhattan)

*New Horizons Reform Democrats (Brooklyn)

*New Leadership Reform Democrats (Brooklyn)

Peoples Regular Democratic Club (Brooklyn)

Pioneer Democratic Club (Brooklyn)

Star Democratic Club (Bronx)

Stars and Stripes Regular Democratic Club (Brooklyn)

United Democratic Club (Queens)

United Political Club (Democratic) (Brooklyn)

United Regular Democratic Organization (Brooklyn)

Washington Heights Progressive Democratic Club (Manhattan)

Youth for an Equal Society (Democratic) (Queens)

United Democratic Club of Co-op City (Brooklyn)

*Phoenix Reform Democrats (Manhattan)

New Directions Democratic Club (Manhattan)

Rutgers New Frontier Democratic Club (Manhattan)

Republican

Century Republican Club (Manhattan)

Community Republican Club of Jackson Heights (Queens)

Evergreen Republican Club (Manhattan)

Metropolitan Republican Club (Manhattan)

Progress Republican Club (Manhattan)

Progressive Republican Club (Queens)

American Eagle Republican Club (Bronx)

Excelsior Republican Club (Bronx)

Ivy Republican Club (Manhattan)

Union Republican Club (Manhattan)

Conservative

Born Free Conservative Club (Queens)

OTHER CLUBS

Black Panther Party (Bronx)

*Independent Citizens for a Better Community (Manhattan)

Jamaica Political Action League, Inc. (Queens)

Liberal Action Club (Staten Island)

HISTORICAL CLUBS

Democratic

New Deal Democratic Club (Manhattan)

New Frontier Democratic Club (Queens)

Republican

Federal Republican Club (Manhattan)

Old Glory Republican Club (Queens)

Conservative

Monitor Conservative Club (Brooklyn)

DEMOGRAPHIC IDENTIFICATION CLUBS

Democratic

Democratic Youth Club of Chinatown (Manhattan)

Young Democrats Affiliate of the Roosevelt Democratic Club
(Bklyn)

Youth For An Equal Society (Democratic) Queens

Republican

Women's Republican Club (Staten Island)

Young Republican Club (Staten Island)

INDIAN CLUBS

Democratic

Amerind Democratic Club (Queens)

Anorac Democratic Club (Queens)

Chippewa Democratic Club (Bronx)

Onodaga Regular Democratic Club of Kings County (Brooklyn)

Powhatan Regular Democratic Club, Inc. (Queens)

Seneca Democratic Club (Brooklyn)

Siwanoy Democratic Club (Bronx)

Taminent Regular Democratic Club (Queens)

Tioga Democratic Club, Inc. (Manhattan)

Pontiac Democratic Club (Bronx)

Kanawha Democratic Club (Manhattan)

ETHNIC CLUBS

Democratic

Aldos Regular Democratic Club, Inc. (Queens)

Caribe Democratic Club (Manhattan)

Filipino American Democratic Club, Inc. (Brooklyn)

John Smolenski Memorial Democratic Club (Brooklyn)

Polonia Democratic Club (Brooklyn)

United Mazzini Democratic Club (Brooklyn)

Carver Democratic Club (Manhattan)

Republican

Janito Republican Club (Manhattan)

* = Reform Club

261

SAMPLE POLITICAL CLUB CONSTITUTION

THE ALEXANDER HAMILTON CONSERVATIVE CLUB
BY-LAWS
NEW YORK STATE CONSERVATIVE PARTY
ADOPTED: NOVEMBER 15, 1966

ARTICLE I - ORGANIZATION

SECTION 1 - BASIC ORGANIZATION

This organization is called the Alexander Hamilton Conservative
Party Club. It is a voluntary, unincorporated association of members
residing in and around the Club area. This Club is chartered by the
Conservative Party, a New York political party, and is subject in all
relevant respects to the rules and regulations of the Conservative
Party, its State Committee and the Queens County Committee
(including the Executive Committees thereof).

SECTION 2 - PURPOSE OF ORGANIZATION

This Club is organized for the purpose of supporting and electing to
public office, candidates nominated by the Conservative Party,
pursuant to law, and of engaging in political action for the promotion
of the principles and policies of the Conservative Party, and of
coordinating all other Conservative Party activities within the Club
area.

ARTICLE II - MEMBERSHIP

SECTION 1 - REQUIREMENTS

Any resident of the state of New York, who is in agreement with the
principles of the Conservative Party and resides in and around the
Club area, may be admitted to membership by the Executive
Committee. A resident 21 years of age and over shall be admitted
to regular membership. Members under 21 years of age shall be
designated "Youth Members." A resident may be admitted to youth
membership at 14 years of age. The applicant must complete the
membership application. Said admission to membership must be
approved by at least a two-thirds (2/3s) vote of the members of the

Executive Committee present, at a meeting at which there is a
quorum. Membership commences as of the date of said approval.
A requirement of admission to membership, is the payment in
advance of the Club membership dues for one year.

SECTION 2 - CONTINUED MEMBERSHIP

Membership in this Club may be continued upon: a) the annual payment of the Club membership dues of $4.00 per person, or $7.00
per married couple, or b) the annual payment of the Club membership dues of $2.00 per person for a "Youth Member," or c) the
payment of $50.00, either in a single payment, or over a twelve
(12) month period, which shall entitle said member to a lifetime
membership.

SECTION 3 - EXPULSION

Any member who engages in conduct detrimental to the best interests
of the Club or the Conservative Party may be expelled, after
reasonable notice and hearing, by the vote of a minimum of sixty
per cent (60%) of the members present, at a meeting at which there
is a quorum, or by the vote of two-thirds (2/3s) of either: a) the
Executive Committee, or b) the Executive Committee of the State
Committee of the Conservative Party, present at a meeting at which
there is a quorum.

ARTICLE III - ELECTION OF OFFICERS
OF THE CLUB AND OF THE EXECUTIVE COMMITTEE

SECTION 1

A)   The officers of the Club shall be i) a President, a First Vice-
     President, a Second Vice-President, a Third Vice-President,
     a Treasurer, a Corresponding Secretary, a Recording Secretary
     and a Sgt.-At-Arms, all of whom shall be elected at the annual
     or special election of officers and shall serve until their
     successors are elected, and ii) members of the Executive
     Committee.

B)   A person may not be elected President, First Vice-President,
     Second Vice-President, Third Vice-President or Treasurer
     unless he is a duly enrolled Conservative and has been so
     enrolled for a minimum of thirty (30) days.

C) A person may not vote in a Club election, nor be elected to any Club office unless he has been a member of the Club for a minimum of thirty (30) days.

SECTION 2

A) The officers of the Executive Committee shall be a Chairman, a First Vice-Chairman, a Second Vice-Chairman, a Third Vice-Chairman, a Treasurer, a Corresponding Secretary, a Recording Secretary and a Sgt.-at-Arms, who shall be the President, First Vice-President, Second Vice-President, Third Vice-President, Treasurer, Corresponding Secretary and Sgt.-at-Arms, of the Club, respectively.

B) The Executive Committee shall be composed of a maximum of twenty (20) members, including 1) the officers as provided in Section 2(A) of Article III and 2) the Youth Member of the Executive Committee.

C) A Youth Member shall serve as a member of the Executive Committee with all duties and obligations thereof. He shall be elected to a six month term of office by a majority vote of the Executive Committee at the meetings of February and August of each year, as soon thereafter as practicable.

D) At the first annual election of officers following the adoption of these By-Laws, one-half (1/2) of the regular members shall be elected to one (1) year terms and the remaining one-half (1/2) of the regular members shall be elected to two (2) year terms. Thereafter, at each annual election, one-half (1/2) of the regular members shall be elected to two year terms. At the annual election of officers, a majority vote may provide that up to two vacancies on the Executive Committee not be filled at that election. The Executive Committee may fill these vacancies at its discretion as provided in Section 3(A) of Article III.

E) If a person is elected to an office as provided in Section 1(A) of Article III, and he is: 1) not a continuing member of the Executive Committee, or 2) not elected to the Executive Committee at the same Election of Officers, he shall be considered a member of the Executive Committee by virtue of his office, and shall serve on the Executive Committee until the expiration of his term of office.

F)   The maximum number of members of the Executive
        Committee as provided in Section 2(B) of Article III, shall
        not be applicable in the case as provided in Section 2(E) of
        Article III, except that in the event of the death, resignation
        or other disqualification of a member of the Executive
        Committee, the vacancy created thereby shall not be filled,
        if the total number of remaining Executive Committee members
        is either the number as provided in Section 2(B) of Article III,
        or a greater number.

SECTION 3 - CLUB ELECTION PROCEDURE

A)   The Club Election Procedure shall be as follows:
        The Chairman of the Nominating Committees shall be
        appointed pursuant to Section 3 of Article V not later than
        the November regular Executive Committee meeting. At
        said meeting subsequent to the appointment of the Chairman,
        the remaining four (4) members of the Nominating Committee
        shall be selected by the Executive Committee. The names of
        the members of the Nominating Committee will be announced
        at the November regular club meeting.

B)   The Nominating Committee shall inquire if each incumbent
        officer wishes to stand for re-election. In such case, such
        officer shall be considered by the Nominating Committee.

C)   Additional recommendations to the Nominating Committee for
        a candidate for particular Club office shall be made in writing
        by two (2) members other than the proposed candidate.

D)   Elections shall be held at the regular January meeting,
        subsequent to the announcement by the Nominating Committee
        Chairman of the recommendations for all offices.

E)   Additional nominations may be made from the floor by members.
        Said nominations must be seconded.

F)   If there are two (2) or more candidates for any office, the
        election shall be by secret paper ballot.

SECTION 4 - VACANCIES

A)   In case of vacancies, or the death, resignation or other
        disqualification of any member of the Executive Committee,
        the Executive Committee shall fill the vacancy created thereby

for the balance of the term of the Executive Committee member in question. The notice of that meeting of the Executive Committee shall specify that an election will be held for the office in question.

B) Any vacancy in a permanent office shall be filled by a special election at the next regular meeting of the membership of the club. Five days written notice shall be given to the membership of the Club of any meeting at which a permanent officer is to be elected.

ARTICLE IV - DUTIES OF OFFICERS

SECTION 1

The President shall be the Chief Executive Officer of the Club and shall preside at all meetings of the Club and of the Executive Committee. He shall maintain liaison with State Headquarters of the Conservative Party, and shall see that such periodical reports, as may be required by State Headquarters, concerning the activities of the Club, are submitted. He shall be ex-officio a member of all standing and special committees unless otherwise provided by these By-Laws. He shall perform the duties ordinarily performed by the Chief Executive Officer of a political party Club, and such other duties as may be prescribed by law, or assigned to him by the Executive Committees of the State, County and Club.

SECTION 2

The First Vice-President, Second Vice-President and Third Vice-President, shall preside, in that order, in the absence of the President. They shall perform the duties of the President in case of his absence or incapacity. They shall be ex-officio members of all standing and special committees unless otherwise provided by these By-Laws. They shall perform the duties ordinarily performed by Vice-Presidents of a Political Party Club and such other duties as may be prescribed by law, or assigned to them by the President, or by the Executive Committees of the State, County and Club.

SECTION 3

The Treasurer shall be the chief financial officer of the Club. He shall be responsible for the collection and custody of all funds for the Club. He shall see that such funds are properly disbursed. He shall be an ex-officio member of all fund raising Committees.

He shall file with the proper officers or departments, all financial reports and statements required by law, the President, and the Executive Committees of the Club, County and State. In general, he shall perform the duties ordinarily performed by the Treasurer of a political party Club, and, in addition thereto, such other duties relating to financial matters as the President or the Executive Committee may require.

SECTION 4

The Corresponding Secretary shall keep the records, files and/or correspondence of the Club and its officers. He shall be responsible for the preparation and filing of all reports required by law and by the Executive Committees of the Club, County and State, except those which have to do with matters financial, or which by law are required to be filed by some other officer. He shall be responsible for the preparation and sending out of all notices of meetings and correspondence. In general, he shall perform the duties of a Corresponding Secretary of a political party Club.

SECTION 5

The Recording Secretary shall take the minutes of all meetings of the Club and the Executive Committee and shall keep said minutes as a permanent record. In general, he shall perform the duties of a Recording Secretary of a Political Party Club. In addition thereto, he shall perform such other duties as the President and the Executive Committees of the Club, County and State may require.

SECTION 6

The Sgt.-at-Arms

ARTICLE V - OTHER COMMITTEES

SECTION 1 - STANDING COMMITTEES

A)   In addition to the Executive Committee there shall be four (4) standing committees of the club.

        THE MEMBERSHIP COMMITTEE
        THE PUBLICITY COMMITTEE
        THE FINANCE COMMITTEE
        THE CLUB COMMITTEE

B)   The Chairman of the standing committees shall be appointed by the President subsequent to the annual election of officers. Only a member of the Executive Committee may be appointed as chairman of a standing committee.

SECTION 2 - DUTIES OF STANDING COMMITTEE

A) It shall be the duty of the Membership Committee to develop
and execute programs to increase the membership of the club,
especially by active solicitation and to conduct a continuous
program of membership retention. The chairman shall have
the responsibility for maintaining records which shall include
the following: Names of members
Address & Telephone No.
Dates of application & approval
Dues payment status

B) It shall be the duty of the Publicity Committee to develop and
execute programs to publicize the club and Conservative
Party in all the medias of communications, especially through
the use of leaflets, posters, and brochures and to enlist
community interest and support for Club and Conservative
Party activities and programs.

C) It shall be the duty of the Finance Committee to develop and
execute programs both to finance the activities of the Club
and to assist in financing other activities of the Conservative
Party.

D) It shall be the duty of the Club Committee to be responsible
for the appearance and housekeeping of the Club. It shall
keep records and coordinate the use of Club facilities. The
Committee will be responsible for Club refreshments and
shall maintain records in connection therewith.

SECTION 3 - TEMPORARY COMMITTEES

Temporary Committees may be constituted and their chairman
appointed by the President. All club members are eligible for such
appointments. Temporary Committee Chairman shall attend
Executive Committee meetings as their Committee duties shall
require.

ARTICLE VI - MEETINGS

SECTION 1 - REGULAR MEETINGS

The regular meetings of
1. The Club
2. The Executive Committee

shall be held monthly at a time and place set by the Executive Committee. Other committees shall meet upon a call of their chairman or the chairman of the Executive Committee.

SECTION - 2 ORDER OF BUSINESS - CLUB MEETINGS

The following shall be recommended order of business at all regular meetings of the club.
- a. Call to order
- b. Reading of Minutes of previous meeting
- c. Treasurer's report
- d. Correspondence and communications
- e. President's remarks
- f. Committee reports
- g. Old business
- h. New business
- i. Adjournment

SECTION - 3 ORDER OF BUSINESS - EXECUTIVE AND OTHER COMMITTEE MEETINGS

The order of business at meetings of the Executive Committee and other committees shall follow the agenda set by the chairman of such committee subject to amendment by the members of such committee.

SECTION - 4 SPECIAL MEETINGS

A) A special meeting of the club or the Executive Committee may be called by the President or the Executive Committee.

B) A special meeting of the club must be called by the president upon written request of either
1. Seven Executive Committee Members or
2. One Third of the club members

C) A special meeting of the Executive Committee must be called by the President upon written request of seven Executive Committee Members.

D) A meeting called upon such written request as provided in paragraphs B and C of this section, shall be held on the date designated therein, provided a minimum of seven days subsequent to said request is allowed to prepare and give appropriate notice.

SECTION - 5 NOTICE OF MEETING

A)   Notice of the time and place of all club meetings must be mailed to each member not less than three days before such meeting, and notice of all adjourned meetings must be mailed to each member at least two days prior thereto.

B)   Notice of the time and place of the Executive Committee and of all standing and other committees may be given either:
   1. By mail at least two days before the meeting, or
   2. By telegraph or telephone twenty four hours before the scheduled time of said meeting.

C)   Whenever mailing is required in these by-laws, it shall be taken to require such mailing by first class mail.

SECTION 6 - QUORUMS

A)   A quorum of the club shall consist of one-fifth of the whole membership or twenty members, whichever shall be less, and may transact the business of the club. Less than a quorum may adjourn a meeting to another time.

B)   A quorum of the Executive Committee shall consist of one half of the membership or eight members, whichever shall be less, and may transact the business of the Executive Committee. Less than a quorum may adjourn a meeting to another time. A quorum shall further consist of a minimum of five members who must be present in person.

SECTION - 7 - PROXIES

A)   At meetings of the Executive Committee a member shall be entitled to the vote in person or by proxy. Such proxy must designate another member of the Executive Committee as the proxy of the member giving the proxy, shall be confined to a specific meeting of the Executive Committee or adjournment thereof, shall be dated and must be evidenced by an authorization in writing on a form to be provided by the Executive Committee, similar to sample form set forth in paragraph B of this section,

B)   Sample form:
   I hereby appoint_____, a member of the Executive Committee, my proxy for the meeting of the Alexander

Hamilton Conservative Club Executive Committee to be
held_____, at _____, Queens, New York.
Dated_____   _____
                                    Signature

or a reasonable facsimile thereof, and to be filed with the
Secretary of the meeting for which the proxy is given.

C)   Members may not vote by proxy at meetings of other committees
or at any club meetings.

SECTION - 8 - SUMMER SUSPENSION

A)   The meetings of the club and/or the Executive Committee may
be suspended only during the months of July and/or August.

B)   At the June meeting, a majority vote of the members present:

        1.   Shall suspend the club meetings.
        2.   (of the Executive Committee) Shall suspend
            the Executive Committee meetings as set
            forth above.

ARTICLE VII - AMENDMENTS

These By-laws shall continue to be the rules for the Alexander
Hamilton Conservative Club until they are amended or new rules are
adopted. These rules may be amended from time to time by a two-
thirds vote of the members of the club present at a meeting at which
there is a quorum, provided that the notice as provided in Section 5,
Article VI shall state:

        "There is to be a vote of the members of the
        Club on an amendment to the By-laws."

members, typical, 64–65
members' characteristics, 62–93; in reform clubs, 173–199
membership qualifications, 58–60
membership totals of clubs, 32
methodology of study, 9–12
Mitchel, John Purroy, 171
Murphy, Charles Francis, 18

Nadjari, Maurice, 149
names of clubs, 101–105; ethnic, 261; geographic, 247–254; historic, 259–260; Indian, 260–261; personality, 254–257; symbolic/ideological, 257–259
Nation, Carrie, 190
nationality clubs, 83, 85
Neal, Clarence, 23
neighborhood factors, effect on reform movement, 177–181
neighborhood nature of clubs, 28
New Chelsea Reform Democratic Club, 174–175
New Democratic Coalition, 10
New York County Democratic Committee, 24
New York Democratic Coalition, 176
number of club members, 32
number of clubs, 9–10, 32–35

occupations of members, 74–82; of reform clubs, 194, 199
O'Dwyer, William, 22–23
officers of clubs, 46–51
Olvany, George W., 18
openness of clubs, 52–58; reform clubs, 216–217
oriental membership, 86

partisan nature of clubs, 28
party organization, relation to clubs, 37–45
party preference, relation to reform club growth, 181, 183

patronage services, 140–141; of reform clubs, 212
Peel, Roy V., 3; significance of his book, 9–12
Perkins, Frances, 190
Perry, Harry, 22
phantom clubs, 10–11
physical property of clubs, 29, 94–114; of reform clubs, 203–205
political activities, 130–133; of reform clubs, 205–206, 209–212
political clubs, activities of, 115–142; conclusions regarding, 222–227; evolution of (1920–1970), 18–26; finances of, 143–169; literature about, 4–9; members' characteristics, 62–93; nature of, 27–61; quarters of, 94–114; reasons for studying, 2–3; reform movement, 170–221; relation to laws, 4
politics, attitudes toward, 170–171; participation in, 1–2
publications of clubs, 129; income from, 153–155; reform clubs, 211

quarters of clubs, 94–114; of reform clubs, 203–205
questionnaire (sample), 228–246

race of members, 82–91; relation to reform club growth, 183–189
reform clubs, 170–221; Brooklyn and Bronx, 180–181; Democratic versus Republican, 181, 183; members' characteristics, 173–199; neighborhood factors affecting formation of, 177–181; in the 1920s and 1930s, 176–177; overall conclusions regarding, 217–218; Peel's

Norman M. Adler, Associate Professor of Political Science
at Hunter College of the City University of New York, is an experienced observer of New York City, and the political party process.
Long active in political clubs in New York City, he has served as
an officer of several "reform" Democratic organizations. A former
speechwriter for Mayor Robert Wagner, he has been a consultant
on campaign organization and on ethnic affairs to the Democratic
National Committee. For the past several years he has been a
consultant to candidates for state and municipal office, as well
as an organizer and consultant for campaign management schools
for candidates and their managers.

Professor Adler has written extensively in the fields of urban
government and political socialization. He has served as consultant
to the New York State Charter Revision Commission for New York
City, as well as the New York State Commission on the Costs,
Efficiency and Quality of Schools. For the past year he has been
helping to spearhead a new organization for citizen participation
in politics, the Center for Policy Through Participation.

Professor Adler received his doctorate from the University
of Wisconsin. He has taught at American University, Pennsylvania
State University, Columbia University and Queens College.

Blanche D. Blank, Dean of Social Sciences and Professor of
Political Science at Hunter College of the City University of New York,
has had experience in teaching, research, consulting, and political
activities. Her teaching and research interests have been in the fields
of American government and politics, public administration, bureau-
cratic theory, and comparative administration. Her book on American
Government and Politics—A Critical Introduction was recently published, and she is the author of numerous articles. She has also
taught at Sarah Lawrence College, The New School for Social Research
and The City College.

Dean Blank has served as Executive Director of the Mayor's
Task Force on New York City Personnel and as a consultant to the
Deputy Mayor's Office and the College-Federal Agency Internship
Program.

Dean Blank studied at Hunter College and at the Maxwell School
of Syracuse University. She received her doctoral degree from
Columbia University. She and her husband live in Scarsdale, New
York and have three daughters.

DECENTRALIZING CITY GOVERNMENT: A Practical
Study of a Radical Proposal for New York City
                Walter G. Farr, Jr.,
                Lance Liebman, and
                Jeffrey S. Wood

LEGISLATIVE POLITICS IN NEW YORK STATE:
A Comparative Analysis
                Alan G. Hevesi

PHILADELPHIA: Neighborhood, Authority, and
the Urban Crisis
                Conrad Weiler

RE-STRUCTURING THE GOVERNMENT OF NEW YORK
CITY: Report of the Scott Commission Task Force on
Jurisdiction and Structure
                Edward N. Costikyan and
                Maxwell Lehman

SUPERCITY/HOMETOWN, USA: Prospects for Two-Tier
Government
                League of Women Voters
                Education Fund